DRAMA CLASSI

These volumes collect together the most popular plays from a single author or a particular period. Both affordable and accessible, they offer students, actors and theatregoers a series of uncluttered texts in impeccable editions, accompanied by concise introductions. Where the originals are in English, there is an end-glossary of unfamiliar words and phrases. Where the originals are in a foreign language, the translations aim to be both actable and accurate – and are made by translators whose work is regularly staged in the professional theatre.

Other Drama Classic Collections

IBSEN – THREE PLAYS

A Doll's House
Ghosts
Hedda Gabler

GREEK TRAGEDY

Antigone
Bacchae
Medea

RESTORATION COMEDY

The Country Wife
The Rover
The Way of the World

CHEKHOV
FOUR PLAYS

The Seagull
Uncle Vanya
Three Sisters
The Cherry Orchard

Anton Chekhov

translated and introduced by
STEPHEN MULRINE

NICK HERN BOOKS
London
www.nickhernbooks.co.uk

A Drama Classic Collection

This edition first published in Great Britain as a paperback original in 2005 by Nick Hern Books Limited, 14 Larden Road, London W3 7ST. Each play originally published in the Drama Classics series.

The Seagull translation copyright © 1997 by Stephen Mulrine
Uncle Vanya translation copyright © 1999 by Stephen Mulrine
Three Sisters translation copyright © 1994 by Stephen Mulrine
The Cherry Orchard translation copyright © 1998
by Stephen Mulrine

Introduction copyright © 2005 by Nick Hern Books

Stephen Mulrine has asserted his moral right to be identified as the translator of this work

Typeset by Country Setting, Kingsdown, Kent CT14 8ES
Printed by Bookmarque Ltd, Croydon, Surrey

ISBN-13   978 1 85459 845 5 / ISBN-10   1 85459 845 7

Contents

Introduction

Anton Chekhov (1860–1904)

Anton Pavlovich Chekhov was born in Taganrog, a seaport in South Russia, in 1860. By his own account, his childhood was far from idyllic. His father Pavel was a domestic tyrant, fanatically religious, and Chekhov and his brothers were forced to rise before dawn to sing in the local church choir, then work long hours after school, in the family grocer's shop.

Taganrog was in decline, but its Greek shipping community was relatively wealthy, and Chekhov was first sent to a Greek-language school, which his father naively regarded as the highway to a lucrative career. After a wasted year, Chekhov was enrolled in the local high school, where he stayed, an unremarkable scholar, until 1879.

His last years at the Taganrog school were spent apart from his family, however, since his bankrupt father had fled to Moscow, where Chekhov's elder brothers were already students. Chekhov completed his studies, entered Moscow University's Faculty of Medicine, and at the age of nineteen became the family's principal breadwinner, writing short comic pieces to supplement his student allowance.

By the time he qualified in 1884, Chekhov's literary ambitions were already in conflict with what he regarded as his true vocation. Indeed, until his own health collapsed, he continued to practise medicine, mostly as an unpaid service to nearby rural communities. Chekhov was almost certainly infected with tuberculosis from childhood, and the disease was in its terminal stages before he would permit an independent diagnosis. In addition to frequent haemorrhaging from the lungs, which forced him to spend the winters in the warm South, Chekhov also suffered from a variety of other chronic ailments, yet his work rate was little short of heroic. In 1899, when he agreed to sell the rights in his works to the publisher Marks, they already filled ten volumes, and the critical consensus is that his short stories are an unparalleled achievement, with the three great plays of his mature dramatic method, *Uncle Vanya*, *Three Sisters*, and *The Cherry Orchard*, no less important.

Human relationships are the substance of all Chekhov's work, and it is perhaps no surprise that this most intimate of writers remained elusive in his own. Although fond of women, and pursued by several, Chekhov characteristically retreated as they advanced, and it is a reasonable assumption that the happiness of his brief married life, with the actress Olga Knipper, depended to an extent on the lengthy periods of separation forced on the couple by the dramatist's poor health, and by Olga's busy metropolitan career.

Finally, in a despairing effort to postpone the inevitable, Chekhov travelled with Olga to Germany for medical treatment, and in July 1904, following a heart attack, he died in the spa town of Badenweiler, at the age of forty-four.

Chekhov the Dramatist

Chekhov might be described as the writer's writer, not only on account of his work, or the fund of wisdom in his correspondence, but also because of the example he presents of the tireless self-improver, grinding his way over a mere two decades from penny-a-line squibs in the comic papers, to the status of modern classic, in both his preferred genres.

In that respect, the year 1887-88 represents a turning-point in his career, with the staging of his first four-act play, *Ivanov* (leaving aside the unplayable epic now known as *Platonov*), and the publication of his short story *The Steppe* in one of the prestige 'thick journals', 'The Northern Herald'. The same year also saw his official recognition as a major Russian writer with the award of the Pushkin Prize, by the Academy of Sciences. Chekhov had arrived, it seems, though the reception given to *Ivanov*, premièred in Moscow to mixed cheering and booing, suggested he had done so some way ahead of his audience.

That is broadly the story of Chekhov's dramatic career, and it is significant that the main bone of contention in *Ivanov*, dividing first-nighters into partisans and scoffers, was the author's seeming abdication of any clear moral stance. After some changes, however, the play was successfully revived in St Petersburg, and Chekhov was emboldened to offer his next play, *The Wood Demon*, for production in Moscow the following year. Alas, *The Wood Demon* was a flop, and in the light of Chekhov's developing method, it is interesting to note that criticism generally centred on its lack of action, and dreary slice-of-life dialogue. Chekhov withdrew the play in disgust and buried it deep within his mysterious creative processes, whence it emerged in 1897, in the radically altered form of *Uncle Vanya*, one of the greatest works of the modern theatre.

Between times, Chekhov endured the catastrophic failure of *The Seagull*, an experience which encapsulated everything that was wrong with the Russian theatre of his day, and which his work did so much to change. *The Seagull* was premièred in October 1896 at the Alexandrinsky Theatre in St Petersburg, which in Chekhov's day was both the administrative and cultural capital of the country, and it was especially important that his new venture should succeed there. Unfortunately, the play spent almost a year in the hands of the censors, which meant that the actors received their scripts a bare week before opening night. Worse still, *The Seagull* had been commissioned from Chekhov as a vehicle for the benefit performance of one of the Alexandrinsky's stars, Levkeyeva, a mature comedienne with a large and vociferous following. She had originally been billed to play Arkadina, but had decided instead to appear in a three-act comedy, ironically titled *This Happy Day*, to be staged immediately after *The Seagull*. The disappointment of her fans, forced to endure four acts of Chekhov, is thus not difficult to imagine, and the play was accompanied with whistling and jeering almost from its opening lines.

After the fiasco of *The Seagull*, Chekhov fled from St Petersburg, and although the play's fortunes improved with 'normal' audiences, the generally hostile reviews made him resolve to quit the theatre for ever. Fortunately, the first great play of his maturity as a dramatist, *Uncle Vanya*, appears to have been already on the stocks, and while the course of its development out of *The Wood Demon* remains unclear, it almost certainly followed the writing of *The Seagull*. At any rate, *Uncle Vanya* first surfaced in 1897, when Chekhov had it published.

The following year, 1898, saw the coming together of Chekhov and the newly-founded Moscow Art Theatre – a meeting commonly presented as a marriage made in theatre heaven. Its founders, Stanislavsky and Nemirovich-Danchenko, shared Chekhov's dissatisfaction with the Russian theatre of the day, its bombastic acting, poor technical standards, and outmoded star system. Stanislavsky, a wealthy merchant's son, ran his own amateur theatre company, and Nemirovich-Danchenko lectured in drama at the Moscow Philharmonic School, where his students included the future director Vsevolod Meyerhold and Olga Knipper, eventually to become Chekhov's wife.

The Moscow Art Theatre was the product of their determination to create a new kind of professional theatre, in which the ensemble, rather than the individual actor, would be paramount, and which would pay close attention not only to the text, but also to scenery, costumes, lighting, incidental music and sound effects – even the design of the programme and the colour of the curtain. There were to be no 'benefit' performances, and no stars; the repertoire, Nemirovich-Danchenko's responsibility, would be chosen on literary merit alone. An actor might play the lead in one production, and carry a spear in the next; in Stanislavsky's famous dictum: 'There are no small parts, only small actors.' The new company also had a mission to educate audiences to a proper respect for the drama: it even excluded latecomers – unheard of in the commercial theatre of the day.

What Chekhov's plays needed – natural, unforced speaking, even-handed ensemble playing and lengthy, painstaking rehearsal – appeared to be exactly what the Moscow Art Theatre could bring to them; indeed it is debatable how much of Stanislavsky's famous 'method' was developed from Chekhov's writing. And if the relationship turned out to be less than wholly blissful, it is to their credit nonetheless that Chekhov continued to write for the stage, including the two masterpieces specially commissioned by the Moscow Art Theatre, *Three Sisters* and *The Cherry Orchard*.

Chekhov had in fact written to Nemirovich-Danchenko in November 1896, soon after the Aleksandrinsky première of *The Seagull*, and his own words describe the trauma he had experienced:

> The theatre breathed malice, the very air was compressed
> with hatred, and in accordance with the laws of physics,
> I shot out of St Petersburg like a bomb!

Not surprisingly, Chekhov's health took a severe downturn at this point, and by the time Nemirovich-Danchenko had managed to convince both Chekhov, and his co-director Stanislavsky, that the new company should stage *The Seagull*, the pattern of Chekhov's relationships with the Moscow Art Theatre was set – fleeting visits for readthroughs and rehearsals, fine tuning by correspondence, and the tense wait by the phone for news of the opening. Indeed, not until 1900, when the Moscow Art Theatre visited Yalta, did Chekhov see the company perform his work.

The rapturous reception accorded to *The Seagull* at its Moscow première on 17 December 1898, has passed into legend. Its success not only restored Chekhov's confidence, it also rescued the fortunes of the Moscow Art Theatre, who were now eager to attempt *Uncle Vanya*, which had already been staged in the provinces. Unfortunately, Chekhov had promised the play to the Maly Theatre, but a number of script changes being demanded by its literary committee gave him a legitimate excuse for withdrawing the offer. *Uncle Vanya* was thus produced by the Moscow Art Theatre in October 1899 – in terms of its reception, more consolidation than triumph, but sufficiently encouraging to focus Chekhov's mind on a new subject: the lives of three sisters in a remote provincial town.

Three Sisters opened in January 1901, and while it was certainly no failure, neither it, nor *The Cherry Orchard* three years later, managed to repeat the smash hit of *The Seagull*. By the spring of 1903, when he began committing *The Cherry Orchard* to paper, Chekhov had little more than a year to live; his health had deteriorated to such an extent that he could write only a few lines a day. Nonetheless, he was able to attend rehearsals at the Moscow Art Theatre in December, and *The Cherry Orchard* was premièred on Chekhov's forty-fourth birthday, 17 January, 1904. Three months later, Chekhov was dead, and the brief span of his career as a dramatist complete. We can only guess at what he might have achieved had he lived as long as Ibsen, say, but in a mere handful of plays Chekhov has given the classic repertoire not only a unique vision, but also, in his off-centre, low-key rhetoric, one of its most compelling modern voices.

The Seagull in Performance

The Seagull is a main source for Chekhov's views as a critic, and it is apt that the play begins with an extended debate, in effect, on the condition of Russian theatre as Chekhov found it. Kostya's Symbolist playlet shows Chekhov's awareness of developments taking place elsewhere in Europe, but the form of *The Seagull* itself was sufficiently innovative to ensure that Russian theatre

would need a radical overhaul to accommodate it. At the height
of his fame, the great Ostrovsky, for example, might hope for
100 roubles per act, for a new play, while the actor who topped
the bill in it received a salary of 10,000 roubles per annum. By
Chekhov's day, two decades later, the repertoire itself had
assumed the status of vehicles for those same stars, supported by
spear-carriers, so that perhaps the most striking innovation in
The Seagull is its even-handed ensemble.

There is no consistently occupied foreground to the play, and
one can imagine the relationships among the principals as an
arrow-strewn diagram, virtually representing its plot. Thus,
Arkadina loves Trigorin; Trigorin, however, falls in love with
Nina, but Kostya also loves Nina, who falls in love with Trigorin.
Masha, meanwhile, loves Kostya, but marries Medvedenko;
Polina is married to Shamraev, but loves Dr Dorn. The
complications are such as to make the head spin, and it is small
wonder that the play's first audience was bewildered.

Chekhov had his own doubts about *The Seagull*, which he
describes in a letter to his friend Suvorin as having 'very little
action, lots of talk, and two hundredweight of love', and the
circumstances of its first performance did little to remove them.
For a start, not all the actors even bothered to turn up for
rehearsals during the bare week allotted to them; the effect on
the ensemble can be easily imagined. Levkeyeva's fans, waiting
impatiently for her to appear in the broad comedy which was
scheduled to follow *The Seagull*, treated Chekhov's play as a
warm-up and roared with laughter on the slightest pretext.
Chekhov left the before the end, hurt and embarrassed, vowing
never to write another line for the theatre. The next day's
reviews only confirmed him in his resolve. Thus an anonymous
notice in the 'Stock Exchange Gazette':

> Never has there been such a breathtaking flop, such a
> stunning fiasco. By the time the curtain came down on the
> first act, the audience was already bemused: scarcely a single
> spectator had the least understanding of what had just taken
> place on stage before them. An ominous, threatening silence
> reigned, and not the slightest attempt at applause could be
> heard. After Act II, there was loud hissing and booing, which
> at the end of Act III became general and quite deafening,
> expressing the unanimous verdict of thousands of spectators
> on this 'new form', and this new idiocy with which our
> talented prose-writer had elected to appear on the stage . . .

And in the same paper, the following day, the critic Selivanov opined that:

> *The Seagull* produces an impression of some sort of creative debility – the literary impotence of a frog, blown up to bullock dimensions . . .

Two months later, Chekhov was still smarting. In a letter to Suvorin he observes: 'It wasn't just my play that failed, it was myself as a person.' He did, however, permit the text of *The Seagull* to be published in the journal 'Russian Thought', though he had every reason to believe that his career as a dramatist was finished. In that, Chekhov was reckoning without the intervention of Stanislavsky and Nemirovich-Danchenko, whose first meeting of May 1897, at the Slavyansky Bazaar – the same hotel, incidentally, in which Trigorin aranges to meet Nina – resulted in the founding of the Moscow Art Theatre.

The new partners had Chekhov in their sights from the outset. Nemirovich-Danchenko, indeed, had been awarded the Griboyedov prize for his play *The Price of Life* in 1896, and had publicly protested, declaring that *The Seagull* was the real triumph of that year's Russian theatre. Not surprisingly, Chekhov took a good deal of persuading to allow it to be staged again, but rehearsals began in September 1898, although the play was not to open until December. That in itself was significant; Stanislavsky's rehearsal method, based on detailed psychological study, and first developed on *The Seagull*, was to become a key influence on later theatre. Chekhov's future wife Olga Knipper played Arkadina, and the great Soviet director-in-waiting Meyerhold played Kostya. Stanislavsky himself played Trigorin, but Chekhov's well-documented objections to Stanislavsky's sound effects extended to the latter's performance, which stereotyped Chekhov's world-weary writer as an elegant *boulevardier*.

Even so, the Moscow Art Theatre production was as resounding a success as the Aleksandrinsky had been a failure. Chekhov's health would not permit him to attend the opening, but a writer friend Tatyana Shchepkina-Kupernik described the remarkable scenes for him in a letter next day:

> By the end of the third act, when the entire audience began calling for the author, Nemirovich, grinning like the cat that got the cream, announced that the author wasn't in the theatre. Shouts went up: 'Send him a telegram!' The noise was terrific, and he asked to make sure: 'You want me to

> send a telegram?' Back came the answer from a hundred
> voices: 'Yes! Yes!' It was an astonishing, deeply touching
> moment . . .

Shchepkina-Kupernik goes on to recount her own impressions,
While she disliked Roksanova in the role of Nina, her analysis is
perceptive:

> There was something wonderful on the stage – it wasn't a
> play being put on, but life itself being created . . . The way
> *The Seagull* was performed last night, you can't talk about
> directors or actors: it was as if the director was life itself, and
> the actors were Trigorin, Arkadina, etc., in the flesh . . . In a
> word, life as it really is, a stupendous drama, while the knives
> and forks are being rattled in the next room . . .

After Chekhov's death, 'his' theatre did not mount another production of the play until 1960, although there was an important
revival at the Moscow Kamerny, directed by Tairov, in 1944.
The Seagull was the first of Chekhov's plays to be performed in
English: the world première took place in 1909, at the Royalty
Theatre in Glasgow, directed by George Calderon, whose
translations of both *The Seagull* and *The Cherry Orchard* were
published in 1911. Since then, many of the most illustrious
names in British theatre have graced Chekhov's notoriously
demanding ensemble. In 1936, the cast of the New Theatre
production included Edith Evans as Arkadina, John Gielgud
as Trigorin, and the young Peggy Ashcroft as Nina. The latter
revisited *The Seagull* at the Queen's Theatre almost thirty years
later, in the role of Arkadina, with Vanessa Redgrave as Nina.
Vanessa Redgrave went on to play Arkadina in the same theatre
in 1985, with her daughter Natasha Richardson as Nina. Paul
Scofield and Mai Zetterling played Kostya and Nina, at the
Lyric Theatre Hammersmith in 1949, and a 1960 production
at the Old Vic featured Judith Anderson as Arkadina, and Tom
Courtenay as Kostya. *The Seagull* has also been adapted for
cinema, and Sidney Lumet's 1968 version starred James Mason
as Trigorin, and Simone Signoret as Arkadina.

Uncle Vanya **and** *The Wood Demon*

Chekhov's first success in the theatre was *Ivanov*, premièred in
Moscow on 4 November, 1887, and its morally inert idealist-
hero, who eventually shoots himself in despair, is a familiar

figure in the later plays. However, although *Ivanov* made enough of an impact to be taken up by the Alexandrinsky Theatre in St Petersburg the following year, Chekhov himself was unhappy with the play, which was frankly melodramatic – part of the reason for its success, no doubt – observing theatrical conventions he was soon to abandon.

It is with *The Wood Demon*, written in late 1889, that Chekhov attempts a new kind of drama, one in which the critical events take place offstage, while the characters get on with the humdrum business of living. *The Wood Demon* can now be seen as a transitional work, however, and its rejection by the Imperial theatres, before a Moscow actors' co-operative offered to produce it, was not entirely due to its innovative character, or the fact that it offended contemporary mores by its disrespectful treatment of a university professor. The Abramova Theatre production opened on 27 December, but by mid-January of 1890 it was already losing money, and was taken off. Chekhov was deeply disappointed, but in truth, the criticism of friend and foe alike, that *The Wood Demon* was a novel manqué, still holds good; a comparison with *Uncle Vanya* shows not only how much work remained to be done, but also how expertly Chekhov managed the task.

Chekhov, who once advised a novice writer to take a pair of scissors to the first and last paragraphs, sight unseen, of his short story, cut *The Wood Demon* with surgical precision, and the nature of the cuts is instructive. While almost every character in *Uncle Vanya* already figures in *The Wood Demon*, though Astrov and Vanya appear as Khrushchev and Uncle Georges, the earlier play has several additional roles, which function as virtual 'shadows' of Serebryakov, Sonya, Astrov, and Vanya himself. Chekhov's extra characters, the Zheltyukhins and the Orlovskys, thicken the play's texture, but they also blur its focus, and their excision streamlines the plot of *Uncle Vanya*, as does its revised setting, reduced from three different estates to one only, that of Serebryakov.

All the plot ingredients of *Uncle Vanya* are present in *The Wood Demon*: the conflict between Serebryakov and Vanya; the latter's infatuation with the Professor's young wife; Sonya's troubled love for the environmentalist-doctor; Yelena's coy interest in him. Much of the incident is also common to both plays: the doctor and Vanya engage in a dispute about forest conservation; Vanya makes a clumsy pass at Yelena; someone walks in on an apparent embrace; Serebryakov outlines his scheme to sell off the estate; Vanya exits in a rage, and an offstage pistol shot is heard. In fact, almost the entire content of Acts II and III of *Uncle Vanya* is recycled from *The Wood Demon*. The difference is that the sequence of events is now purposefully connected, and the obscuring detail cut away. In *The Wood Demon*, for example, it is the doctor, Khrushchev, and not Uncle Georges, who chances upon what he interprets as a lovers' tryst, but which is quite innocent, certainly on Yelena's part. However, Uncle Georges' suicidal depression, which culminates in the fatal pistol shot, is later revealed to have been partly fuelled by the slanderous rumours circulating about his relationship with the Professor's wife.

That revelation is made in Act IV of *The Wood Demon*, through a narrated account of the discovery of Uncle Georges' diary, and Chekhov would never again employ so transparently unconvincing a device. Given that Act III closes on a genuinely tragic note, the picnic atmosphere of Act IV is also discordant, and the formulaic happy ending, in which three couples are paired off or re-united, including Sonya and her 'wood demon' doctor, is almost farcical. Chekhov here is scarcely recognisable; indeed, this conclusion to the play is generally explained by the influence of Tolstoy. Almost the only enthusiast for *The Wood Demon* in Chekhov's own day was the Tolstoyan disciple Prince Urusov, who repeatedly urged him to publish it, regardless of its failure in the theatre. Chekhov's response, even ten years on, in a letter dated 16 October, 1899, could scarcely have been more emphatic:

> I can't publish *The Wood Demon*. I hate this play and I'm trying to forget it. Whether it's the fault of the piece itself, or the circumstances in which it was written and staged, I don't know, but it would be a real blow to me if it were somehow forcibly dragged into the light of day and revived.

The most penetrating critique of *The Wood Demon* is of course Chekhov's own, in the form of the great work which it eventually became. Among the more important changes, the 'reversal' of the interrupted embrace, in which it is now Vanya, clutching his peace-offering of autumn roses, who walks in on Astrov, is at once both comical, and inexpressibly poignant. The genius of the mature Chekhov is shown again in the scene of the offstage pistol shot. Given Vanya's state of mind, we have every reason to expect suicide, so that when he re-enters in pursuit of Serebryakov, the shock is palpable. In that context, Vanya's outburst of 'Bang! Missed? Missed again!?' is funny, of course, but painful to behold – the unedifying spectacle of a man so inept that not even a gun in his hand can give him an advantage.

Chekhov's most radical alteration, however, was to discard Act IV of *The Wood Demon* almost completely, and the new, much shorter Act IV of *Uncle Vanya* is a masterpiece of anti-climax. There is a reconciliation of sorts, but it is very far from Tolstoyan. Serebryakov and Yelena go off to continue their half-life in grimy Kharkov, while Vanya and Sonya undertake to slave for them as before, and the brief, tantalising glimmer of hope, or any prospect of change, is extinguished forever. Chekhov's Act IV is as close to music as drama gets, with its studied recapitulation of themes and sustained diminuendo. Sonya's long closing speech, consoling Vanya, and herself, with a vision of an after-life in which they will at last find rest, is like an aria, but it is sung to the accompaniment not only of Telegin's guitar, but also the nightwatchman's tapping, Marina's knitting-needles, and Maria Vasilievna's demented scribbling, as she annotates her absurd pamphlets, diluting any hope it offers.

Ironically, but for the persistence of Urusov, who appears to have been besotted by *The Wood Demon*, Chekhov might well have succeeded in trying to forget it; it is our great good fortune that he did not, and *Uncle Vanya* is perhaps the most concentrated of all his plays, with its arrow-straight plot, and emotional power.

Uncle Vanya in Performance

Chekhov published *Uncle Vanya* in a collection of his plays in 1897, but the invitation to submit it to the prestigious Maly Theatre did not come until February 1899. Meanwhile, it had been staged in a number of provincial towns, including Kiev, Odessa, and Tiflis, and been generally well received. When the script changes requested by the Maly authorities proved unacceptable, Stanislavsky and Nemirovich-Danchenko eagerly acquired the rights for the Moscow Art Theatre, and promised Chekhov it would be performed exactly as he had written it. This turned out to be less than the whole truth, and Stanislavsky indeed believed Chekhov to be a poor interpreter of his own works. Chekhov for his part thought Stanislavsky, in the role of Astrov, completely misunderstood the nature of his relationship with Yelena, and failed to convey his ironic detachment. The Moscow Art Theatre's obsession with naturalistic detail and sound effects also disturbed him, and while the introduction of live chickens, barking dogs, chirruping crickets, etc., could be classed as a minor irritant, Stanislavsky also added a piano duet for Yelena and Sonya, defeating Chekhov's purpose in the symbolism of the silent piano.

Chekhov's criticisms, however, tended to be expressed obliquely, and often in the form of costume notes – his insistence that Vanya should wear a silk necktie, for example, was a coded instruction on how the character should be played, that is, as an elegant, cultured man, not a stereotyped provincial. Chekhov also bore with some fortitude Stanislavsky's treatment of his dialogue, in which the effect of significant pauses, marked as such in the script, was diminished by the snail's-pace approach the Moscow Art Theatre believed his work required.

At any rate, *Uncle Vanya* opened in Moscow on 26 October, 1899, and although the production failed to repeat the success of *The Seagull*, it did well enough to interest the Alexandrinsky Theatre in St Petersburg. *Uncle Vanya* also remained a fixture in the Moscow Art Theatre repertoire until the late 1920s, when Chekhov's drama entered on a long period of neglect, falling as it did beyond the narrow ideological bounds of Socialist Realism. In 1958, the Moscow Art Theatre toured three major plays to the UK, including *Uncle Vanya*, which had a profound influence on later British productions. The Moscow Art Theatre also revisited *Uncle Vanya* in an important production by Oleg Yefremov in 1985. A filmed version of the play, directed by Andrei Konchalovsky in 1972, with Sergei Bondarchuk as Astrov, and Innokenty Smoktunovsky as Vanya, is regarded as one of the finest cinematic adaptations of Chekhov.

In the UK, the first English staging of *Uncle Vanya* at the Aldwych in 1914 was greeted with bewilderment for the most part, and it was not until 1926, with the emigré Fyodor Komissarzhevsky's production, that the play made any real impact on English audiences, though the emphasis was on the lachrymose, rather than the comic. *Uncle Vanya* was given another notable outing in 1945, by the Old Vic Company, with Laurence Olivier as Astrov, Margaret Leighton as Yelena, and Ralph Richardson as Vanya, but while the production was much admired, the star-studded cast apparently found it difficult to submerge themselves fully in Chekhov's demanding ensemble.

Olivier, again playing Astrov, directed a production for the
newly-founded National Theatre in 1963, with Michael
Redgrave as Vanya, and worthy of note also is the Royal Court
production of 1970, with Paul Scofield as Vanya and Colin
Blakely as Astrov. The UK première of *The Wood Demon*,
incidentally, was staged at the Arts Theatre, Cambridge, in
1973, with Ian McKellen as Khrushchev. Two major
productions of *Uncle Vanya* took place in 1982: at the National
Theatre, with Michael Bryant and Dinsdale Landen, and Cherie
Lunghi as Yelena, and at the Theatre Royal, Haymarket, with
Donald Sinden, Ronald Pickup, and Sheila Gish. More recently,
Mike Alfreds directed Ian McKellen as Vanya and Antony Sher
as Astrov, in a version by Pam Gems at the National Theatre in
1992, and Sam Mendes directed Simon Russell Beale as Vanya,
Mark Strong as Astrov, Helen McCrory as Yelena and Emily
Watson as Sonya in a version by Brian Friel at the Donmar in
2002. Chekhov's masterly exercise in recycling thus continues
to be an inexhaustible repertoire favourite.

Three Sisters in Performance

Chekhov describes *Three Sisters* as a 'drama', the only play he so
designates, and in a letter written soon after its completion, he
speaks of it having 'an atmosphere more gloomy than gloom
itself'. Its central theme, that of the creeping usurpation of the
Prozorovs' house and patrimony by Natasha, is prefigured in a
short story of 1899, 'In the Ravine', in which the lively and
industrious Aksinya eventually drives her husband's family out of
their own house, having earlier killed her sister-in-law's baby in
an act of casual savagery. Aksinya also has a long-running affair
with a local mill-owner, and there are enough other similiarities
between this grimly un-Tolstoyan peasant idyll and *Three Sisters*
to suggest that Chekhov was revisiting the subject for his first
Moscow Art Theatre commission.

Three Sisters is, however, a masterpiece of free-standing construction,
and even the most cursory inspection of its intricate mechanisms,
the complex interconnected lives of its ten major players, gives
the lie to the persistent notion that Chekhov's drama lacks plot.
In abstract terms, there is an element of folk-tale symmetry about
the play, and it is perhaps not too fanciful to extend this to a
crude typology of the sisters themselves – the solidly domestic
Olga, the sensual Masha, the virginal Irina – like facets of some
idealised Woman. These, and the relentless forward movement

of the play, as Natasha colonises room after room in the Prozorov house, furnish the scaffolding of *Three Sisters*, but Chekhov's is an art of concealment, such that we are aware only of the detail, the civilised table-talk for the most part, of a community in which onstage violence is represented by Natasha's rudeness to the servants, while Masha and Vershinin conduct their extra-marital indiscretions for the most part in discreet code.

Chekhov's declared intention was to banish 'drama' to the wings, and *Three Sisters* achieves this in more than the offstage pistol shot which wrecks Irina's hopes. Protopopov, for example, a prime mover in the sisters' downhill slide, appears only by passing mention – the absent cake-giver at Irina's name-day party, Natasha's gentleman caller in his waiting troika, and, when the usurpation is finally complete, little Sophie's putative father. Protopopov's cake, in the context of later developments, has a distinctly bitter aftertaste.

Likewise, in a play which repeatedly exposes the gap between the characters' pretensions and their true situation, the offstage presence of Vershinin's wife and daughters subtly undermines his credibility, though he is as much of a hero as the play can muster. Despite his charm, and the ringing optimism of his 'philosophising', the last word on Vershinin is not Masha's, but rather his own request to Olga, to watch over his emotional left luggage for a month or two, until he's settled into the next garrison town, with doubtless another flower-filled room in the offing.

Moreover, the telling contribution, in Chekhov's drama, of unseen characters is matched by that of unspoken lines and implicit connections. Tuzenbakh's final conversation with Irina, for example, is achingly incomplete, and not only because of what he must conceal. In a play which wears its plot lightly, there is scarcely a word or deed, however casual-seeming, that is not purposefully linked to another. Thus Natasha's grand design, mistress of all she surveys, to cut down the Prozorovs' cherished trees and plant flowers in their stead, recalls not only Tuzenbakh's emotional farewell to those same trees a short while before, but also Vershinin's first impressions of the Prozorov house, interior and exterior, at the beginning of the play.

Again, the sisters' unkind observations on Natasha's dress sense come full circle in the final act, when she repays the compliment to Irina. Much of our sympathy, indeed, is engaged by Irina, but she is a particular focus of Chekhov's irony, just as she most embodies the sisters' illusory hopes. Is it possible, for example, as she finally dedicates her life to teaching, that she can have forgotten her elder sister's experience?

In the light of later developments, the serial debate between the two amateur futurologists, Vershinin and Tuzenbakh, holds a particular fascination, and Chekhov has suffered from attempts to locate the author's voice in this work especially. On balance, if there is a message to be got from the *totality* of the play, as distinct from individual speeches, then that is most plausibly presented in Tuzenbakh's analysis of an existence whose laws we cannot fathom, and which will remain fundamentally unchanged, in all but the most superficial details.

That is not to deny hope, and indeed the very rhythms of Vershinin's great operatic arias surely convey the intensity of Chekhov's feeling. However, hope is not faith, and the author's belief (as articulated more reliably, perhaps, in his letters) is coloured by his own experience of the left and right ideologues of the day. Chekhov's vision, indeed, set out in a famous letter to the poet Pleshcheyev, of a Russia which, 'Beneath the banner of science, art and oppressed freedom of thought . . . will one day be ruled by toads and crocodiles, of a sort unknown even in Spain under the Inquisition . . . ' is infinitely more chilling than Tuzenbakh's 'fierce, cleansing wind', to which the twentieth century has supplied its own subtext. Tuzenbakh seeks salvation through toil in a brickworks, and Solzhenitsyn's first labour camp, at 'New Jerusalem' on the outskirts of Moscow, was a brickyard: an irony which he develops at some length in the second volume of the *Gulag Archipelago*.

Despite that, the experience of *Three Sisters* in the theatre is both intensely moving and uplifting. The sisters' closing speeches, however they may appear to be subverted by Chebutykin's killing indifference, represent a hymn to human endurance scarcely to be matched in the modern theatre. Of course we know that even if Chekhov's people were to achieve their hearts' desire, it would turn instantly to ashes. What model, for example, does he offer of domestic bliss that any of his characters, Natasha included, should even contemplate marriage? As for Andrei's academic yearnings, the career of Serebryakov, in *Uncle Vanya*, or the narrator's reflections in 'A Boring Story', hint at the likely outcome, in Chekhov's world, had Andrei satisfied that ambition.

The sisters' Moscow, the repository of all their hopes, is likewise a dream landscape, a symbol of the unattainable, and Irina's outburst, to the effect that there's no place like Moscow on this earth, is comical even without benefit of hindsight. Among the major characters, in fact, only the rapacious Natasha actually lives in the present, or realises her aims. She is happy and fulfilled, in the manner of a predatory animal sleeping off a successful kill on some featureless provincial prairie.

It is that very gulf, between aspiration and realisation, into which we pour our sympathy for Chekhov's often absurd characters; it is the piercing view he affords us of our own plight that moves us, and Stanislavsky's tears were scarcely out of place, even if the playing demands a healthy comic detachment. And in the long run, Chekhov's bleakest play still warms us with the consolation of love, the deep affection of the sisters, shining out like a beacon from the play's closing tableau.

Three Sisters remains one of the most popular plays in the classic repertoire, and benchmark productions include Sir Laurence Olivier's 1967 Old Vic National Theatre staging, with Robert Stephens, Derek Jacobi and Joan Plowright. Jonathan Miller's 1976 production for the National Theatre, with Janet Suzman and Nigel Davenport, was also widely acclaimed. A new version by Michael Frayn was premièred at the Manchester Royal Exchange in 1985, and directed by Caspar Wrede. Niamh Cusack, who played Irina in that production, reprised her role in an intriguing family affair at the Dublin Gate Theatre in 1990, when the three Cusack sisters, Sorcha, Niamh and Sinead, appeared onstage with their father, Cyril, as Chebutykin. More recently, two important productions were staged in 2003: at the Playhouse Theatre, directed by Michael Blakemore, with Kristen Scott Thomas as Masha, and at the National Theatre, in a version by Nicholas Wright, directed by Katie Mitchell. The translation published in this collection was first performed in 1995, by the Bristol Old Vic/Out of Joint company, directed by Max Stafford-Clark.

The Cherry Orchard in Performance

Like all Chekhov's major plays, *The Cherry Orchard* is constructed on a pattern of arrival – sojourn – departure: a newcomer or returning absentee enters a hitherto stable community, and brings about a series of changes, generally for the worse, in the characters' lives. In purely abstract terms, this pattern is at its most schematic in *The Cherry Orchard*: almost the whole of Act I is taken up with Ranevskaya's return; Act IV, perhaps fittingly in

Chekhov's last work, is one long process of leave-taking; and between these, Acts II and III are effectively static – no major plot developments, no significant shift in relationships.

The main event, of course, the enforced sale of Ranevskaya's estate, takes place offstage, and that gives the drama its forward movement, while the characters look on, for the most part helplessly. As the clock ticks down through the lazy summer months, they might be flippantly described as 'setting out the deck-chairs on the Titanic', but their apparent inertia, their failure either to understand their situation, or act purposefully to change it, is by turns tragic and funny, and this accounts both for the play's continuing fascination, and its chequered stage history.

The Cherry Orchard has more than its share of boisterous comedy, the kind of character and incident which was Chekhov's speciality in his early years, writing comic fillers for the Moscow papers. Yepikhodov, with his squeaky boots, choking down his cockroach-contaminated *kvas*; Simeonov-Pishchik, descended from Caligula's horse, foolhardy swallower of other people's pills; Charlotta Ivanovna, acrobat-ventriloquist-conjuror, whose little dog even eats nuts – more than in any other play, Chekhov peoples the stage with two-dimensional eccentrics. They engage our attention, but not our sympathies.

At a higher level of realisation, the undoubted suffering of the principals is muted by the same comic touch: Gaev, for example, is an important channel for the family's sense of loss, as their inheritance melts away, but his absurd obsession with billiards aligns him with the likes of Yepikhodov, while his rhetorical posturing tends to undermine him as a serious commentator – rather in the way that old Firs' ramblings obscure the truth in much of what he says. Lopakhin, moreover, though his back-ground gives him every right to do so, does not descend on Ranevskaya's estate like the wolf on the fold – this is no rapacious *arriviste*, like Natasha in *Three Sisters*, and such philistinism as he displays is counterposed to the pretensions of Trofimov, rather to Lopakhin's benefit. *The Cherry Orchard*'s only villain of sorts, barring the unseen Deriganov, whom Lopakhin outbids at the auction, is the obnoxious Yasha, too insignificant to cast much of a shadow.

Chekhov's treatment of the love interest in the play is especially noteworthy. In outline, *The Cherry Orchard* is as intricately choreographed as any of his works: Ranevskaya is pining for her worthless lover, whose name we never learn; Lopakhin, it is hinted, carries a torch for Ranevskaya, but is himself the object of Varya's affections, which he only half-heartedly returns; Anya and Trofimov are in love, beyond question, but their notions of the blessed state differ markedly; Yepikhodov loves Dunyasha, but her pretty head has been turned by the 'sophisticated' Yasha. In each case, the outcome is potentially tragic, but at the end of the play, Ranevskaya is returning to her lover, with enough money to ensure his loyalty, at least for a few months; Anya and Trofimov have yet to discover their profound incompatibility; the abandoned Dunyasha may well be pregnant, but that is purely speculation. The most painful rejection, Lopakhin's failure to propose to Varya at the crucial moment, is almost wordless, and one need only compare Vershinin's parting from Masha in *Three Sisters* to see how Chekhov lowers the emotional temperature here.

Chekhov's intentions in that regard may be illustrated by another comparison: the fierce Act III row between Trofimov and Ranevskaya over her decision to go back to her lover. The scene bears a close resemblance to the confrontation between Arkadina and Konstantin in Act III of *The Seagull*; yet where the latter ends in tearful reconciliation, Trofimov's stormy exit in *The Cherry Orchard* is followed by an offstage crash, and hoots of laughter, as he tumbles downstairs.

However, the comic texture of the play cannot disguise its tragic undertow; Chekhov's characters stand effectively as types for an entire society in transition, and no matter what temporary folly they may be engaged in, it is the passing of a world we are witnessing, the extinction of a species. In the finale of *Three Sisters*, when Natasha declares her intention to cut down an alley of fir-trees and plant flowers in their stead, it is the whim of one destructive individual; when Lopakhin's workers take the axe to the cherry orchard, it is the judgement of history.

In the light of the above, it is little wonder that Stanislavsky and Chekhov found themselves at odds as to how *The Cherry Orchard* was to be played. Indeed, from the very outset, Chekhov was at such pains to emphasise its comedic nature that one might imagine he had written a sequel to his one-act farce *The Bear*, but past experience with the Moscow Art Theatre had taught him which way Stanislavsky was likely to jump. He even advised the great actor-director to take the part of Lopakhin himself, perhaps to ensure that the play's positive elements got a fair hearing; Stanislavsky, however, played Gaev, and by all accounts moved the action at a snail's pace, to milk every drop of sympathy for these charming but feckless individuals.

In his letter of 10 April 1904, to Olga Knipper, Chekhov unequivocally rejects that interpretation: Stanislavsky and Nemirovich-Danchenko have got it wrong, he says, and it is quite clear that neither of them has read the play with due attention. Unfortunately, the Moscow Art Theatre's elegiac and lachrymose approach became the standard, and helped establish Chekhov as the sad-eyed chronicler of 'twilight Russia', which went some way to ensuring his relative neglect during the Soviet period. And not surprisingly, when *The Cherry Orchard* was revived in the 1930s, the focus was on Lopakhin, as the 'positive hero' demanded by Socialist Realism.

In England, George Bernard Shaw was an early convert to Chekhov, and his *Heartbreak House* (1917) pays direct homage to *The Cherry Orchard*. Between the wars, a series of important productions of the major plays was staged by Fyodor Komissarzhevsky, with distinguished casts including John Gielgud, Peggy Ashcroft, and Edith Evans; Tyrone Guthrie's 1933 production of *The Cherry Orchard*, which featured Charles Laughton as Lopakhin, also won considerable acclaim, although the Stanislavskian approach to the play has proved remarkably resilient. In more recent times, however, notable departures from the tradition include Richard Eyre's 1977 Nottingham Playhouse production, in which Trevor Griffiths's adaptation gave more authority to Trofimov, emphasising the class divisions among the characters. And though less occupied with social issues, Mike Alfreds' 1985 production for the National Theatre, with Ian McKellen as Lopakhin, attracted high praise for its freshness and balance.

Translating Chekhov

Literary Russian has undergone much less change since Chekhov's day than has English, and there is little justification for using a period style in translation, particularly with a writer whose declared aim was to bring conversation to the stage, the common speech of the educated classes of his day, uttered in more or less commonplace contexts. For ease of playing, I have also for the most part simplified the Russian polite mode of address, i.e., first name and patronymic, which English speakers sometimes find difficult. A guide to pronunciation of proper names appears at the end of the volume.

There follow some notes on particular problems thrown up by individual plays.

THE SEAGULL   Chekhov's plays are strewn with odd ends of song and poetry, and while these do not always furnish a sub-text, they are important for the atmosphere of the scene, and often as markers of the character's state of mind. *The Seagull* has fewer of these lyrical inserts than other of his works, but they perhaps need some comment. Thus, in Act I, Sorin exits singing 'Die beiden Grenadiere', Schumann's setting of a poem by Heine, which presents two French grenadiers, survivors of the 1812 retreat from Moscow, lamenting Napoleon's defeat and capture. The Schumann ballad was a parlour warhorse in its day, and for Sorin to sing it as the curtain is about to rise on Kostya's play suggests that his audience isn't wholly attuned to 'new forms'.

Later in the same act, Dr Dorn sings snatches of two now-forgotten Russian ballads, one a setting of a poem by Nekrasov, and while their relevance may be obscure, the effect, in a scene in which Polina reveals their long-standing relationship, is to underline Dorn's casual treatment of her, and his general all-round insouciance. In Act II, likewise, his quotation of Ziebel's aria from Gounod's *Faust*: 'Oh, speak to her, my flowers . . . ' prefigures Polina's tearing up the flowers he has just been given by Nina, in a fit of jealous pique. Dr Dorn also breaks into song in Act IV, with a serenade by Shilovsky, and it is again arguably a device to suggest his emotional detachment from the turmoil going on around him.

The Seagull also features some extended literary quotation, and in Act II, Arkadina's reading from Maupassant's book of travel sketches, *Sur l'eau*, has obvious relevance to her relationship with Trigorin. Likewise the quotation from Shakespeare, in which Hamlet confronts Gertrude in her bedchamber, is a thematic echo of Kostya's own situation, as he perceives it, and at least one critic describes him as: 'this Hamlet of the steppes'. Nina's little medallion, with which she offers her life to Trigorin, bears what is in fact a twice-coded message, linked to an intriguing relationship between Chekhov himself, and a certain Lydia Avilova. The details can be found in any good biography, but the engraved lines are taken from Chekhov's short story *Neighbours* of 1892. And Trigorin's technique for imaging a moonlit night, which Kostya glumly envies in Act IV, is put to work by Chekhov in his own short story *The Wolf*, of 1886. In passing, Shamraev's Latin tag in Act I: *De gustibus aut bene aut nihil* is an absurd conflation of *De gustibus non est disputandum*, and *De mortuis, aut bene aut nihil* – what Shamraev in effect says, is: 'If you can't say anything good about taste, say nothing!'

Finally, Chekhov had some difficulty with the censor over the text of *The Seagull* for its first production, and a number of lines in Acts I and III, making plain Kostya's awareness of his mother's relationship with Trigorin, had to be altered. These have been restored in line with Chekhov's first thought in the most recent Russian edition of his Collected Works, and are accordingly included here.

UNCLE VANYA   In comparison with *The Seagull, Uncle Vanya* is notably sparing in its use of quotation, and the only song, as distinct from the music here and there supplied by Telegin's guitar, is an absurd little folk ditty on a hearth and home theme, of no apparent significance, ventured by the drunken Astrov in Act Two. Rather more pointedly, in his opening salvo against the pretensions of Serebryakov, Vanya quotes a few lines of a late 18th-century satire by Ivan Dmitriev, attacking the second-rate poets of the day, who 'write and write and write' to no good purpose. And although scholarship is discussed at some length in the play, only two Latin tags are cited – Astrov's *quantum satis*, 'as much as I need', referring to his sleep requirements, in Act One, and the Professor's quotation from Horace, *Manet omnes una nox*, 'One night (i.e., death) awaits us all', decorating the Act Three exposition of his plans for the estate, which also opens with a ponderous reference to the Mayor's speech in Gogol's *Government Inspector*, in a vain attempt to lighten the atmosphere. Elsewhere, there are passing mentions of Ostrovsky, the great realist playwright of the generation before Chekhov's, and of Dostoevsky and Schopenhauer, and also the painter Aivazovsky, though the latter, famed for his sea-battles, is scarcely the ideal interpreter of the previous day's domestic uproar, as Telegin fatuously suggests at the beginning of Act Four. In the Russian, Telegin's conversation is also occasionally marked by the use of '-s', an obsolete form of respectful address, tacked on to the end of certain words, and underlining his status as permanent house-guest and general dogsbody. Furthermore, while university professors in Chekhov's day were entitled to be called 'Your Excellency', it is significant that only Telegin addresses Serebryakov so without irony.

THREE SISTERS   Chekhov's occasional use of snatches of song
and poetry here warrants special mention. Thus, in Act One,
Masha quotes the opening lines of the prologue to Pushkin's
mock-heroic poem 'Ruslan and Lyudmila', familiar to every
educated Russian: 'By a curving shore stands a green oak tree/
Hung with a golden chain . . . ' The unspoken next line of
Pushkin's poem introduces a learned cat, doubtless a concealed
ironic hit at Kulygin, and Masha's marital fetters, but she does
not refer to the cat until Act Four, and then only in a garbled
form.

Soliony's lines: 'Before he had time to gasp/The bear had him
in its grasp . . . ' come from a fable by the Russian Aesop, Ivan
Krylov, titled 'The Peasant and the Workman', and in Act
Three, Soliony again quotes Krylov: 'This moral I might make
more clear/But that would vex the geese, I fear', from his fable
'The Geese'. Soliony's lines in Act Two: 'I am strange, but who
is not? Be not angry, Aleko!', and 'Forget, forget thy dreams!',
roll together a quotation from Griboyedov's verse comedy *Woe
from Wit*, and a reference to the hero of Pushkin's poem, 'The
Gipsies', although not a direct quotation. The Captain's pretensions as a latter-day Lermontov incline him to utterances of this
kind, and he aptly dramatises his own exit to fight the duel with
the concluding lines of Lermontov's poem 'The Sail': 'But he,
rebellious, seeks the storm/As if in storms lay peace . . . '
Pushkin's *Eugene Onegin*, or rather the Tchaikovsky libretto, is the
source of Vershinin's lines, 'To Love all ages humbly bow/Her
promptings do each heart endow', sung in the opera by
Gremin, celebrating love in the autumn of one's life.

Chebutykin is also much given to quoting snatches of song, and
his lines: 'For love alone did Nature/Bring us forth upon this
earth', in Act One, and 'Oh, lady, please accept this fruit', ('date'
in the Russian) in Act Three, derive from forgotten operettas.
His insouciant 'Ta-ra-ra-boom-dee-ay' in Act Four tempts the
translator with a second line, which means literally 'I'm sitting
on a kerbstone', but it's perhaps best simply repeated, as in the
original song. Near the end of Act Two, Tuzenbakh, Chebutykin
and Andrei join in a traditional folk ditty about a new
maplewood porch, difficult to translate, and impossible to sing,
and I have left it as a stage direction. The bizarre exchange in
the same act, over Chebutykin's meal of 'chekhartmà', which
Soliony wilfully mishears as 'cheremshà', might have come from
Ionesco, but the Caucasian words mean what each claims, and
are as exotic in Russian as they are in English.

THE CHERRY ORCHARD   *The Cherry Orchard* is notable for the
wide spectrum of social classes represented on stage, and
Chekhov naturally characterises these by speech, ranging very
approximately from Anya at the upper end, to old Firs at the
bottom, with a fair degree of confusion in between, e.g., in the
affectations of the servants Yasha and Dunyasha. Chekhov also
employs speech mannerisms as a kind of nervous tic, for comic
purposes, in the clichéd repetitions of Simeonov-Pishchik, or
Gaev's billiards jargon, or the bookish excesses of Yepikhodov.
Any translator must reconcile these with a consistent 'voice' for
the play as a whole, and this I have attempted to do.

One or two oddities are perhaps worth remark: Charlotta
Ivanovna very occasionally lapses into 'Germanic' syntax, notably
in her little ventriloquial discourse in Act III. And when Lopakhin
quotes *Hamlet* in Act II, addressing Varya as 'Okhmelia', he is
almost certainly making an untranslatable pun, on the Russian
verb '*okhmelet*', meaning 'to become tipsy'. In fact, there are very
few quotations in *The Cherry Orchard*, and Chekhov's comic
purposes seem not to have included the snatches of song and
verse often found in the earlier plays. Exceptions are the couple
of lines uttered by the drunken vagrant in Act II, taken from
the 'socially aware' poets Nadson and Nekrasov. Finally,
Chekhov's Act III stage direction requires the stationmaster to
begin reciting Aleksei Tolstoy's long Biblical poem *The Sinner*
(1857), the story of Christ's conversion of a sinful woman,
during a banquet at a wealthy merchant's house. Roughly
translated, the first few lines are as follows:

> A throng of people, merrily laughing,
> The sound of lutes, of cymbals crashing,
> Palm leaves and flowers all around;
> Betwixt the pillars, richly draped,
> The portals bear a heavy weight
> Of finely patterned silk brocade;
> The chamber, gorgeously attired,
> With gold and crystal seems afire . . .

Chekhov: Key Dates

1860   Born 17 January in Taganrog, a port on the Sea of Azov.

1875   Father's grocery business fails, family flees to Moscow, leaving Chekhov behind.

1879   Completes his education at the local high school, and sets off for Moscow, to enter the Medical Faculty of Moscow University.

1880   First comic story published in 'The Dragonfly', a St Petersburg weekly.

1884   Graduates from University, begins medical practice in Moscow. First symptoms of tuberculosis.

1885   Contributes short stories to the 'St Petersburg Gazette' and 'New Time'.

1886   First collection: *Motley Tales*.

1887   Second collection: *In the Twilight*. First performance of *Ivanov* at Korsh's Theatre, Moscow, 19 November.

1888   First major story, *The Steppe*, published in the 'Northern Herald'. Awarded Pushkin Prize for Literature, by the Imperial Academy of Sciences.

1889   First performance of *The Wood Demon* at Abramov's Theatre, Moscow.

1890   Travels across Siberia to carry out research on the penal colony of Sakhalin Island.

1896   Disastrous first performance of *The Seagull*, at the Aleksandrinsky Theatre in St Petersburg, 17 October.

1898   Begins association with the Moscow Art Theatre. Worsening tuberculosis forces him to move to Yalta. On 17 December, first successful performance of *The Seagull*, by the Moscow Art Theatre.

Further Reading

Among the several biographies of Chekhov, Ronald Hingley's *A New Life of Chekhov*, Oxford University Press, 1976, is outstanding not only for its wealth of detail, but also the care the author takes to disentangle the man from the work. Other useful sources include Henry J. Simmons' *Chekhov*, University of Chicago Press, 1962, and Donald Rayfield's *Anton Chekhov*, Harper Collins, 1997. Maurice Valency's *The Breaking String*, Oxford University Press, 1966, and David Magarshack's *The Real Chekhov*, George Allen & Unwin, 1972, remain among the most readable studies of the plays, while Harvey Pitcher's *The Chekhov Play: a new interpretation*, Chatto and Windus, 1973 is also worth tracking down. Nick Worrall's contribution to Methuen's Writer-Files series: *File on Chekhov*, Methuen, 1986, is both a compact introduction to Chekhov's theatre, and a handy source of review material. *Anton Chekhov Rediscovered*, edited by Senderovich and Sendich, Russian Language Journal, 1987, includes a bibliography of works in English relating to Chekhov, and *A Chekhov Companion*, edited by Toby W. Clyman, Greenwood Press, 1985, contains useful articles on themes ranging from social conditions in late 19th-century Russia, to the critical tradition, both native and Western. Chekhov's reception in the West, over the period roughly 1900-1945, is also documented in detail by Viktor Emeljanow, in *Chekhov, the Critical Heritage*, Routledge & Kegan Paul, 1981. Patrick Miles' excellent *Chekhov on the British Stage*, Cambridge University Press, 1993, is a collection of essays by several hands, accompanied by a chronology of British productions of Chekhov up to 1991. Also recommended are Richard Peace's *Chekhov: a Study of the Four Major Plays*, Yale University Press, 1983, and Laurence Senelick's *The Chekhov Theatre – a Century of the Plays in Performance*, Cambridge University Press, 1997.

THE SEAGULL

Dramatis Personae

ARKADINA, Irina Nikolaevna, *an actress*

KOSTYA, Konstantin Gavrilovich Treplev, *her son*

SORIN, Pyotr Nikolaevich, *her brother*

NINA, Nina Mikhailovna Zarechnaya, *daughter of a wealthy landowner*

SHAMRAEV, Ilya Afanasyevich, *a retired lieutenant, Sorin's estate manager*

POLINA Andreevna, *his wife*

MASHA, *his daughter*

TRIGORIN, Boris Alekseevich, *a writer*

DORN, Yevgeny Sergeevich, *a doctor*

MEDVEDENKO, Semyon Semyonovich, *a schoolmaster*

YAKOV, *a workman*

COOK

MAID

The action takes place on Sorin's estate.
There is an interval of two years between Acts III and IV.

For a Guide to Pronunciation of Names, see page 279.

ACT ONE

A section of the park on SORIN's *estate. A broad avenue leads away from the audience towards a lake in the background. The avenue is screened off by a makeshift stage, for amateur theatricals, obscuring the view of the lake. There are bushes on either side of the stage. A few chairs, and a small table.*

The sun has just set. YAKOV *and some other workmen are busy behind the stage curtain; sounds of coughing and hammering.* MASHA *and* MEDVEDENKO *enter left, returning from a walk.*

MEDVEDENKO. Why do you always wear black?

MASHA. I'm in mourning for my life. I'm unhappy.

MEDVEDENKO. Why? (*Thinking it over.*) I don't understand it. You're in good health, your father might not be rich, but he's comfortably off. My life's much harder than yours. I earn a measly twenty-three roubles a month, and there's superannuation to come off that, but you don't see me in mourning.

They sit down.

MASHA. It's not a question of money. Even a pauper can be happy.

MEDVEDENKO. Yes, in theory, but in practice it's a different story. I've got my mother, two sisters, and a younger brother to support, all on a salary of twenty-three roubles. And we need to eat and drink, don't we? We need tea and sugar, right? Tobacco? Things are tight, I don't mind telling you.

MASHA (*looking round at the stage*). They'll be starting the play soon.

MEDVEDENKO. Yes. Nina's going to be in it, and Kostya's written it. They're in love with one another, and tonight their souls will merge to create a single, unified work of art. But between your soul and mine there's no such point of contact. I love you, I can't sit at home because I miss you so much. I walk four miles here every day and four miles back, and I meet with nothing but indifference on your part. Well, that's understandable. I've no money, we have a large family. Who'd want to marry a man who can't even feed himself?

MASHA. Oh, that's rubbish. (*Takes a pinch of snuff.*) I'm really quite touched by your affection, I just can't return it, that's all. (*Offers him the snuff-box.*) Have some.

MEDVEDENKO. No, thanks.

A pause.

MASHA. It's very close, there's going to be thunder tonight. You're always droning on about something – either that or complaining about money. You think there's no greater unhappiness than poverty, but the way I see it, it's a thousand times better to go about in rags and beg for your living, than to . . . Oh, you wouldn't understand.

SORIN *and* KOSTYA *enter right.*

SORIN (*leaning on his walking-stick*). No, country life just doesn't suit me, old chap, and I'll never get used to it now, that's obvious. I went to bed last night at ten, and woke up this morning at nine, with the distinct feeling my brains were glued to my skull, after all that sleeping. (*Laughs.*) And I dozed off again by chance after lunch, so now I'm completely wrecked, it's a nightmare, all things considered.

KOSTYA. Yes, you certainly ought to live in town. (*Catching sight of* MASHA *and* MEDVEDENKO.) Excuse me – you'll be called when it's due to begin, but you can't stay here just now. Please go away.

SORIN (*to* MASHA). Masha dear, if you'd be so kind – ask your father to let the dog off its chain, to stop it howling. My sister didn't get a wink of sleep again last night.

MASHA. You can speak to my father yourself, I shan't. Leave me out of it, please. (*To* MEDVEDENKO.) Come on, let's go.

MEDVEDENKO (*to* KOSTYA). You'll send somebody to tell us when it's ready, won't you?

They exit.

SORIN. That means that dog's going to be howling all night again. Anyway, as I was saying, I've never lived in the country, the way I'd like to. I used to take a month's leave, come down here for a rest, that sort of thing, but they'd start plaguing you with all manner of nonsense, you'd feel like clearing off the first day. (*Laughs.*) Yes, I was always glad to leave. Well, now I'm retired and I don't know what to do with myself, by and large. Still, got to put up with it.

YAKOV (*to* KOSTYA). Sir, we're going for a swim now.

KOSTYA. Fine, just make sure you're back here in ten minutes. (*Looks at his watch.*) We'll be starting soon.

YAKOV. Right, sir. (*Exits.*)

KOSTYA (*looking over at the stage*). Now, this is what you call a theatre. A curtain, a wing at either side, and open space beyond. No scenery whatsoever. A view straight onto the lake and the horizon. We'll raise the curtain at exactly half-past eight, when the moon comes up.

SORIN. Splendid.

KOSTYA. Of course, if Nina's late, it'll spoil the whole effect. She ought to be here by now. Her father and stepmother keep her on such a tight rein, slipping out of the house is like breaking out of prison. (*Fixes his uncle's tie.*) Your hair and beard are a mess. You should have them trimmed, honestly . . .

SORIN (*combing his beard*). That's the story of my life. Even when I was young I looked as if I drank like a fish. Never had any luck with the ladies, either. (*Sitting down.*) So, why is your mother in such a mood?

KOSTYA. Why? She's bored. (*Sits beside him.*) And she's jealous. She's got it in for me to start with – and the performance, and my play – because that writer of hers might take a fancy to Nina. She doesn't even know the piece, but she hates it already.

SORIN (*laughs*). Oh, come on, you're imagining things . . .

KOSTYA. No no, she's annoyed because it'll be Nina who gets all the applause on this tiny little stage, and not her. (*Glances at his watch.*) She's a psychologist's dream, my mother. She's talented all right, she's intelligent, she'll weep buckets over some book, and reel off the whole of Nekrasov by heart. Oh yes, she'll tend the sick like a ministering angel, but you just let her hear you praising Eleanora Duse. Oh, no. You must worship her alone, she's the only one you can write or shout about – you've got to go into ecstasies over her wonderful acting in *The Lady of the Camellias* or *The Fumes of Life*. Well, there's none of that intoxicating brew here in the country, so she becomes bored and irritable, and we're all her enemies, it's all our fault. She's superstitious, too – terrified if she sees three candles, or the number thirteen. And she's miserly. She's got seventy thousand in a bank in Odessa, I know that for a fact. But you ask her for a loan, and she bursts into tears.

SORIN. You've got it into your head that your mother won't like your play, that's what's really bothering you. Oh, come on – your mother adores you.

KOSTYA (*pulling the petals off a flower*). She loves me – she loves me not, she loves me – she loves me not, she loves me – she loves me not. (*Laughs.*) You see? My mother doesn't love me. No wonder. She wants to live, have affairs, wear bright clothes, and I'm twenty-five already, a constant reminder to her that she's no longer young. She's thirty-two when I'm not here, and forty-three when I am, that's why she hates me. And she knows I've no time for the theatre. She loves the theatre, she thinks she's serving humanity, a sacred art, but as far as I'm concerned the theatre of today's stuck in a rut, boring and conventional.

When the curtain goes up on that room with its three
walls, and its artificial light, and we see those great
geniuses, those high priests of the sacred art, miming how
people eat, drink, make love, walk, wear their jackets –
when they try to fish some sort of moral out of the most
banal scenes and lines, some pathetic reach-me-down
maxim that'll come in handy around the house – when
they serve up the same thing over and over again, in a
hundred-and-one variations – well, I just take to my heels,
the way Maupassant fled from the Eiffel Tower, which
weighed down his brain with its sheer vulgarity.

SORIN. We can't do without the theatre.

KOSTYA. It's new forms we need. We need new forms of
theatre, and if we can't have them, we'd be better off with
nothing. (*Looks at his watch.*) I love my mother, I love her
very much, but look at her: smoking, drinking, living in
sin with that writer of hers, her name constantly bandied
about in the papers – I find that all so tiresome. Sometimes
I feel a twinge of selfishness, like any ordinary mortal, and
I actually regret having a famous actress for a mother –
I think I'd be much happier if she were just an ordinary
woman. I mean, can you imagine a more desperate situation? It's so stupid. She'd be entertaining, a whole room
full of celebrities, actors and writers, and I'd be stuck in
the middle of them, an utter nonentity, tolerated only
because I'm her son. Who am I? What am I? I left
university in third year, due to circumstances beyond our
control, as they say, with no talents of any kind, and not a
kopeck to my name. My passport says I'm a tradesman,
from Kiev. That was my father's official status, though he
was also a famous actor. Anyway, when all those actors and
writers in her drawing-room deigned to notice me, I'd feel
they were simply taking stock of my insignificance – I
could read their minds, and I suffered terrible humiliation.

SORIN. By the way, what sort of chap is this writer of hers?
I can't make him out. He never opens his mouth.

KOSTYA. He's intelligent and unassuming, a bit on the
melancholy side, in fact. A decent type. He's still some

way off forty, but he's already famous, and doing rather
nicely, thank you. These days he drinks nothing but beer,
and goes in for older women. As for his writing, well,
what can I say? It's charming, clever . . . but after Tolstoy
or Zola, you won't feel like reading Trigorin.

SORIN. You know, I'm rather fond of writers. Two things I
used to be absolutely passionate about: I wanted to get
married, and I wanted to be a writer, but I didn't manage
either. Yes. Must be nice to be even a minor writer, all
things considered.

KOSTYA (*listening*). I hear footsteps . . . (*Flings his arms round*
SORIN.) I just can't live without her . . . Even the sound
of her footsteps is beautiful. I feel deliriously happy.
(*Rushes to meet* NINA, *as she enters*.) Oh, my enchantress, my
dream . . .

NINA (*agitated*). I'm not late, am I? I can't be.

KOSTYA (*kissing her hands*). No, of course not.

NINA. I've been worried the whole day, it's been dreadful! I
was so afraid father wouldn't let me come, but he's gone
out now with my stepmother. The sky was red, and the
moon was already rising, I had to ride like the wind,
honestly. (*Laughs.*) I'm so glad I've made it. (*Warmly shakes*
SORIN's *hand.*)

SORIN (*laughs*). Looks as though you've been crying, too.
Dear me – that'll never do!

NINA. It's all right. Look at me, I'm completely out of
breath. And I'll have to leave in half an hour, we'd better
hurry. I can't stay, I really can't, please don't keep me
back. Father doesn't know I'm here.

KOSTYA. Actually, it's time we got started. We'll have to go
and call everybody.

SORIN. I'll go, I'll go. This very minute. (*Makes to exit right,*
singing Schubert's 'Die beiden Grenadiere'. Turns to look round.)
You know, I started singing like that once, and a colleague
of mine, the public prosecutor, said to me: 'You have
a powerful voice, Your Excellency.' Then he thought for

a minute and added: 'But not a very good one!' (*Exits laughing*).

NINA. My father and stepmother won't let me come here. They say you're all bohemians, and they're afraid I might go on the stage. Even so, I feel drawn to this lake, like a seagull . . . I've quite lost my heart to you. (*Looks round.*)

KOSTYA. We're alone now.

NINA. There's somebody there . . .

KOSTYA. It's nobody. (*They kiss.*)

NINA. What sort of tree's that?

KOSTYA. It's an elm.

NINA. Why is it so dark?

KOSTYA. It's evening, everything's getting dark. Don't leave early, please.

NINA. I've got to.

KOSTYA. Well, what if I come over to your house, Nina? I'll stand in the garden the whole night, gazing up at your window.

NINA. You can't, the watchman would see you. Trésor's still not used to you, and he'd start barking.

KOSTYA. I love you.

NINA. Ssshh!

KOSTYA (*hearing footsteps*). Who's there? Yakov, is that you?

YAKOV (*from behind the stage*). Yes, sir.

KOSTYA. Everyone get into position. It's time. Is the moon coming up?

YAKOV. Yes, sir.

KOSTYA. Have you got the methylated spirits? What about the sulphur? There has to be a smell of sulphur, when the red eyes appear. (*To* NINA.) Off you go, everything's ready back there. Feeling nervous?

NINA. Yes, very. Your mother's all right, I'm not frightened of her, but Trigorin's here. I'll feel terribly embarassed, acting in front of him. A famous writer! Is he quite young?

KOSTYA. Yes.

NINA. He writes such wonderful stories!

KOSTYA (*coldly*). I wouldn't know, I've never read them.

NINA. You know, it's quite difficult acting in your play. There aren't any real people in it.

KOSTYA. Real people! We've got to represent life not how it is, but how it should be, the way it appears in our dreams.

NINA. There's not enough action in it, it's all just speeches. And I think there really ought to be some love interest in a play . . .

They both exit behind the stage. Enter POLINA *and* DOCTOR DORN.

POLINA. It's getting damp. You should go back and put your galoshes on.

DORN. I'm too hot.

POLINA. You don't look after yourself. It's sheer obstinacy. You're a doctor, you know perfectly well damp air's bad for you, but you want to make me suffer. You sat out on the terrace the whole evening yesterday quite deliberately.

DORN (*sings*). 'Oh, never say thy youth was ruined . . . '

POLINA. You were so taken up with Madame Arkadina . . . you didn't even notice the cold. Now, admit it, you're quite fond of her, aren't you.

DORN. I'm fifty-five.

POLINA. What of it? That's not old for a man. You're extremely well preserved, women still find you attractive.

DORN. So what would you have me do?

POLINA. You're all dying to bow down and worship the great actress – you're all the same!

DORN (*sings*). 'Once more I stand before thee . . . ' Yes, people in this world do admire actors and actresses. They treat them quite differently from shopkeepers, for example, – that's in the nature of things. It's called idealism.

POLINA. And women were forever falling in love with you, and running after you. Was that idealism too?

DORN. Who cares? There was a lot of good in what women felt for me. I was a first-rate physician, that's the main reason they loved me. Ten, fifteen years ago, if you remember, I was the only decent obstetrician in this entire province. Besides which, I've always dealt honestly with them.

POLINA (*takes his hand*). My dearest!

DORN. Ssshh. They're coming.

Enter ARKADINA, *on* SORIN's *arm, with* TRIGORIN, SHAMRAEV, MEDVEDENKO, *and* MASHA.

SHAMRAEV. She gave a wonderful performance in '73, at the Poltava Fair. An absolute triumph. Superb acting. You wouldn't happen to know what became of that comic actor Chadin, Pavel Chadin? He was marvellous as Rasplyuev, even better than Sadovsky, dear lady, I swear. Where is he now?

ARKADINA. You keep asking about all these old has-beens. How should I know? (*Sits down.*)

SHAMRAEV (*sighs*). Yes, the great Pavel Chadin. You don't get actors like that nowadays. Theatre's not what it used to be, dear lady. Used to be mighty oak-trees, now we see nothing but stumps.

DORN. It's true, there isn't much real talent around, but your average actor's distinctly improved.

SHAMRAEV. I can't agree. Still, it's a matter of taste. *De gustibus aut bene, aut nihil.*

KOSTYA *emerges from behind the stage.*

ARKADINA (*to her son*). Kostya darling, when is it going to begin?

KOSTYA. In a minute. Please be patient.

ARKADINA (*recites from 'Hamlet'*).
O Hamlet! Speak no more:
Thou turn'st mine eyes into my very soul;
And there I see such black and grainèd spots
As will not leave their tinct.

KOSTYA (*from 'Hamlet'*).
Nay, but to live
In the rank sweat of an enseamèd bed,
Stew'd in corruption, honeying and making love
Over the nasty sty . . .

A horn is sounded behind the stage.

Ladies and gentlemen! We are about to commence – your attention, please!

A pause.

I shall begin. (*Taps with a stick and recites in a loud voice.*) O honoured shades of yore, that hover nightly o'er this lake, lull us to sleep, that we may dream of what will be, two hundred thousand years from now!

SORIN. Two hundred thousand years from now there'll be nothing.

KOSTYA. Then let them show us that nothing.

ARKADINA. Yes, let them. We're asleep anyway.

The curtain rises, to reveal a view of the lake. The moon is above the horizon, reflected in the water. NINA *is seated on a large stone, dressed all in white.*

NINA. Men, lions, eagles and partridges, the antlered deer, geese, spiders, silent fish that roam the deep, the starfish and all creatures unseen by the eye – in brief, all life, all living things, their mournful cycle ended, are extinct. For many thousand years, the earth has borne no living creature, and in vain does this poor moon now light its lamp. No longer does the meadow crane awaken with a cry, the may-bug in the lime grove hums no more. Cold, cold, cold. Empty, empty, empty. Terrible, terrible, terrible.

A pause.

The bodies of all living things have turned to dust, Eternal Matter has transmuted them to stone, to water, clouds, their spirits all are merged into one. I am that Universal Spirit, I . . . In me are met the souls of Alexander, Caesar, Shakespeare and Napoleon – and the vilest leech. In me the thoughts of men are blended with the instincts of the beasts, and I remember all things, all, each life within myself I live anew.

Will-o'-the-wisps appear.

ARKADINA (*sotto voce*). This is some sort of avant-garde piece.

KOSTYA (*reproachfully*). Mother!

NINA. I am alone. Once in a hundred years I open my mouth to speak, my voice sounds doleful in this void, and no-one hears . . . You too, pale fires, you hear me not . . . Born of the rotting marsh before first light, you wander aimlessly till dawn, without a thought, without free will, without the quivering of life. And fearing lest you bring forth life, the Devil, father of Eternal Matter, causes in you at each moment, as in stones and water, interchange of atoms, endless flux. In all the universe, one spirit only stands unchanged, immutable.

A pause.

Like a prisoner, flung into a deep and empty well, I know not where I am or what awaits me. All things are hidden from me save my destiny, in stubborn, bitter conflict, to defeat the Devil, prime agent of material force, then matter shall with spirit merge in perfect harmony, and Universal Will begin his reign. But this shall only come to pass when step by step, through many long millennia, this moon, bright Sirius and earth shall turn to dust . . . Until that day, oh, horror, horror . . .

A pause. Against the background of the lake, two red eyes appear.

Behold, my mighty enemy the Devil comes. I see his fearsome, blood-red eyes . . .

ARKADINA. There's a smell of sulphur. Is that intentional?

KOSTYA. Yes.

ARKADINA (*laughs*). Quite an effect.

KOSTYA. Mother!

NINA. He wearies without man . . .

POLINA (*to* DORN). You've taken your hat off. Put it on again before you catch cold.

ARKADINA. The doctor's taken off his hat to the Devil, the father of Eternal Matter.

KOSTYA (*flaring up, loudly*). Right, the play's over! That's enough! Drop the curtain!

ARKADINA. What are you so angry about?

KOSTYA. That's enough! Curtain! Drop the curtain! (*Stamping his foot.*) Curtain!

The curtain is lowered.

I'm sorry! It quite slipped my mind that only a select few are allowed to write plays and perform on the stage. I've broken their monopoly! I . . . I . . . (*He is about to say something, waves his hand dismissively and exits left.*)

ARKADINA. What's the matter with him?

SORIN. Irina my dear, that's not how to deal with a young man's *amour propre.*

ARKADINA. What did I do?

SORIN. You hurt his feelings.

ARKADINA. He told us himself it was a joke, so I treated his play as a joke.

SORIN. All the same . . .

ARKADINA. And now it turns out he's written a great work of art! Well, honestly! So, he's put on this performance and practically choked us all with sulphur, not for fun, but as some sort of protest. He wants to teach us how to write, and how to act. Well, this is becoming a bore. These constant sideswipes at me, these pinpricks of his, say what you like, they'd get on anyone's nerves. He's a headstrong, arrogant boy.

SORIN. He only wanted to please you.

ARKADINA. Really? Then why didn't he choose some normal play, instead of forcing us to sit through this Symbolist rubbish? I don't mind listening to rubbish for a laugh, but this claims to present new forms, a new era in art. Frankly, I don't think there are any new forms on display here, only bad temper.

TRIGORIN. People write what they want to, what they're capable of.

ARKADINA. Well, he can do likewise, as long as he leaves me in peace.

DORN. Jupiter, thou art angry . . .

ARKADINA. I'm not Jupiter, I'm a woman. (*Lights up a cigarette.*) And I'm not angry, I'm just annoyed that a young man should be wasting his time like that. I didn't mean to offend him.

MEDVEDENKO. No-one has any real grounds for separating spirit from matter — quite possibly, the spirit itself is a combination of material atoms. (*Animatedly, to* TRIGORIN.) You know, somebody ought to write a play about the life of a schoolmaster, put it on the stage. It's a hard life, I can tell you.

ARKADINA. No doubt it is, but let's have no more talk of plays, or atoms. Oh, it's such a glorious evening! Listen, everybody, isn't that someone singing? (*Listens.*) How lovely!

POLINA. It's coming from the other side of the lake.

A pause.

ARKADINA (*to* TRIGORIN). Sit down beside me. You know, ten or fifteen years ago there would be music and singing here on this lake, without fail, almost every evening. There are six different estates round its shores. I remember the laughter, the noise, the shooting, oh, and the endless love affairs. The romantic lead in those days, the idol of all those estates, was a certain young – allow me to introduce him (*Nods towards* DORN.) – Doctor Yevgeny Dorn. He's charming even now, but back then he was utterly irresistible. Actually, my conscience is beginning to bother me. Why did I hurt my poor boy's feelings? I'm really quite worried. (*Loudly.*) Kostya! Kostya darling!

MASHA. I'll go and have a look for him.

ARKADINA. If you would, my dear.

MASHA (*goes off left*). Cooeee! Kostya! Cooeee! (*Exits.*)

NINA (*emerging from behind the stage*). It doesn't seem as if we're going on, so I can come out now. Hello! (*Kisses* ARKADINA *and* POLINA.)

SORIN. Bravo! Well done!

ARKADINA. Yes, bravo! You were wonderful, my dear. With your looks, and that divine voice it's a shame to bury yourself in the country. I'm sure you have talent. You really ought to go on the stage.

NINA. Oh, it's the dream of my life! (*Sighs.*) But it'll never come true.

ARKADINA. Well, who knows? You must allow me to introduce you – this is Boris Trigorin.

NINA. Oh, I'm so delighted . . . (*Embarrassed.*) I read your books all the . . .

ARKADINA (*sitting her down beside them*). Now don't be shy, my darling. He's a famous person, but he's a simple soul at heart. See, he's embarrassed too.

DORN. Presumably we can raise the curtain now. It's a bit eerie.

SHAMRAEV (*loudly*). Yakov, pull up the curtain, will you!

The curtain is raised.

NINA (*to* TRIGORIN). It's a strange play, don't you think?

TRIGORIN. I didn't understand a word. I enjoyed watching it, though. You played your part with real feeling. And the scenery was excellent.

A pause.

There'll be plenty of fish in that lake, I suppose.

NINA. Yes.

TRIGORIN. I love fishing. Nothing gives me more pleasure than sitting by a river in the late afternoon, watching a float.

NINA. I should think that for someone who has experienced the joy of creative work, all other pleasures cease to exist.

ARKADINA (*laughing*). Don't say that. When people say nice things to him, he doesn't know where to look.

SHAMRAEV. I remember at the opera in Moscow once, the great Silva managed to hit bottom C. And as it happened, the bass from our church choir was sitting in the gallery. Well, you can imagine our astonishment when we hear this voice coming from the gallery: 'Bravo, Silva!', a full octave lower! Like this: (*In a deep bass.*) 'Bravo, Silva!' The audience was absolutely stunned.

A pause.

DORN. Somebody's stepped on my grave.

NINA. Well, it's time I was going. Goodbye.

ARKADINA. Going where? It's much too early. We shan't let you.

NINA. My father'll be expecting me.

ARKADINA. Honestly, what a man . . .

They kiss.

Well, it can't be helped. But it's a shame we have to let you go.

NINA. If you only knew, I really hate having to leave!

ARKADINA. We ought to see you home at least, my darling.

NINA (*alarmed*). Oh no, no!

SORIN (*imploring her*). Do stay, please!

NINA. I can't.

SORIN. Stay for another hour, that's all. I mean, surely you . . .

NINA (*hesitates, then tearfully*). No, I mustn't! (*Shakes hands with him and hurriedly exits.*)

ARKADINA. Actually, she's a most unfortunate young woman. They say her mother left the whole of her huge fortune to her husband, right down to the last kopeck, and now the poor girl's got nothing, because her father's already willed it to his second wife. It's an absolute scandal.

DORN. Oh yes, give the man his due, her dear papa is a thoroughgoing swine.

SORIN (*rubbing his hands to warm them*). Let's go inside, everybody, it's getting damp. My legs are aching.

ARKADINA. They're like lumps of wood, you can barely get about on them. All right, let's go, you poor old thing. (*Takes him by the arm.*)

SHAMRAEV (*offering his arm to his wife*). Madame?

SORIN. I can hear that dog howling again. (*To* SHAMRAEV.) Be a good chap, Shamraev, tell them to let it off the chain.

SHAMRAEV. Sorry, can't be done – I don't want thieves breaking into the barn. I've got millet in there. (*To* MEDVEDENKO, *walking alongside.*) Yes, a full octave lower: 'Bravo, Silva!' And he wasn't a professional, just an ordinary choir member.

MEDVEDENKO. So how much does he get paid for that?

Exit everyone except DORN.

DORN (*alone*). I don't know, maybe I'm stupid or crazy, but I liked the play. It really has something. When that young girl was talking about loneliness, and afterwards, when the Devil's red eyes appeared, my hands were honestly trembling. It was so fresh, and unaffected . . . Ah, here he comes now. There's a few things I'd like to say to him.

KOSTYA (*entering*). They've all gone.

DORN. I'm here.

KOSTYA. Masha's been hunting for me all over the park. Insufferable creature.

DORN. You know, Kostya, I enjoyed your play enormously. It's a bit strange, and I haven't heard the ending, but I found it impressive even so. You're a talented young man, you must keep on writing.

KOSTYA *warmly shakes his hand and embraces him impulsively.*

Heavens, you *are* in a state. Tears in your eyes . . . May I say something? You took your subject matter from the realm of abstract ideas. And that's as it should be, because a work of art absolutely must express some sort of grand idea. Only serious things are truly beautiful. You look so pale!

KOSTYA. You don't think I should give up, then?

DORN. No. But you should portray only what is significant and permanent. You know, I've led a pretty full life, I'm a contented man, but if I'd ever felt that spiritual uplift, which artists experience when they create, I think I'd have treated this bodily shell, and everything pertaining to it, with contempt. Yes, I'd have soared to the very heights, away from this earth altogether.

KOSTYA. Excuse me, but where's Nina?

DORN. And another thing. A work of art needs to have a clear, well-defined idea. You must know why you're writing. If you stroll down this image-strewn path without any definite aim, you'll lose your way, and your talent will be the ruin of you.

KOSTYA (*impatiently*). Where's Nina?

DORN. She's gone home.

KOSTYA (*in despair*). What am I going to do? I want to see her. I must see her. I'll ride over there . . .

MASHA *enters.*

DORN (*to* KOSTYA). Take it easy, my dear chap.

KOSTYA. I'm going anyway. I've got to.

MASHA. Kostya, come indoors. Your mother's waiting for you. She's very worried.

KOSTYA. Tell her I've gone. And please, all of you, leave me alone! Do you hear? Stop following me around!

DORN. Now now, my dear chap . . . you can't go on like this, it's not right.

KOSTYA (*tearfully*). Goodbye, Doctor. And thank you . . . (*Exits.*)

DORN (*sighs*). Ah, the joys of youth!

MASHA. That's what people say when they can't think of anything else: the joys of youth. (*Takes a pinch of snuff.*)

DORN (*snatches the snuffbox from her and flings it into the bushes*). That's disgusting!

A pause.

I think that's someone playing the piano. We'd better go in.

MASHA. No, wait.

DORN. What is it?

MASHA. I want to tell you again. I need to talk to you. (*Agitated.*) I don't like my father, but I have a soft spot for

you. I feel we've a lot in common, I don't know why.
Help me, please. Help me before I do something stupid,
before I make a mess of my life, and ruin it completely.
I can't go on like this.

DORN. What do you mean? Help in what way?

MASHA. I'm in agony. Nobody knows how I'm suffering.
(*Lays her head on his chest, then softly.*) I'm in love with
Kostya.

DORN. What a state they're all in! What a state! And so
much love! The lake's bewitched! (*Gently.*) But what can I
do, my child? What can I do? Eh?

Curtain.

ACT TWO

A croquet lawn. In the background to the right, a house with a large terrace; to the left, the lake can be seen, sparkling in the sunlight. Flowerbeds. It is midday and hot. ARKADINA, DORN *and* MASHA *are sitting on a bench beside the lawn, in the shade of an old lime tree.* DORN *has a book open on his lap.*

ARKADINA (*to* MASHA). Let's stand up. (*They both rise.*) Stand next to me. You're twenty-two, and I'm almost twice your age. Now, Doctor, which of us looks younger?

DORN. You do, of course.

ARKADINA. There, you see? And why is that? It's because I work, I feel things, I'm always on the go, and you're stuck here in the same old place, you've no life. And I have a strict rule – never try to see into the future. I never think about old age, or death. *Que sera, sera.*

MASHA: And I feel as if I'd been born ages ago, and I'm dragging my life along behind me, like an endless train. Sometimes I don't feel like living at all. (*Sits down.*) That's silly, of course it is. I'll just have to give myself a shake, and put it out of my mind.

DORN (*begins softly singing*). 'Oh, speak to her, my flowers . . . '

ARKADINA. What's more, when it comes to my appearance, I'm as fussy as an Englishman. I keep myself up to the mark, as they say, my dress and hair are always *comme il faut*. I wouldn't dream of stepping out of doors, not even as far as the garden, in a blouse, or with my hair not done. Never. And that's why I've kept my looks, I've never been sloppy, or let myself go, like some people . . . (*Paces up and down the lawn, her hands on her hips.*) You see? Fresh as a daisy. I could play a girl of fifteen, easily.

DORN. Anyway, I'll carry on reading if you don't mind. (*Picks up the book.*) We'd got as far as the corn merchant and the rats . . .

ARKADINA. Yes, the rats. Read on. (*Sits down.*) No, give it to me, I'll read. It's my turn. (*Takes the book and searches for the place.*) The rats . . . Ah, here we are . . . (*Reads.*) 'And of course it is as dangerous for society people to pamper novelists, and take them to their hearts, as it is for corn merchants to breed rats in their granaries. Yet they love them notwithstanding. Thus, when a woman has her eye on a writer she wishes to captivate, she lays siege to him with compliments, flattery and favours . . . ' Well, that may be true of the French, but we don't do that here, there's no plan of campaign whatsoever. If a woman sets out to captivate a writer in this country, she's usually head over heels in love with him already, believe me. And you don't have to look any further than myself and Trigorin.

Enter SORIN, *leaning on his walking-stick, with* NINA *by his side.* MEDVEDENKO *follows, pushing the empty bath-chair.*

SORIN (*fondly, as if to a child*). Now then, are we happy? We're in a good mood today, are we? (*To his sister.*) Well, we're delighted! Her father and stepmother have gone off to Tver, and we're free now for three whole days!

NINA (*sits beside* ARKADINA *and hugs her*). Oh, I'm so happy! I belong to you now.

SORIN (*sits in his bath-chair*). She's looking so pretty today.

ARKADINA. Yes, nicely dressed, quite attractive . . . You're a very clever girl. (*Kisses* NINA.) But we mustn't praise you too much, it's bad luck. Where's Trigorin?

NINA. He's fishing down by the bathing-hut.

ARKADINA. Honestly, you'd think he'd be bored by now. (*Makes to continue reading.*)

NINA. What's that?

ARKADINA. It's Maupassant's 'Sur l'eau', my dear. (*Reads a few lines to herself.*) Well, the next bit's rather dull, it's also not true. (*Closes the book.*) You know, I'm very worried. Tell me, what's the matter with my son? Why is he so moody and bad-tempered? He's out on the lake for days on end, I scarcely ever see him.

MASHA. He's feeling depressed. (*To* NINA, *timidly.*) Please, recite something from Kostya's play.

NINA (*shrugs*). Do you want me to? It's not very interesting.

MASHA (*trying to restrain her rapture*). Whenever he reads something, his eyes glow, and his face turns pale. He has such a beautiful, sad voice – like a true poet.

SORIN *can be heard snoring.*

DORN. Sweet dreams!

ARKADINA. Petya!

SORIN. Eh?

ARKADINA. Are you asleep?

SORIN. Of course not.

A pause.

ARKADINA. You know, you're not getting any treatment, Petya, that's bad.

SORIN. I'd be quite happy to have some, but the doctor won't give me any.

DORN. What, treatment at sixty?

SORIN. People want to live even at sixty.

DORN (*testily*). Well, take some valerian drops, then.

ARKADINA. I think it would do him good to take the waters somewhere.

DORN. Why not? He can go if he likes. Or not, if he doesn't.

ARKADINA. What's that supposed to mean?

DORN. It's not supposed to mean anything. It's perfectly clear.

A pause.

MEDVEDENKO. Mr Sorin really ought to give up smoking.

SORIN. Rubbish.

DORN. It's not rubbish. Alcohol and tobacco rob you of your personality. After a cigar or a glass of vodka you're no longer Mr Sorin, but Mr Sorin plus somebody else. Your real self simply dissolves, and you think of yourself in the third person, as 'him'.

SORIN (*laughs*). Well, it's all right for you. You've lived life to the full, but what about me? I worked in the Justice Department for twenty-eight years, but I've never really lived, by and large, never experienced anything. So it goes without saying that I want to live, very much. You've had your fill, you've lost interest, that's why you've taken to philosophy, but I want to live. That's why I enjoy a sherry at dinner and smoke cigars and all that. So there you are.

DORN. We ought to take life seriously. But to go to your doctor at sixty, and complain because you didn't enjoy yourself when you were young – well, I'm sorry, that's downright childish.

MASHA (*rises*). It must be lunch time. (*Walks off insouciantly, with a slight limp.*) I think my foot's gone to sleep . . . (*Exits.*)

DORN. She's off to sink a couple of vodkas before lunch.

SORIN. The poor thing's desperately unhappy.

DORN. Excuse me, Your Excellency, that's nonsense.

SORIN. See? You're bored with life. That's why you think like that.

ARKADINA. Ah, what could be more boring than this delightful country boredom! It's so hot, and still, nobody does a stroke, everybody just talks. Yes, I do enjoy listening to you, my dears, but I'd much rather be in a hotel room somewhere, learning my lines!

NINA (*rapturously*). Oh yes, yes! I know what you mean.

SORIN. Of course, it's not so bad in town. You're shut away in your study, the footman won't let anybody in unannounced, you have a telephone, there are cabs outside in the street, and so forth . . .

DORN (*sings*). 'Oh, speak to her, my flowers . . . '

Enter SHAMRAEV, *followed by* POLINA.

SHAMRAEV. Here they are. Good morning! (*Kisses* ARKADINA's *hand, then* NINA's.) I'm delighted to see you looking so well. (*To* ARKADINA.) My wife tells me you and she are going into town today, is that correct?

ARKADINA. Yes, it is.

SHAMRAEV. Hm. Well, that's splendid, but how do you plan to get there, dear lady? We're bringing in the rye today, and all the men are busy. And begging your pardon, but which horses were you going to take?

ARKADINA. Which horses? How should I know which horses?

SORIN. We have carriage horses, surely.

SHAMRAEV (*agitated*). Carriage horses? And where'll I find the harness? Where'll I take the collars from, eh? This is incredible! It passes belief! My dear lady! Forgive me, I have the greatest respect for your talent, I'd sacrifice ten years of my life for you, but I can't let you have any horses!

ARKADINA. And what if I've *got* to go? Really, this is most peculiar.

SHAMRAEV. My dear lady! You have no idea what running an estate means!

ARKADINA (*angrily*). Oh, don't give me that! If that's the case I'm leaving for Moscow this very day. Tell them to hire horses for me in the village, or I'll walk to the station.

SHAMRAEV. And if that's the case I resign! Find yourself another manager! (*Exits.*)

ARKADINA. Every summer it's the same thing, I come here to be insulted every summer! I'll never set foot in this place again!

Exits left, in the direction of the bathing-hut. A few moments later she is seen entering the house, followed by TRIGORIN, *carrying fishing rods and a bucket.*

SORIN (*angrily*). What damn cheek! The absolute limit. I'm fed up with this, and that's the truth of it. Have all the horses brought here this minute!

NINA (*to* POLINA). Fancy refusing a famous actress, like Madame Arkadina! Surely her slightest wish, even if it's just a whim, is more important than farm business? It's quite incredible!

POLINA (*in despair*). But what can I do? Put yourself in my place – what can I do?

SORIN (*to* NINA). We'll go and see my sister. We'll all beg her not to leave. Shall we do that? (*Looking in the direction in which* SHAMRAEV *went off.*) Insufferable man! Tyrant!

NINA (*prevents him rising*). No no, sit there. We'll take you. (*She and* MEDVEDENKO *wheel the bath-chair.*) This is dreadful, it really is!

SORIN. Yes, it is, quite dreadful. But he won't resign, I'll have a word with him.

They exit, leaving only DORN *and* POLINA.

DORN. People make me sick. Quite frankly, your husband should be flung out on his ear, but it'll end up with that old woman Sorin and his sister apologising to him. You wait and see!

POLINA. He's sent the carriage-horses out on farm work. There are rows like this every day, you've no idea how it upsets me. It's making me ill – see, I'm trembling all over . . . I can't stand his rudeness. (*Imploringly.*) Oh, Yevgeny, my dearest, my darling, take me away with you. Time's running out, we're no longer young, surely we don't need to lie, and hide any more, at the end of our lives . . .

A pause.

DORN. I'm fifty-five. It's too late to change now.

POLINA. I know why you're refusing me. It's because you have other women in your life, besides me. And you can't take all of us. I understand. I'm sorry for being a nuisance.

NINA *appears beside the house. She is picking flowers.*

DORN. That's all right.

POLINA. I get terribly jealous. You're a doctor, of course, you can't avoid seeing women. I realise that . . .

DORN (*to* NINA, *approaching*). What's going on?

NINA. Madame Arkadina is crying, and Mr Sorin's had an asthma attack.

DORN (*stands up*). I suppose I'd better give them some valerian drops . . .

NINA (*hands him the flowers*). These are for you.

DORN. *Merci bien.* (*Walks towards the house.*)

POLINA (*accompanying him*). What beautiful flowers! (*As they near the house, in a thick voice.*) Let me have those flowers! Give me those flowers! (*He hands them to her, she tears them to shreds and flings them away. They enter the house.*)

NINA. It's strange to see a famous actress crying, and over nothing, really! Then there's a famous writer, hugely popular, his name in all the papers, his picture on sale everywhere, his books translated into foreign languages, yet he spends the whole day fishing, and he's ecstatic because he catches two chub! I used to think famous people were proud and aloof, that they despised the common herd. I thought they somehow used their fame, their glamour, to take revenge on people who think birth and wealth are all that matters. And here they are crying, catching fish, playing cards, laughing and losing their temper, same as the rest of us.

KOSTYA (*enters hatless, carrying a shotgun and a dead seagull*). Are you alone?

NINA. Yes.

KOSTYA *lays the seagull at her feet.*

What does this mean?

KOSTYA. I did something vile today. I killed this seagull. I'm laying it at your feet.

NINA. What's the matter with you? (*Picks up the seagull and looks at it.*)

KOSTYA (*after a pause*). I'll kill myself soon, in the same way.

NINA. I don't know you any longer.

KOSTYA. Yes, but that's only since I stopped knowing you. You've changed towards me, you look at me coldly, my presence is obviously an embarrassment to you.

NINA. You're so irritable lately, half the time you talk in symbols, I don't know what you mean. I suppose this seagull's some kind of symbol too, but I'm sorry, I can't work it out. (*Puts the seagull down on the bench.*) I'm too simple, I don't understand you.

KOSTYA. It all started that evening, when my play was such a stupid flop. Women can't forgive failure. I've burned the lot, every last scrap of paper. If you only knew how miserable I am! Your coldness towards me is terrible, it's unbelievable – it's like waking up one day and finding the lake has suddenly dried up, or soaked into the earth. You say you're too simple to understand me. Oh, come on, what is there to understand? They didn't like my play, so you despise my inspiration, you think I'm mediocre, worthless, just one more nonentity. (*Stamping his foot.*) Yes, I can see that all right, I'm well aware of it. It's as if a nail's been driven into my brain, damn it, and damn my stupid pride along with it, sucking the blood out of me, like a serpent! (*Catches sight of* TRIGORIN *approaching, reading a book.*) Now here's true genius, coming on like Hamlet, book in hand. (*Mockingly.*) 'Words, words, words!'

The sun hasn't even reached you yet, and you're already smiling, your eyes are melting in its rays. Well, I won't disturb you. (*Hurriedly exits.*)

TRIGORIN (*making notes in a pocket-book*). Takes snuff and drinks vodka . . . Always wears black . . . Schoolmaster in love with her . . .

NINA. Good morning, Mr Trigorin!

TRIGORIN. Good morning. An unexpected turn of events, I think we'll be leaving today. So I don't suppose we'll see each other again. That's a pity. I don't often get the chance to meet young girls – interesting young girls, that is. I've forgotten what it feels like to be eighteen or nineteen, can't get a clear picture of it at all. That's why the young girls in my novels and short stories are unconvincing, for the most part. I wouldn't mind changing places with you for an hour, even, to see what goes on in your head, just generally what makes you tick.

NINA. And I wouldn't mind changing places with you.

TRIGORIN. Why?

NINA. To see what it feels like being a famous, talented writer. What's it like to be a celebrity? What does it feel like?

TRIGORIN. Eh? Nothing in particular. I've never given it much thought. (*After a pause.*) Which means one of two things – either you're exaggerating my fame, or else it's something you just don't feel.

NINA. But when you read about yourself in the papers?

TRIGORIN. Well, it's nice when they're praising you, but you feel rotten for a day or two when they attack you.

NINA. What a wonderful life! You can't imagine how I envy you. People have such different destinies. Some barely drag out their existence in total obscurity. They're all alike, and all miserable. Other people, like you, for instance – you're one in a million – lead the most brilliant, interesting lives, full of meaning. You're so lucky.

TRIGORIN. Me? (*Shrugs*). Hm . . . You're talking about fame, about happiness, about some sort of brilliant, interesting life, but to me all these fine words, sad to say, are like jam, which I never eat. You're very young, and very kind.

NINA. But you have a marvellous life!

TRIGORIN. What's so great about it? (*Looks at his watch.*) I've got to do some writing now. I'm sorry, but I've no time . . . (*Laughs.*) You've touched me on a sore spot, as they say, and I'm starting to get heated now, and slightly irritated. Yes, all right, let's have a talk. Let's talk about my wonderful, brilliant life. Where shall we begin? (*Thinks for a moment.*) You know, some people have what's termed an *idée fixe* – for example, when a person thinks about nothing but the moon, day and night. Well, I have my own moon. Day and night I'm obsessed with one compelling thought: I must write, I must write, I must . . . No sooner have I finished one novel, than I've got to write another, I don't know why, then a third, and after that a fourth. I write incessantly, without a break, I can't help it. So what's wonderful and brilliant about that, eh? It's a hellish life. Here I am with you, I feel excited and happy, yet at the same time, I can't get it out of my mind that I have an unfinished novel waiting for me. I look at that cloud there, shaped like a grand piano. And I think: I'll have to mention that somewhere in a story, that a cloud floated by, shaped like a piano. And there's a scent of heliotrope. So I make another mental note: sickly-sweet perfume, colour of widow's weeds, use it in a description of a summer evening. I try to catch every word, every phrase that passes between us, and quickly lock all these words and phrases away in my literary larder: they might come in handy! When I stop work, I dash off to the theatre or go fishing – I should be able to relax, forget everything, but no! There's a heavy iron ball already on the move in my head – a new subject, and it's dragging me back to my desk, so I've got to hurry and start writing again. It's like that all the time, I give myself no peace. I feel as if I'm devouring my own life: that in order to deliver honey to someone out there somewhere, I have to gather pollen from all my finest flowers, then tear those same flowers up by the roots and trample on them. I must be mad, surely? I mean, do my family and friends treat me like a normal person? 'What are you writing now?' 'What have you got in store for us?' It's always the same, it never stops, and I have the distinct feeling that all the attention they pay me, all that praise and admiration, is nothing but a sham. I'm being deceived, the way people deceive a sick man, and occasionally I have this fear that someone will steal up from behind and grab me, then whisk me off to an asylum, like Gogol's madman. In my young days, when I was at my best, just starting out, writing was a form of torture. A minor writer, particularly if he's not having much luck, feels clumsy and awkward, no use to anybody. He's on edge the whole time, a bag of nerves. He's irresistibly drawn to people involved in literature and the arts, he hangs around them unrecognised and unnoticed, afraid to look anybody in the eye, like a compulsive gambler with no money. I couldn't see my readers, but somehow I thought of them as hostile and sceptical. I was afraid of audiences, really terrified. Whenever I had a new play staged, I would imagine all the dark-haired people hated it, and the fair-haired people couldn't care less! It was absolutely dreadful. Sheer torture!

NINA. But what about your inspiration, and the actual process of writing? Surely that must give you some moments of genuine happiness?

TRIGORIN. Oh yes. I enjoy the writing. And I like reading the proofs, but . . . well, it's no sooner in print than I can't abide it, it's all wrong, a big mistake, I should never have written it, and I get annoyed and depressed. (*Laughs.*) And the public read it and say: 'Yes, charming, very clever, but not a patch on Tolstoy,' or else: 'A wonderful piece, but not as good as Turgenev's 'Fathers and Sons'.' It'll be like that till my dying day – charming and clever, end of story. And when I die, people'll walk past my tomb and read: 'Here lies Trigorin. He was a good writer, but not as good as Turgenev.'

NINA. No, I'm sorry, I can't accept that. You've simply been spoiled by success.

TRIGORIN. What success? I've never liked my work. I don't like myself as a writer. Worst of all is the fact that I'm in some sort of daze, often I don't even understand what I'm writing. I love this lake, the trees, the sky – I have a real feeling for nature, it inspires me with passion, an overwhelming desire to write. But I'm not just a landscape painter, I'm also a citizen, I love my country, and its people. And as a writer, I feel I have a duty to speak about the people, about their sufferings, and their future, to speak about science, and the rights of man and so forth. So I write about everything, always in a hurry, people driving me on from all sides, raging at me. I dart all over the place, like a fox with a pack of hounds at his heels. I see life and science constantly forging ahead, while I'm left further and further behind, like a man who's missed his train, and I end up feeling all I'm good for is nature descriptions. In every other respect I'm a fake, false to the marrow of my bones.

NINA. You've been working too hard, you haven't had either the time or the inclination to see how important you really are. You're not satisfied with yourself, but to other people you're a great man, a wonderful writer! If I were a writer like you, I'd give my whole life to the people, but I'd be aware that they would only find happiness by rising up to my level, and they'd harness themselves to my chariot.

TRIGORIN. A chariot, indeed! So I'm Agamemnon, then?

They both smile.

NINA. If I was lucky enough to be a writer, or an actress, I wouldn't care about upsetting my family, I'd willingly put up with poverty, disappointment, I'd live in a garret, and eat nothing but rye bread. I'd suffer terribly, I'd be so dissatisfied with myself, so aware of my own shortcomings, but in return I'd demand fame . . . yes, genuine, resounding fame . . . (*Covers her eyes with her hands.*) Oh, I feel quite dizzy . . . phew!

ARKADINA (*from the house*). Trigorin!

TRIGORIN. They're calling me. To pack my things, no doubt. I don't want to leave, you know. (*Looks round at the lake.*) This is a lovely spot. Wonderful!

NINA. You see that house and garden, the other side of the lake?

TRIGORIN. Yes.

NINA. That was my mother's estate. I was born there. I've lived beside this lake all my life, I know every tiny island on it.

TRIGORIN. It's a lovely spot. (*Notices the seagull.*) What's this?

NINA. A seagull. Kostya killed it.

TRIGORIN. Beautiful bird. I honestly don't want to leave. Try and talk Madame Arkadina into staying, eh? (*Writes something in his notebook.*)

NINA. What's that you're writing?

TRIGORIN. Just making a note . . . An idea for a plot. (*Puts away his notebook.*) A plot for a short story. It's about a young girl, not unlike you, who has lived all her life beside a lake. She loves the lake, the way a seagull does, and she's as happy and free as a seagull. Then a man comes along, catches sight of her, and in an idle moment, destroys her – just like that seagull of yours.

A pause. ARKADINA *appears at the window.*

ARKADINA. Trigorin, where are you?

TRIGORIN. I'm coming! (*Walks away and looks round at* NINA. *Calls to* ARKADINA.) What is it?

ARKADINA. We're staying.

TRIGORIN *goes into the house.*

NINA (*comes downstage to the footlights. After some thought*). It must be a dream!

Curtain.

ACT THREE

The dining-room in SORIN's *house. Doors to right and left.*
A sideboard. A medicine cabinet. A table in the middle of the room.
A trunk and some hat-boxes indicate preparations for departure.
TRIGORIN *is having breakfast,* MASHA *is standing by the table.*

MASHA. I'm telling you all this because you're a writer.
You'll be able to use it. I'll tell you the truth, if he'd
seriously hurt himself I wouldn't have gone on living
another minute. Still, I'm a brave person. I've made my
mind up: I'm going to tear this love out of my heart, just
tear it out by the roots.

TRIGORIN. And how will you do that?

MASHA. I'm getting married. To Medvedenko.

TRIGORIN. The schoolmaster?

MASHA. Yes.

TRIGORIN. I don't see any need for that.

MASHA. Loving without hope, constantly waiting for something, years on end . . . Once I'm married there'll be no
more time for love. I'll have new cares to drown out the
old. Anyway, it'll be a change, you know? Shall we have
another?

TRIGORIN. Do you think we should?

MASHA. Oh, come on. (*Pours them both a glass.*) Don't look at
me like that. Women drink a lot more than you imagine.
A few do it openly, like me, but most women drink on the
sly. And it's always either vodka or cognac. (*They clink glasses.*)
Cheers! You're a decent man, I'll be sad to see you go.

They drink.

TRIGORIN. I don't really want to leave.

MASHA. So why don't you ask her to stay?

TRIGORIN. No, she won't stay now. Kostya's behaving extremely tactlessly. First he tries to shoot himself, now I hear he wants to challenge me to a duel. And what for? He's in a constant sulk, snarling all the time, going on about new forms. But there's room for both, surely, the old and the new. Why all this pushing and shoving?

MASHA. Well, that's jealousy, isn't it. Anyway, it's none of my business.

A pause. YAKOV *crosses from left to right, carrying a suitcase.* NINA *enters and stands by the window.*

My schoolmaster isn't particularly clever, and he's poor, but he's a kind man, and he loves me very much. I feel sorry for him. And his old mother. Well, I wish you all the best. Don't think badly of me. (*Shakes his hand warmly.*) I'm most grateful to you for all your kindness. Please send me your books, and make sure you sign them. Don't write the usual 'To my dear so-and-so . . . ', just put: 'To Masha, origin unknown, and no purpose in life'. Goodbye! (*Exits.*)

NINA (*holding out her clenched fist to* TRIGORIN). Odd or even?

TRIGORIN. Even.

NINA (*sighs*). Wrong. I've only one pea in my hand. I'm trying to decide whether I should go on the stage or not. If only someone would advise me.

TRIGORIN. Nobody can advise you about that.

A pause.

NINA. So, you're leaving . . . we probably won't see each other again. I'd like you to take this little medallion as a keepsake. I had your initials engraved on it, and the title of your book 'Days and Nights' on the other side.

TRIGORIN. How charming! (*Kisses the medallion.*) What a delightful present.

NINA. You'll think of me sometimes?

TRIGORIN. I shall indeed. I'll think of you just as you were that sunny day – you remember? – about a week ago, you were wearing a white dress, and we had a long talk . . . there was a white bird, a seagull, lying on the bench.

NINA (*thoughtfully*). Yes, the seagull . . .

A pause.

We'd better not say any more, someone's coming. Let me have two minutes with you, please, before you leave.

Exits left. ARKADINA *simultaneously enters right, with* SORIN, *wearing a frock-coat, and a star decoration, then* YAKOV, *busy with the packing.*

ARKADINA. You should stay at home, old chap. You shouldn't be gadding about visiting people with that rheumatism of yours. (*To* TRIGORIN.) Who was that just now? Was it Nina?

TRIGORIN. Yes.

ARKADINA. And we've disturbed you – I'm so sorry. (*Sits down.*) That's everything packed, I think. I'm absolutely worn out.

TRIGORIN (*reads the inscription on the medallion*). 'Days and Nights', page 121, lines 11 and 12.

YAKOV (*clearing the table*). D'you want me to pack the fishing-rods too, sir?

TRIGORIN. Oh yes, I'll need them again. But you can give away the books.

YAKOV. Yes, sir.

TRIGORIN (*to himself*). Page 121, lines 11 and 12. What's in those lines? (*To* ARKADINA.) Are any of my books in the house?

ARKADINA. Yes, in my brother's study, in the corner bookcase.

TRIGORIN. Page 121 . . . (*Exits.*)

ARKADINA. Honestly, Petya, you ought to stay indoors.

SORIN. You're leaving, it's going to be awful here without you.

ARKADINA. And what is there in town?

SORIN. Nothing very much, but all the same . . . (*Laughs.*) They're laying the foundation stone for the new Council building and all that. I need cheering up – get away from this stagnant pond, even for an hour or two, otherwise I'll grow stale, like an old cigarette-holder. I've ordered the horses for one o'clock, so we can leave together.

ARKADINA (*after a pause*). Anyway, you stay on here, don't mope around the house, and don't catch cold. Look after my son. Take care of him, and see he behaves.

A pause.

Here I am leaving, and I won't even know why Kostya tried to shoot himself. I think it was jealousy, that's the main reason, and the sooner I take Trigorin away from here the better.

SORIN. I'm not so sure. There were other things too. It stands to reason, a bright young man, stuck out here in the wilds, no money, no position, no prospects. Nothing to occupy him. He's ashamed and afraid of being so idle. I'm very fond of him, and he's quite attached to me, but by and large he feels out of place here, feels he's sponging off us, living on charity. It's a question of pride, stands to reason.

ARKADINA. He's a real worry. (*Thoughtfully.*) Maybe if he got some sort of a job . . .

SORIN (*starts whistling, then hesitantly*). I think the best thing would be if you were to . . . well, let him have some money. I mean, in the first place, he needs some decent clothes and so forth. Look at him, he's been wearing the same old jacket for three years now, and he hasn't got a coat . . . (*Laughs.*) Yes, and it'd do the lad no harm to have a bit of fun. Take a trip abroad, why not? It wouldn't cost that much.

ARKADINA. Well . . . I might manage a new suit for him, but a trip abroad . . . No, actually, I can't even afford a suit at the moment. (*Firmly.*) I haven't any money.

SORIN *laughs.*

I haven't!

SORIN (*whistles*). If you say so. No, I'm sorry, my dear, don't be angry. I believe you. You're a fine, generous woman.

ARKADINA (*tearfully*). I haven't any money!

SORIN. I'd give it him myself, if I had it, that goes without saying, but I haven't any, not a bean. (*Laughs.*) That manager takes all my pension and squanders it on farming – raising cattle, beekeeping, and so on, it all just disappears. The bees die, the cows die, they won't even let me have the horses.

ARKADINA. I do have money, of course, but I'm an actress, good heavens, I've spent a fortune on dresses alone.

SORIN. You're a dear, kind woman. I admire you, yes. Goodness, I think I'm having another of my . . . (*Sways slightly.*) My head's spinning. (*Holds onto the table.*) I feel quite ill, actually.

ARKADINA (*alarmed*). Petya! (*Tries to support him.*) Petya, my dearest . . . (*Shouts.*) Help! Somebody help!

Enter KOSTYA, *with a bandage round his head, and* MEDVEDENKO.

He's ill!

SORIN. It's all right, it's nothing . . . (*Smiles and takes a drink of water.*) It's passed off already, honestly.

KOSTYA (*to* ARKADINA). Don't be alarmed, mother, it's not serious. Uncle has these attacks quite often nowadays. (*To* SORIN.) You'd best lie down for a bit, Uncle.

SORIN. For a little while, yes. But I'm still going into town. I'll have a lie down, then I'll be off . . . goes without saying . . . (*Walks off, leaning on his stick.*)

MEDVEDENKO (*taking his arm*). Here's a riddle for you: what goes on four legs in the morning, on two in the afternoon, and on three in the evening?

SORIN (*laughs*). I know, I know! And lies on its back at night. Thank you, I can manage by myself . . .

MEDVEDENKO. Come on now, don't stand on ceremony. (*He and* SORIN *exit.*)

ARKADINA. He really frightened me!

KOSTYA. It's bad for his health, living in the country. He gets depressed. Now, mother, if you were to have a sudden fit of generosity, and loan him a couple of thousand, he'd be able to live in town all year round.

ARKADINA. I've no money. I'm an actress, not a banker.

A pause.

KOSTYA. Mother, will you change my bandage, please? You do it so well.

ARKADINA (*takes some iodine and a box of bandages out of the medicine cabinet*). The doctor's late.

KOSTYA. He said he'd be here by ten, and it's already noon.

ARKADINA. Sit down. (*Removes his bandage.*) You look as if you're wearing a turban. Someone came into the kitchen yesterday and asked what nationality you were. It's almost completely healed. Hardly anything left. (*Kisses him on the forehead.*) You won't fiddle around with guns again, will you, when I'm not here?

KOSTYA. No, mother. It was a moment of despair, sheer madness – I just couldn't control myself. It won't happen again. (*Kisses her hand.*) You have magic hands. I remember, a long time ago, when you were still acting in the State theatres – I was quite small then – and there was a fight in our yard, and one of the tenants, a washerwoman, got badly beaten. D'you remember? She was unconscious when they picked her up . . . you kept going to see her, taking medicines to her, washing her children in the tub. You don't remember?

ARKADINA. No. (*Applies a fresh bandage.*)

KOSTYA. There were two girls, ballet dancers, living in the same block. They used to drop in for coffee.

ARKADINA. Yes, that I do remember.

KOSTYA. They were very religious.

A pause.

You know, these past few days, I've loved you just as tenderly and as devotedly as when I was a child. There's no-one left for me now, except you. But why, tell me why has this man come between us?

ARKADINA. You don't understand him, Kostya. He's a very noble character.

KOSTYA. Yes, and when he heard I was about to challenge him to a duel, his nobility didn't stop him taking the coward's way out. He's leaving. Saving his skin!

ARKADINA. Oh, what rubbish! I'm taking him away myself. Kostya, you may not like our relationship, but you're an intelligent boy, and I have the right to demand that you respect my freedom.

KOSTYA. I respect your freedom, yes, but you must allow me *my* freedom to treat this man how I please. Noble character, huh! Look at us, we're practically falling out over him, and he's sitting right now in the drawing-room or the garden somewhere, laughing at the pair of us . . . working on Nina, trying to convince her he's a genius!

ARKADINA. You take a delight in being nasty to me. I respect that man, and I'll ask you not to speak ill of him in my presence.

KOSTYA. Well, I don't respect him. You want me to think he's a genius too, but I'm sorry, I can't lie, his writing just makes me sick.

ARKADINA. That's pure envy. People with no talent, but plenty of pretension – that's all they can do, run down genuine talent. Well, that's scant consolation, I'd say.

KOSTYA (*sarcastically*). Genuine talent! (*Fiercely.*) If it comes to that, I've got more talent than the whole lot of you! (*Tears the bandage from his head.*) You people with your stale conventions, you've got the art world in your pocket, you think what you do is the only legitimate, real work, everything else you try to stifle and suppress! Well, I don't acknowledge you! I don't acknowledge either you or him!

ARKADINA. Decadent! . . .

KOSTYA. Go back to your cosy little theatre and act in your pathetic, rubbishy plays!

ARKADINA. I've never acted in rubbish. Leave me alone! You couldn't even write a third-rate farce. Provincial philistine! Sponger!

KOSTYA. Miser!

ARKADINA. Tramp!

KOSTYA *sits down and begins quietly weeping.*

Nonentity! (*paces up and down in agitation.*) Look, don't cry. There's no need for that. (*Begins to weep also.*) Don't, please. (*Kisses his forehead, his cheeks.*) Oh, my darling boy, forgive me, please. Forgive your sinful mother. Forgive me, I'm so unhappy.

KOSTYA (*embraces her*). Oh, if you only knew! I've lost everything. She doesn't love me, I can't write any more. I've nothing left to live for.

ARKADINA. Don't give up hope. It'll all turn out right. I'm taking him away now, she'll come to love you again. (*Wipes away his tears.*) Don't cry. We're friends again, right?

KOSTYA (*kisses her hands*). Yes, mother.

ARKADINA (*tenderly*). Kostya, make it up with him. We don't want any duels, do we.

KOSTYA. All right. Only please don't make me face him. That's too hard. I haven't the strength . . .

Enter TRIGORIN.

Anyway . . . I'll go now. (*Hurriedly puts the dressings back in the medicine cabinet.*) The doctor'll see to the bandage.

TRIGORIN (*leafing through the book*). Page 121 . . . lines 11 and 12 . . . Ah, here we are . . . (*Reads.*) 'If ever you need my life, come and take it . . . '

KOSTYA *picks up the bandage from the floor and exits.*

ARKADINA (*glances at her watch*). The horses'll be here soon.

TRIGORIN (*to himself*). 'If ever you need my life, come and take it.'

ARKADINA. I trust you've got everything packed.

TRIGORIN (*impatiently*). Yes, yes . . . (*Musing.*) Why do I hear such sadness in this appeal from an innocent girl, why does it wring my heart so painfully? . . . 'If ever you need my life, come and take it.' (*To ARKADINA.*) Why don't we stay here one more day?

ARKADINA *shakes her head.*

Let's stay!

ARKADINA. Darling, I'm well aware what's keeping you here, but do try and control yourself. You're a little tipsy, you ought to sober up.

TRIGORIN. You should sober up too, be sensible and reasonable. Please, I'm asking you to look on all this as a true friend. (*Presses her hand.*) You're capable of making sacrifices. Be my friend, let me go . . .

ARKADINA (*deeply disturbed*). You're so infatuated?

TRIGORIN. I feel drawn to her. Maybe it's what I need.

ARKADINA. What, the love of some provincial miss? How little you know yourself!

TRIGORIN. People sometimes walk in their sleep. That's how I feel now. I'm talking to you, but it's as if I'm asleep, and dreaming about her. I'm caught up in the sweetest, most wonderful dreams. Let me go, please.

ARKADINA (*trembling*). No, no. I'm just an ordinary woman, you shouldn't say these things to me. Don't torture me, Boris. I'm so frightened . . .

TRIGORIN. You can be extraordinary, if you wish. Young love, enchanting, poetic love, the sort that transports us to the land of dreams – that's the only happiness this life has to offer us! I've never known love like that. When I was young I had no time, hanging around editors' offices, battling with poverty. Now it's here at last, this love, and it's calling to me. What's the sense of running away from it?

ARKADINA (*furiously*). You're out of your mind!

TRIGORIN. What if I am?

ARKADINA. This is a conspiracy, you all want to torture me today! (*Weeps.*)

TRIGORIN (*clutches his head*). She doesn't understand! She doesn't *want* to understand!

ARKADINA. Am I really so old and ugly, that you can talk to me about other women without embarrassment? (*Embraces him and kisses him.*) Oh, you've gone crazy! My marvellous, wonderful . . . You're the last page of my life! (*Kneels before him.*) My joy, my pride, my bliss . . . (*Embraces his knees.*) If you leave me for even one hour, I won't survive, I'll go mad, my astonishing, magnificent master . . .

TRIGORIN. Someone might come in. (*Helps her to her feet.*)

ARKADINA. Let them. I'm not ashamed of my love for you. (*Kisses his hands.*) Oh, my treasure, my reckless boy, you want to run wild, but I won't let you, I won't. (*Laughs.*) You're mine, you're all mine. This forehead's mine, these eyes are mine, this beautiful silky hair's mine too. Every bit of you, mine. You're so talented and clever, the best of all the modern writers, you're Russia's only hope. You have so much sincerity, simplicity, so much freshness and humour. You can convey the essentials of a person or a landscape, with one stroke of the pen. The characters in your books are so alive, people can't fail to be delighted by them. You think I'm insincere? You think that's flattery? All right, look into my eyes . . . go on. Do I look like a liar? There, you see? I'm the only one who appreciates you. I'm the only one who'll tell you the truth, my darling, wonderful . . . You'll come with me? Yes? You won't leave me?

TRIGORIN. I've no will of my own. Never have had. I'm inert and spineless, I always give in – is that really what women like? All right, take me, carry me off, only don't let me out of your sight . . .

ARKADINA (*to herself*). He's mine now. (*Casually, as if nothing had happened.*) You know, you can stay if you wish. I'm leaving, of course, but you can come on later, in a week's time. There's no great hurry, is there.

TRIGORIN. No, we'll leave together.

ARKADINA. It's up to you. Together, then.

A pause. TRIGORIN *writes something in his notebook.*

What's that?

TRIGORIN. I heard a nice phrase this morning: 'Virgin forest'. It'll come in handy. (*Stretches.*) So, we're off again? More railway carriages, stations, buffets, veal cutlets, conversations . . .

SHAMRAEV (*enters*). I have the honour to inform you, with regret, that the horses are ready. It's time you were leaving for the station, dear lady. The train's due at five past two. Do me a favour, Madame Arkadina – don't forget to ask where the actor Suzdaltsev is these days. Find out if he's still alive and well. We used to go drinking together. He was absolutely superb in 'The Mail Robbery'. The great tragedian Izmailov played alongside him, as I recall, in Yelisavetgrad – he was a remarkable character too. There's no rush, dear lady, you've another five minutes yet. One time they they were playing a pair of conspirators in some melodrama, and when they were discovered, they were supposed to say: 'We're caught in a

trap!' And Izmailov said: 'We're trapped in a cot!'
(*Guffaws.*) Trapped in a cot!

While he is speaking, YAKOV *is fussing around the suitcases; the*
MAID *brings* ARKADINA *her hat and coat, umbrella and*
gloves; everyone helps ARKADINA *to put them on. The* COOK
peeps round the door at left, then enters hesitantly a little later.
POLINA *enters, followed by* SORIN *and* MEDVEDENKO.

POLINA (*carrying a small basket*). These are some plums for
the road. They're quite sweet. You might feel like
something nice to eat . . .

ARKADINA. You're very kind, Polina.

POLINA. Goodbye, my dear. Please forgive us if anything
wasn't to your liking. (*Weeps.*)

ARKADINA (*embraces her*). Everything was just fine, honestly.
There's no need to cry.

POLINA. Our life's slipping away.

ARKADINA. Well, that can't be helped.

SORIN (*crosses the room wearing a caped overcoat and hat, and*
carrying a stick). It's time we were going, sister – mustn't be
late, after all. I'll go and sit in the carriage. (*Exits.*)

MEDVEDENKO. I'll walk on ahead to the station, to see
you off. It won't take long. (*Exits.*)

ARKADINA. Goodbye, my dears. If all goes well, we'll meet
again next summer.

The MAID, YAKOV, *and the* COOK *kiss her hand.*

Don't forget me. (*Gives the* COOK *a rouble.*) Here's a
rouble. That's for the three of you.

COOK. Thank you very much, ma'am. Have a safe journey.
You've been so good to us.

YAKOV. God bless you, ma'am!

SHAMRAEV. If you'd drop us a line or two, we'd be
delighted. Goodbye, Mr Trigorin!

ARKADINA. Where's Kostya? You'd better tell him I'm leaving. We've still to say goodbye. Well . . . think kindly of me. (*To* YAKOV.) I've given a rouble to cook. It's for the three of you.

All exit right. The stage is empty. Sounds of people being seen off. The maid comes back in, to collect the basket of plums from the table, then goes out again.

TRIGORIN (*re-entering*). I've forgotten my cane. I think it's on the terrace. (*Walks over to the door left, and meets* NINA *coming in.*) It's you! We're just leaving.

NINA. I knew we'd see each other again. (*Excitedly.*) Mr Trigorin, I've made up my mind once and for all – the die is cast, I'm going on the stage. By tomorrow I'll be gone, I'm leaving my father, leaving everything, starting a new life . . . I'm going away to Moscow, just like you. We'll see each other there.

TRIGORIN (*glancing behind him*). Look, take a room at the Slavyansky Bazaar. Let me know the minute you arrive. Molchanovka, Grokholsky's house. I've got to rush.

A pause.

NINA. One minute . . .

TRIGORIN (*in a low voice*). You're so beautiful. Oh, I'm so happy to think we'll meet again soon!

She leans her head against his chest.

I'll see those wonderful eyes again, that inexpressibly lovely, tender smile . . . those gentle features, that look of angelic purity. Oh, my darling . . .

A prolonged kiss.

Curtain.

Two years elapse between Acts III and IV.

ACT FOUR

A drawing-room in SORIN's *house, converted into a study for* KOSTYA. *Doors right and left, leading to inner rooms. A French window in the centre, giving onto a terrace. Besides the usual drawing-room furniture, a writing-desk in the corner, right, an ottoman by the door left, a book-case, and books on the window-sills and on the chairs. It is evening. The room is in semi-darkness, lit only by a table lamp. The sound of of trees rustling, and the wind howling in the chimney. The nightwatchman is tapping. Enter* MEDVEDENKO *and* MASHA.

MASHA (*calls out*). Kostya! Kostya! (*Has a look round.*) There's nobody here. The old man keeps asking, 'Where's Kostya? Where's Kostya?' He can't live without him.

MEDVEDENKO. He's afraid of being alone. (*Listening.*) What terrible weather! That's two whole days now.

MASHA (*turns up the lamp*). There are waves on the lake. Enormous.

MEDVEDENKO. It's dark in the garden. They should get somebody to pull that old stage down. It's like a skeleton standing there, so bare and ugly, and the curtain flaps in the wind. When I was walking past yesterday evening, I thought I heard somebody crying on it.

MASHA. Well, anyway . . .

A pause.

MEDVEDENKO. Masha, let's go home.

MASHA (*shakes her head*). I'm spending the night here.

MEDVEDENKO (*pleading*). Come on, Masha, let's go. The baby'll be hungry.

MASHA. Nonsense. Matryona can feed him.

A pause.

MEDVEDENKO. It's a shame. This'll be the third night running without his mother.

MASHA. You know, you've got really boring. You used to have something to say, at least, now it's nothing but baby, and home – that's all we ever hear these days.

MEDVEDENKO. Masha, let's go home, please!

MASHA. Go yourself.

MEDVEDENKO. Your father won't let me have a horse.

MASHA. Yes, he will. Just ask him.

MEDVEDENKO. Well, I suppose I could. Anyway, you'll come home tomorrow?

MASHA (*takes a pinch of snuff*). Yes, yes. Don't annoy me.

Enter KOSTYA and POLINA. KOSTYA is carrying pillows and a blanket, and POLINA bed-linen. They lay them on the ottoman, then KOSTYA goes over to his desk and sits down.

Who's that for, mother?

POLINA. Mr Sorin wants his bed made up here, in Kostya's room.

MASHA. Let me do that . . . (*Begins making up a bed.*)

POLINA (*sighs*). Old people are like children . . . (*Goes over to the writing-desk, leans on it and looks at a manuscript.*)

A pause.

MEDVEDENKO. Well, I'll be off then. Goodbye, Masha (*Kisses his wife's hand.*) Goodbye, mother. (*Makes to kiss his mother-in-law's hand.*)

POLINA (*irritated*). Oh, for heaven's sake, go.

MEDVEDENKO. Goodbye, Kostya.

KOSTYA offers him his hand in silence. MEDVEDENKO exits.

POLINA (*looking at the manuscript*). No-one ever thought you'd make a real writer, Kostya, they'd never have believed it.

And now, praise be, the magazines have even started paying you. (*Runs her hand through his hair.*) And you've grown so handsome . . . Dear, good Kostya – try to be a little nicer to my Masha.

MASHA (*making up the bed*). Mother, leave him alone.

POLINA (*to* KOSTYA). She's a lovely girl.

A pause.

That's all a woman wants, Kostya, just a little affection. I know that myself.

KOSTYA *gets up from his desk and silently exits.*

MASHA. You see? You've made him angry. Why d'you keep pestering him?

POLINA. I'm sorry for you, Masha, I really am.

MASHA. That's all I need!

POLINA. My heart aches for you. I can see everything, I know what's going on.

MASHA. That's nonsense. Unrequited love belongs in novels. It's all rubbish. You just don't give in to it, that's all, you don't sit twiddling your thumbs, hoping. The minute love creeps into your heart, you have to get rid of it. My husband's been promised a job in another district. Once we move there, I'll forget everything – just tear it out of my heart by the roots.

Someone is playing a melancholy waltz, two rooms away.

POLINA. That's Kostya playing. That means he's depressed.

MASHA (*dances a few waltz steps in silence*). The main thing is not to have him in view all the time. If they'd just give my Semyon that transfer, I'd get over him in a month, believe me. It's all so silly.

The door left opens; DORN *and* MEDVEDENKO *wheel in* SORIN *in his bath-chair.*

MEDVEDENKO. We've six mouths to feed now. And flour's seventy kopecks a bag.

DORN. Well, you'll just have to get by.

MEDVEDENKO. You can laugh. You're rolling in money.

DORN. Me? Listen, my friend, after thirty years in practice, and extremely bothersome practice at that, on call night and day, not a minute to myself, I managed to save two thousand, that's all, and I've just blown that on a trip abroad. I haven't a bean.

MASHA (*to her husband*). Haven't you gone yet?

MEDVEDENKO (*guiltily*). How can I? They won't give me a horse!

MASHA (*bitterly, sotto voce*). I wish to God I'd never clapped eyes on you!

The bath-chair comes to a halt down left. POLINA, MASHA *and* DORN *sit down beside it.* MEDVEDENKO *moves apart, miserable.*

DORN. Well, you've certainly made some changes here. Converted the drawing-room into a study, I see.

MASHA. Kostya finds it more convenient for his work. He can go out into the garden to think, whenever he feels like it.

The night-watchman is heard tapping.

SORIN. Where's my sister?

DORN. She's gone to the station to meet Trigorin. She'll be back shortly.

SORIN. So, if you had to send for my sister, I presume I'm seriously ill. (*After a pause.*) You know, it's funny – I'm seriously ill, but I'm not getting any medicine.

DORN. Well, what would you like? Valerian drops? Bicarbonate? Quinine?

SORIN. You see? There he goes again. What have I done to deserve this? (*Nods towards the ottoman.*) Is this made up for me?

POLINA. It is, sir.

SORIN. Thank you.

DORN (*sings*). 'The moon floats by, in the evening sky . . . '

SORIN. I'm going to give Kostya an idea for a novel. It should be titled: 'The Man Who Wanted' – *'L'homme qui a voulu'*. When I was young, I wanted to be a writer – never managed it, though. I'd have liked to be a good speaker, but I was absolutely appalling – (*Mimics himself.*) 'And er . . . as I was saying . . . er . . . so to speak . . . er . . . ' Frightful. When I was trying to sum up a case, I used to drone on and on, till I broke out in a sweat. I wanted to get married, and didn't. I wanted to live in town, and here I am, ending my days in the country, and all that.

DORN. Well, you wanted to be a State Councillor, and you managed that.

SORIN (*laughs*). I didn't particularly want that. That just happened.

DORN. Moaning about your life at the age of sixty-two – it's rather mean-spirited, don't you think?

SORIN. Will you listen to the man? I want to live, that's all!

DORN. That's plain foolishness. It's the law of Nature, every life must come to an end.

SORIN. You've bored with life, you can afford to talk like that. You've had your fill, so you don't care, it's all one to you. But you'll be afraid of death just the same.

DORN. The fear of death is an animal fear. We need to suppress it. The only people who consciously fear death are those who believe in eternal life, and they're afraid because of their sins. But as for you – in the first place, you're not a believer, and in the second place, what sins have you committed? You worked in the Ministry of Justice for twenty-five years, and that's about it.

SORIN (*laughing*). Twenty-eight . . .

KOSTYA *enters and sits down on a stool at* SORIN's *feet.* MASHA *can't take her eyes off him.*

DORN. We're keeping Kostya from his work.

KOSTYA. Not at all.

A pause.

MEDVEDENKO. Doctor, may one ask which foreign city you liked best?

DORN. Genoa.

KOSTYA. Why Genoa?

DORN. The street life there's simply wonderful. When you step outside your hotel in the evening, the whole street's jammed with people. You drift along in the crowd, aimlessly, here, there and everywhere – you live with the crowd, you merge with it psychologically, and you start believing that there might actually be a World Spirit, like the one Nina acted in that play of yours. By the way, where is Nina these days? How's she getting on?

KOSTYA. Fine, I suppose.

DORN. I was told she's been leading a rather strange life. What's all that about?

KOSTYA. It's a long story, Doctor.

DORN. Well, shorten it.

A pause.

KOSTYA. She ran away from home and had an affair with Trigorin. Did you know that?

DORN. Yes.

KOSTYA. She had a baby. The baby died. Trigorin tired of her and went back to his former attachments, as one might have expected. Actually, he'd never given them up – he's so spineless he'd somehow managed to string them both along. As far as I can make out, Nina's personal life has been a disaster.

DORN. And what about the theatre?

KOSTYA. Even worse, apparently. She made her debut in

summer season outside Moscow somewhere, then went to
the provinces. At that time I never let her out of my sight
– wherever she went, that's where I'd be. She took on
leading roles, but her acting was terribly crude and
tasteless, one long rant, with very awkward gestures.
There were moments when she showed talent, if she had
to scream or die – she had some talent for that – but they
were only moments.

DORN. So, she has some ability nonetheless?

KOSTYA. It's hard to tell. I suppose she must have. I saw
her, but she refused to see me, and they wouldn't let me
into her hotel room. I could understand her feelings, so I
didn't insist on a meeting.

A pause.

What more can I tell you? Afterwards, when I went back
home, I started getting letters from her. Intelligent, warm,
interesting letters. She didn't complain, but I could sense
she was deeply unhappy. Every line was like a tense,
aching nerve. And her mind seemed rather disturbed. She
used to sign herself 'Seagull'. In Pushkin's 'Rusalka', the
miller calls himself a raven, and it was like that in her
letters. She kept repeating she was a seagull. She's here
now.

DORN. Here? What d'you mean?

KOSTYA. She's in town, staying at an hotel. She's been
there the past four or five days. I was going to visit her,
and Masha here actually went to see her, but she's not
receiving anybody. Medvedenko swears he saw her in the
fields yesterday afternoon, about a mile from here.

MEDVEDENKO. Yes, I did. She was headed in the other
direction, towards town. I said hello, and asked her why
she hadn't come to see us. She said she would.

KOSTYA. She won't.

A pause.

Her father and stepmother won't have anything to do
with her. They've got lookouts posted everywhere, to

make sure she doesn't even come near the estate. (*Walks off with* DORN *over to the writing-desk.*) It's easy to be philosophical on paper, Doctor, but a sight harder in real life.

SORIN. She was a delightful girl.

DORN. I'm sorry?

SORIN. I said, she was a delightful girl. State Councillor Sorin was even a little in love with her.

DORN. Old lecher.

SHAMRAEV *is heard laughing offstage.*

POLINA. I think that's them arrived from the station.

KOSTYA. Yes, I can hear my mother.

Enter ARKADINA *and* TRIGORIN, *followed by* SHAMRAEV.

SHAMRAEV (*entering*). We're all getting old, the elements are taking their toll of us, but you, dear lady, are still young. Bright, cheerful blouse, lively, graceful . . .

ARKADINA. You'll bring me bad luck again, you tiresome man!

TRIGORIN (*to* SORIN). Good evening, sir. What's all this about you being ill? That's not good enough, you know. (*Catching sight of* MASHA, *delightedly.*) Masha!

MASHA. You recognised me? (*Shakes hands with him.*)

TRIGORIN. You're married?

MASHA. Ages ago.

TRIGORIN. And are you happy? (*Bows to* DORN *and* MEDVEDENKO, *then hesitantly goes up to* KOSTYA.) Your mother tells me you've forgotten the past, and stopped being angry with me.

KOSTYA *holds out his hand.*

ARKADINA (*to her son*). Look, Boris has brought a magazine with your new short story.

KOSTYA (*taking it, to* TRIGORIN). Thank you. You're most kind.

They sit down.

TRIGORIN. Your admirers send their regards. There's a lot of interest in you in St Petersburg and Moscow, people keep asking me about you. They want to know what you're like, what age you are, whether you're fair or dark. For some reason or other, everybody seems to think you're not a young man. And you publish under a pseudonym, so nobody knows your real name. You're as mysterious as the Man in the Iron Mask.

KOSTYA. Will you be staying long?

TRIGORIN. No, I think I'll go back to Moscow tomorrow. Needs must. I have a novel to finish, and I've promised to do something for an anthology. In a word, the same old story.

While they are talking, ARKADINA *and* POLINA *place a card-table in the middle of the room and open it out;* SHAMRAEV *lights some candles and sets out the chairs. A game of lotto is brought from the cupboard.*

The weather hasn't been too kind. That's a fierce wind. If it's died down by morning I'll do a spot of fishing on the lake. By the way, I must have a look at the garden, and that place – you remember? – where that play of yours was performed. I have an idea for a story, I just need to refresh my memory of the setting.

MASHA (*to her father*). Father, please let Semyon have a horse. He's got to go home.

SHAMRAEV (*mimicking her*). Let him have a horse . . . got to go home . . . (*Sternly.*) You can see for yourself, they're only just back from the station. I'm not sending them out again.

MASHA. But surely there are other horses . . . (*When her father says nothing, she waves her hand in irritation.*) Oh, there's no use talking to you.

MEDVEDENKO. Masha, I'll walk. Honestly.

POLINA (*sighs*). Walk, in this weather! (*Sits down at the card-table.*) Now, everybody, please . . .

MEDVEDENKO. I mean, it's only four miles . . . Goodbye . . . (*Kisses his wife's hand.*) Goodbye, mother.

His mother-in-law reluctantly holds out her hand for him to kiss.

I really wouldn't have bothered anyone, but it's the baby . . . (*Bows to the company.*) Goodbye . . . (*Exits, looking rather sheepish.*)

SHAMRAEV. Let him walk. He's not a general.

POLINA (*rapping the table*). Come on, everybody. Let's not waste time, they'll be calling us for supper soon.

SHAMRAEV, MASHA *and* DORN *sit down at the table.*

ARKADINA (*to* TRIGORIN). Once the long autumn evenings draw in, people around here play lotto. Have a look – it's an extremely old set. It's the one my mother used, when she played it with us as children. Why not join in, have a game till supper-time? (*She sits down at the table with* TRIGORIN.) It's pretty boring, but not too bad once you get used to it. (*Deals everyone three cards.*)

KOSTYA (*leafing through the magazine*). He's read his own story, but he hasn't even cut the pages of mine. (*Puts the magazine down on the desk, then walks towards the door at left. As he passes his mother, he kisses her on the head.*)

ARKADINA. What about you, Kostya?

KOSTYA. Sorry, I don't feel like it. I'm going for a stroll. (*Exits.*)

ARKADINA. The stake is ten kopecks. Put it down for me, Doctor, will you?

DORN. Certainly.

MASHA. Now, has everybody put in? Right, I'll start . . . twenty-two!

ARKADINA. Got it.

MASHA. Three!

DORN. Yes.

MASHA. Have you put three down? Eight! Eighty-one! Ten!

SHAMRAEV. Don't go so fast.

ARKADINA. Anyway, that was some reception I got in
Kharkov – heavens, my head's still spinning from it!

MASHA. Thirty-four!

A melancholy waltz is being played offstage.

ARKADINA. The students gave me a standing ovation. Three
baskets of flowers, two bouquets, and this – look . . .

Takes off a brooch and throws it onto the table.

SHAMRAEV. Very nice, indeed . . .

MASHA. Fifty!

DORN. Fifty, was that?

ARKADINA. I wore the most stunning outfit. Say what you
like, I do know how to dress.

POLINA. That's Kostya playing. The poor boy's so
depressed.

SHAMRAEV. He's been getting a lot of abuse in the papers.

MASHA. Seventy-seven!

ARKADINA. Nobody takes any notice of them.

TRIGORIN. He's unlucky. He just can't seem to find his
own voice. There's something strange about his work, it's
so vague – at times it's like someone raving. And not a
single real character.

MASHA. Eleven!

ARKADINA (*Looks round at* SORIN). Petya dear, are you
bored?

A pause.

He's asleep.

DORN. State Councillor Sorin is asleep.

MASHA. Seven! Ninety!

TRIGORIN. If I lived on an estate like this, beside a lake, do you think I'd write? No, I'd simply suppress the urge, and do nothing but fish, the whole day.

MASHA. Twenty-eight!

TRIGORIN. Catching a ruff, or a perch – sheer bliss!

DORN. Well, I have faith in Kostya. He's got something, there's definitely something there. He thinks in images, his stories are full of colour, they're so vivid. I feel them very strongly. It's just a pity he hasn't any definite aim. He makes an impression, but that's all, and you won't get far on just making an impression. Irina, are you pleased your son is a writer?

ARKADINA. D'you know, I haven't read anything of his yet? I never have the time.

MASHA. Twenty-six!

KOSTYA *enters quietly, and walks over to his desk.*

SHAMRAEV (*to* TRIGORIN). By the way, Mr Trigorin, we've got something of yours.

TRIGORIN. Oh? What's that?

SHAMRAEV. That time Kostya shot a seagull – you asked me to have it stuffed.

TRIGORIN. Did I? (*After some thought.*) I don't remember.

MASHA. Sixty-six! One!

KOSTYA (*flings open the window and listens*). How dark it is! I feel so restless, I don't know why.

ARKADINA. Kostya, close the window, please, there's a draught.

KOSTYA *closes the window.*

MASHA. Eighty-eight!

TRIGORIN. It's my game, ladies and gentlemen!

ARKADINA (*gaily*). Bravo! Bravo!

SHAMRAEV. Bravo!

ARKADINA. This man has all the luck, always. (*Rises.*) Now, let's go and have a bite to eat. Our celebrity hasn't had any lunch today. We'll carry on after supper. (*To her son.*) Kostya, put your writing away, come and have something to eat.

KOSTYA. No thanks, mother, I don't feel like eating.

ARKADINA. Please yourself. (*Wakes* SORIN.) Petya dear, supper! (*Takes* SHAMRAEV*'s arm.*) I'll tell you all about the reception I got in Kharkov . . .

POLINA *extinguishes the candles on the table, then she and* DORN *wheel out the bath-chair. Everyone exits left, leaving* KOSTYA *alone on stage at his desk.*

KOSTYA (*Preparing to write, reads over what he has already written*). I've talked so much about new forms, and now I feel myself gradually slipping into the same old rut. (*Reads.*) 'The notice on the fence proclaimed' . . . 'A pale face, framed with dark hair . . . ' Proclaimed, framed . . . That's rubbish. (*Crosses it out.*) I'll start from where the hero is awakened by the sound of rain, and cut all the rest. The description of the moonlit night's too long and stilted. Trigorin's got all his little tricks, it's easy for him. He'd have the neck of a broken bottle glinting on top of the dam, the black shadow of the mill-wheel, and there's your moonlit night ready-made, whereas I've got to go on about the shimmering light, the gently twinkling stars, the distant sounds of a piano, fading away in the soft, scented air . . . Frightful.

A pause.

Yes, I'm becoming more and more convinced that it's got nothing to do with old forms or new forms. The thing is to write, without thinking about forms of any kind − just write, because it pours freely from your heart.

Someone taps at the window nearest to his desk.

What was that? (*Looks out of the window.*) I can't see anything. (*Opens the French window and looks out into the garden.*) Someone ran down the steps. (*Calls out.*) Who's there? (*Exits. He is heard walking quickly along the terrace; a minute later, he re-enters with* NINA.) Nina! Nina!

NINA *lays her head on his chest and begins quietly sobbing.* KOSTYA *is deeply moved.*

Oh, Nina, Nina, it's you! It's as if I had a premonition – all day long I've had a terrible ache in my heart. (*Takes off her hat and cape.*) Oh, my angel, my darling, she's come. Don't cry, we mustn't cry.

NINA. There's someone here.

KOSTYA. No, there isn't.

NINA. Lock the doors, in case they come in.

KOSTYA. No-one'll come in.

NINA. Your mother's here, I know she is. Lock the doors.

KOSTYA (*locks the door at right, goes up to the one at left*). This one doesn't lock. I'll put a chair against it. (*Places an armchair against the door.*) Don't worry, no-one'll come in.

NINA (*stares intently at him*). Let me look at you. (*Gazing round the room.*) It's warm in here, very nice. This used to be the drawing-room. Have I changed much?

KOSTYA. Yes. You're thinner, and your eyes are bigger. Nina, it's so strange, seeing you like this. Why didn't you let me visit you? Why didn't you come before now? You've been in town almost a week, I know. I've been to your hotel several times each day, and stood under your window, like a beggar.

NINA. I was afraid you hated me. Every night I dream you look at me and don't recognise me. Oh, if you only knew! I've been coming here ever since I arrived, walking round the lake. I've been past your house several times, but I didn't dare come in. Let's sit down.

They sit down.

Let's sit down, and just talk and talk. It's so nice here, warm and cosy. Can you hear the wind? There's a passage in Turgenev: 'Happy the man who on nights like this has a roof over his head, a warm corner of his own.' I'm a seagull. No, that's wrong. (*Rubs her forehead.*) What was I saying? Oh yes, Turgenev. 'And God help all homeless wanderers . . . ' Well, no matter. (*Begins sobbing.*)

KOSTYA. Nina, you're crying again . . . Nina!

NINA. It's all right, I feel better for it. I haven't cried in over two years. Late last night I came to have a look at the garden, to see if our little theatre was still there. It is, it's still standing. I cried then, for the first time in two years, and I felt better, my mind seemed clearer. See, I've stopped crying. (*Takes his hand.*) So, you're a writer now. You're a writer, and I'm an actress. We've both ended up in the thick of it. I used to be so happy, like a child. I'd wake up in the morning and start singing. I loved you, and dreamed of being famous, but now . . . I've got to leave for Yelets tomorrow morning, travel third class, with the peasants. And in Yelets, all those educated shop-keepers'll force their attentions on me. It's a rough life.

KOSTYA. What are you going to Yelets for?

NINA. I've taken an engagement there for the winter. It's time I went.

KOSTYA. Oh, Nina, I cursed you, I hated you, I tore up all your letters and photographs, but I knew, every single minute, that my heart was yours forever. I can't stop loving you, Nina. Ever since I lost you, and began to have my work published, my life's been unbearable – I'm in agony. It's as if my youth had suddenly been snatched from me, I feel like an old man of ninety. I call your name, I kiss the very ground you walked on. Wherever I look, I see your face, that sweet smile that lit up the best years of my life.

NINA (*distractedly*). Why is he saying these things? Why is he saying these things?

KOSTYA. I'm all alone, I haven't anyone's affection to warm me. I'm cold, it's as if I were in a dungeon, and no matter what I write, it all comes out dry and soulless, steeped in gloom. Nina, stay here, please, or let me go with you!

NINA *hurriedly puts on her hat and cape.*

Nina, what are you doing? For God's sake, Nina . . . (*Watches her dressing. A pause.*)

NINA. There's a carriage waiting at the gate. Don't come with me, I'll find my own way. (*Tearfully.*) Give me some water, please . . .

KOSTYA (*gives her a drink of water*). Where are you going now?

NINA. Into town.

A pause.

Is your mother here?

KOSTYA. Yes. My uncle was very ill on Thursday, and we sent her a telegram.

NINA. Why do you say you kiss the ground I walked on? I'm not fit to live. (*Droops over the table.*) Oh, I'm so tired! If I could just rest . . . rest. (*Raises her head.*) I'm a seagull. No, that's wrong. I'm an actress. Yes, I am!

Hearing ARKADINA and TRIGORIN laughing, she listens a moment, then runs over to the door at left and looks through the keyhole.

He's here, too. (*Returning to KOSTYA.*) Yes, I am. And that's all right. Yes. He didn't believe in the theatre, he laughed at my dreams, and gradually I stopped believing too, and lost heart. Then all the troubles of love, jealousy, the constant fear for my baby. I became petty and smallminded, I hadn't a clue what I was doing. I'd no idea what to do with my hands, how to stand, I couldn't control my voice. You can't imagine what it feels like, to know you're giving a dreadful performance. I'm a seagull. No, that's wrong. D'you remember shooting that seagull?

'Then a man comes along, catches sight of it, and in an idle moment, destroys . . . ' An idea for a short story. No, that's wrong. (*Rubs her forehead.*) What was I saying? Yes, I was talking about the stage. I'm not like that now. I'm a real actress, I enjoy performing, I revel in it, I feel intoxicated on stage, I feel wonderful. And while I've been staying here, I've been going for walks, walking and thinking, thinking and feeling myself grow stronger, spiritually, with every day that passes. Kostya, I know now, I understand that what's important about our work – whether we act on the stage or write – isn't fame, it isn't glory, it's none of those things I used to dream of, it's simply the capacity to endure. To bear your cross, and have faith. I have faith, and it doesn't hurt so much – when I think of my profession, I'm no longer afraid of life.

KOSTYA (*sadly*). You've found your way, you know where you're going, but I'm still drifting in a chaos of dreams and images, I've no idea what for, or for whom. I've no faith, I don't even know what my profession is.

NINA (*listening*). Ssshh . . . I'm going now. Goodbye. You'll come and see me, when I'm a great actress, won't you. Promise? Anyway . . . (*Presses his hand.*) It's getting late. I can hardly stand up. I'm so tired, and hungry.

KOSTYA. Stay, please. I'll get you some supper.

NINA. No, no. And don't come with me, I'll find my own way. My carriage is quite near. So, she brought him with her? Well, what does it matter? When you see Trigorin, don't say anything to him. I love him. I love him even more than before. An idea for a short story . . . I love him, love him passionately, desperately. Life used to be so good, Kostya! Do you remember? Everything was so clear and warm, life was so joyous, so innocent – and such feelings we had, like delicate, exquisite flowers. Do you remember? (*Recites.*) 'Men, lions, eagles and partridges, the antlered deer, geese, spiders, silent fish that roam the deep, the starfish and all creatures unseen by the eye – in brief, all life, all living things, their mournful cycle ended, are extinct. For many thousand years, the earth has borne no living creature, and in vain does this poor moon now light its lamp. No longer does the meadow crane awaken with a cry, the may-bug in the lime grove hums no more . . . ' (*Impulsively embraces* KOSTYA *and runs out through the French window.*)

KOSTYA (*after a pause*). I hope nobody meets her in the garden and tells mother. It might upset her.

KOSTYA *spends the next two minutes tearing up his manuscripts and flinging them under his desk, then he unlocks the door at right and exits.*

DORN (*trying to open the door at left*). That's odd. The door appears to be locked . . . (*Enters and returns the armchair to its place.*) A veritable obstacle race.

Enter ARKADINA *and* POLINA, *followed by* YAKOV *with some bottles, and* MASHA, *then* SHAMRAEV *and* TRIGORIN.

ARKADINA. Put the red wine, and the beer for Mr Trigorin here on the table. We'll have a drink while we play. Now, let's sit down, everybody.

POLINA (*to* YAKOV). And bring in the tea as well.

SHAMRAEV (*leads* TRIGORIN *over to the cupboard*). See, here's the thing I was telling you about . . . (*Takes out the stuffed seagull.*) As you ordered.

TRIGORIN (*looking at the seagull*). I don't remember. (*Thinks for a moment.*) No, I don't remember.

A shot is heard offstage right. Everyone gives a start.

ARKADINA (*alarmed*). What was that?

DORN. Oh, nothing. I expect something's gone off in my medicine bag. Not to worry. (*Exits right, re-enters half a minute later.*) Yes, as I thought. A bottle of ether's burst. (*Sings.*) 'Once more I stand before thee, enchanted . . . '

ARKADINA (*sitting down at the table*). My goodness, that gave me a fright. It reminded me of the time . . . (*Covers her face with her hands.*) I almost fainted . . .

DORN (*leafing through a magazine, to* TRIGORIN). There was an article in here a couple of months ago. A letter from America, and I was meaning to ask you . . . (*Takes* TRIGORIN *by the waist and leads him downstage to the footlights.*) since I'm extremely interested in this matter . . . (*Lowers his voice, in a hushed tone.*) Get Madame Arkadina away from here. The thing is, Kostya's shot himself.

Curtain.

UNCLE VANYA

Scenes from country life in four acts

Dramatis Personae

SEREBRYAKOV, Alexander Vladimirovich, *a retired professor*

YELENA Andreyevna, *his wife, aged 27*

SONYA (Sofya Alexandrovna), *his daughter by his first marriage*

MARIA VASILIEVNA Voinitskaya, *widow of a Privy Councillor, mother of the professor's first wife*

VANYA, Ivan Petrovich Voinitsky, *her son*

ASTROV, Mikhail Lvovich, *a doctor*

TELEGIN, Ilya Ilyich, *an impoverished landowner*

MARINA, *an old nurse*

A WORKMAN

The action takes place on Serebryakov's country estate.

For a Guide to Pronunciation of Names, see page 279.

ACT ONE

A garden. Part of the house and a veranda can be seen. Under an old poplar tree in the avenue, a table is set for tea. Benches and chairs; on one of the benches lies a guitar, and a little way off from the table is a swing. It is between two and three in the afternoon, cloudy and overcast. MARINA, a stout, slow-moving old woman, is sitting by the samovar, knitting a stocking, and ASTROV is walking up and down nearby.

MARINA (*pouring a glass of tea*). Have some tea, my dear.

ASTROV (*accepts it reluctantly*). I don't really feel like it.

MARINA. Maybe you'd take a drop of vodka?

ASTROV. No. No, I don't drink vodka every day. Besides, it's rather close. (*A pause.*) Nanny, how long have we known each other?

MARINA (*pondering*). How long? Goodness, let me think . . . You came here, to these parts, when was it . . . ? Sonya's mother, Vera Petrovna, was still alive. And you were coming to us for two winters, while she was here . . . so, that would make it about eleven years. (*After some thought.*) Maybe more . . .

ASTROV. Have I changed much since then?

MARINA. Oh, a lot. You were young in those days, and handsome, and now you've aged. You're not as good-looking. And you like a drop of vodka now.

ASTROV. Yes . . . In ten years I've become a different person. And what's the cause? Too much hard work, Nanny. I'm on my feet the whole day, I don't know the meaning of rest. I hide under the blanket at night, afraid I'm going to be hauled out to see a patient. In all the time we've known each other, I haven't had a single day off. No wonder I've aged. And life's boring in itself, mindless and squalid . . . It drags you down, this life. You're surrounded by the strangest people, cranks, all of them; you live amongst them two or three years, and gradually, without even noticing it, you become a crank yourself. It's inevitable. (*Twirling his long moustache.*) And this huge moustache I've grown . . . it's so stupid. Yes, I've become a crank, Nanny . . . I haven't gone completely ga-ga yet, thank God, my brain's still in one piece, but my feelings have somehow got blunted. I don't want anything, I don't need anything, I don't love anybody . . . Apart from you, of course. (*Kisses her on the forehead.*) When I was a child, I had a nanny just like you.

MARINA. Would you like something to eat?

ASTROV. No, thanks. In the third week of Lent, I had to go to Malitskoye. There was an epidemic . . . typhus . . . People stretched out in rows in the huts . . . Filth, stench, smoke everywhere, calves lying on the floor among the sick . . . young pigs too . . . I was on the go all day, didn't sit down, not even a bite to eat, and when I finally arrived home I got no rest either – they brought in a signalman from the railway; I laid him out on the table, and was about to operate, when he upped and died on me, under the chloroform. And just when I didn't need it, some sort of feeling awoke in me, and my conscience started to nag at me, as if I'd killed him deliberately . . . I sat down, closed my eyes – like this, and started thinking: the people who come after us, in two or three hundred years' time, the people we're now clearing the way for – will they remember us, d'you think? They won't, Marina, will they.

MARINA. People won't remember, but God will.

ASTROV. Thank you. That was well said.

VANYA *enters, emerging from the house. He has had a nap after lunch and looks a little dishevelled; he sits down on a bench and fixes his fashionable tie.*

VANYA. Yes . . . (*A pause.*) Yes . . .

ASTROV. Had a good sleep?

VANYA. Yes . . . very. (*Yawns.*) You know, ever since the
Professor and his spouse came to stay, my life's been out
of joint . . . I sleep at the wrong time, eat all sorts of
spicy food at lunch and dinner, drink wine . . . it's not
healthy! We never used to have a spare minute, Sonya
and I worked non-stop – but now, Sonya does all the
work, and I do nothing but eat, drink and sleep . . . It's
unhealthy!

MARINA (*shaking her head*). Such goings-on! The Professor
doesn't get up till twelve, but the samovar's kept boiling
the whole morning, waiting for him. Before they came we
used to have dinner at one, same as everybody else, and
now they're here it's at seven. The Professor reads and
writes all night, and you'll suddenly hear the bell at about
two . . . Heavens, what is it? Tea! So the servants have to
be wakened, to put on the samovar . . . What a carry-on!

ASTROV. Will they be staying here much longer?

VANYA (*whistles*). A hundred years. The Professor's made up
his mind to settle down.

MARINA. Look at this now. The samovar's been on the
table the past two hours, and they've gone out for a walk.

VANYA. They're coming, they're coming . . . Don't worry.

Voices are heard offstage. From the far end of the garden come
SEREBRYAKOV, YELENA, SONYA *and* TELEGIN,
returning from their walk.

SEREBRYAKOV. Splendid, absolutely splendid . . . The
scenery's wonderful.

TELEGIN. Quite remarkable, Your Excellency.

SONYA. We'll go to the plantation tomorrow, papa – would
you like that?

VANYA. Ladies and gentlemen – tea's ready!

SEREBRYAKOV. Dear friends, be so kind as to have tea
sent up to my study. I've a few things still to do today.

SONYA. I'm sure you'll enjoy it at the plantation . . .

YELENA, SEREBRYAKOV *and* SONYA *exit into the house.*
TELEGIN goes over to the table and sits down beside
MARINA.

VANYA. It's stiflingly hot, yet our great scholar's wearing a
coat and galoshes, and carrying his umbrella and gloves.

ASTROV. Taking good care of himself.

VANYA. And she's so lovely. So lovely! In my entire life, I've
never seen a more beautiful woman.

TELEGIN (*to* MARINA). You know, dear lady, whether I'm
riding through the fields, or walking in the shade in the
garden, or just looking at this table, I experience a feeling
of such bliss, I can't explain it! The weather's enchanting,
the little birds are singing, we all live in peace and
harmony here – what more could we ask? (*Accepts a glass of
tea.*) Thank you most kindly!

VANYA (*dreamily*). Those eyes . . . A wonderful woman!

ASTROV. Tell us something, Vanya.

VANYA (*listlessly*). What've I got to tell you?

ASTROV. What, nothing new?

VANYA. No. All old stuff. I'm just the same as I was, except
maybe worse, now that I've become lazy, and do nothing
– apart from grumble, like some old fogey. And that old
magpie of mine, my dear *maman*, still prattles on about the
emancipation of women. She's got one eye fixed on her
grave, while the other searches through her learned tomes,
looking for the dawn of a new life.

ASTROV. And the Professor?

VANYA. The Professor, as ever, sits in his study from morn
till dead of night, writing. 'With anxious mind and
furrowed brow, we write and write and write, And no
praise ever comes our way, our labours to requite.' I feel
sorry for the paper! He'd do better to write his
autobiography. Now there's a superb subject! A retired
professor, you see, a dry old stick, a sort of scholarly
kipper . . . Gout, rheumatism, migraine, his liver bloated

with jealousy and envy . . . And this dried fish lives on his
first wife's estate, stays there against his will, because he
can't afford to live in town. He's forever going on about
his misfortunes, although in point of fact he's been
extraordinarily lucky. (*Excitedly.*) Yes, just think, what luck
he's had! The son of a humble sacristan, he trains as a
priest, somehow manages to get university degrees and a
professorship, goes on to become 'Your Excellency', and
the son-in-law of a Senator, etc., etc. All that's neither
here nor there, but consider this. A man spends twenty-
five years, no less, lecturing and writing about art, and
doesn't understand the first thing about it. For twenty-five
years he's been chewing over other people's ideas about
realism, naturalism, and all manner of nonsense; for
twenty-five years he's been lecturing and writing about
things that any intelligent person already knows, and no
stupid person cares to know. In a word, for twenty-five
years he's been pouring water into a sieve. And the self-
importance of the man! The pretensions! So now he's
retired, and nobody's ever heard of him, he's completely
unknown; which means that for twenty-five years he's
been keeping somebody else out of a job. And look at
him – strutting around, half-man, half-god!

ASTROV. Oh, come on, you envy him.

VANYA. Of course I envy him! Look at his success with
women! No Don Juan ever experienced a more complete
triumph! His first wife, my sister, a beautiful, gentle
creature, as pure as that blue sky, a noble, generous
woman, who had more admirers than he had students –
she loved him the way only the angels can love beings as
pure and beautiful as themselves. My mother, his mother-
in-law, worships him to this day, and he still inspires her
with a feeling of devout awe. His second wife, a beautiful,
clever woman – you've just seen her – married him when
he was already old, surrendered her youth, her beauty,
her freedom, her radiance to him. What for? Why?

ASTROV. Is she faithful to the Professor?

VANYA. Unfortunately, yes.

ASTROV. What do you mean, unfortunately?

VANYA. Because that kind of faithfulness is a sham from
beginning to end. It's got plenty of rhetoric, but no logic.
To deceive an old husband, whom you can't abide – that's
immoral; but to attempt to stifle your wretched youth,
every living emotion you possess – that's not immoral?

TELEGIN (*tearfully*). Vanya, I don't like it when you say
these things. It's the truth, you know . . . If somebody
deceives their wife or husband, well, that means they're
not to be trusted, they'd even betray their country!

VANYA (*irritated*). Oh, give it a rest, Waffles!

TELEGIN. Vanya, let me speak. My wife ran off with the
man she loved, the day after our wedding, on account of
my unprepossessing appearance. But I've never failed in
my duty. I still love her, and I've stayed true to her. I
help as much as I can, and I've given up everything I
owned for her children's education, the ones she had by
the man she loved. I've had to do without happiness, but
I still have my pride. But what about her? She's lost her
youth now, her beauty, in accordance with the laws of
nature, has faded, and the man she loved is dead. What
does she have left?

Enter SONYA *and* YELENA, *followed a moment later by*
MARIA VASILIEVNA, *holding a book. She sits down and
begins to read. A cup of tea is handed to her, and she drinks it
without looking up.*

SONYA (*hurriedly, to* MARINA). Nanny dear, some peasants
have come. Go and have a word with them, I'll look after
the tea . . . (*Pours out the tea.*)

MARINA *exits,* YELENA *takes her cup of tea and drinks it
sitting on the swing.*

ASTROV (*to* YELENA). I've actually come to see your
husband. You wrote me that he was very ill, rheumatism
and something else, but he seems perfectly fit.

YELENA. He was a bit depressed yesterday evening,
complaining of pains in his legs, but he's all right today . . .

ASTROV. And I've galloped twenty miles at breakneck speed. Oh well, it's not the first time. I'll stay here overnight to make up for it – at least I'll be able to sleep *quantum satis.*

SONYA. That's wonderful. It's such a rare event, having you stay the night with us. You won't have had any dinner, I suppose?

ASTROV. No, I haven't.

SONYA. Then that's settled, you'll dine with us. We have dinner about seven these days. (*Drinks.*) This tea's cold!

TELEGIN. Yes, the temperature of the samovar has fallen significantly.

YELENA. Never mind, Ivan Ivanych, we can drink it cold.

TELEGIN. Forgive me, ma'am, but it's not Ivan Ivanych, it's Ilya Ilyich . . . Ilya Ilyich Telegin, or, as certain people call me on account of my pockmarked face – Waffles. I stood godfather at dear Sonya's christening, and His Excellency your husband knows me quite well. I live here now, ma'am, on this estate . . . If you've been kind enough to notice, I dine with you here every day.

SONYA. Mr Telegin helps us out – he's our right-hand man. (*Tenderly.*) Come on, godfather, I'll pour you another glass.

MARIA. Oh!

SONYA. What's the matter, grandma?

MARIA. I forgot to tell Alexander . . . my mind's going . . . I had a letter today from Pavel Alexeyevich in Kharkov . . . He's sent his new pamphlet.

ASTROV. Is it interesting?

MARIA. It is, but it's rather strange. He's now trying to disprove the very thing he was defending seven years ago. It's dreadful!

VANYA. There's nothing dreadful about it. Drink your tea, *maman.*

MARIA. But I want to talk!

VANYA. And we've been talking and reading pamphlets for fifty years now. It's time we called it a day.

MARIA. For some reason or other, you don't like listening when I talk. I'm sorry, *Jean*, but this past year you've changed so much I simply don't recognise you . . . You used to be a man of such firm convictions, a truly enlightened individual . . .

VANYA. Oh yes! I used to be an enlightened individual, only I never managed to enlighten anybody . . . (*A pause.*) An enlightened individual . . . you couldn't have come up with a more venomous jibe! I'm forty-seven years old now. And up until last year I made every effort, as did you, to blind myself with all this pedantic rubbish of yours, quite deliberately, to avoid seeing life as it really is – and I was doing rather well, I thought. But now – oh, if you only knew! I can't sleep at nights for sheer vexation, for resentment at having so stupidly wasted my time – that time when I might've had everything which my old age now denies me!

SONYA. Uncle Vanya, please, this is boring.

MARIA (*to her son*). It's almost as if you were accusing your former principles. But those aren't to blame, you are. You seem to have forgotten that principles are nothing in themselves, a dead letter . . . You should've been doing something.

VANYA. Doing something? It isn't everybody that can be a non-stop writing machine, like your Herr Professor.

MARIA. What's that supposed to mean?

SONYA (*imploringly*). Grandma! Uncle Vanya! Please!

VANYA. Right, right, I'll shut up. I'll shut up and apologise.

A pause.

YELENA. It's a lovely day. Not too hot . . .

A pause.

VANYA. A lovely day for hanging yourself . . .

TELEGIN *tunes his guitar.* MARINA *walks up and down near the house, calling the chickens.*

MARINA. Cheep, cheep, cheep . . .

SONYA. Nanny dear, what did those peasants want?

MARINA. Oh, same as usual, they're still after that bit of waste ground. Cheep, cheep, cheep . . .

SONYA. Which one are you calling?

MARINA. The speckled one, she's gone off somewhere with her chicks . . . Don't want the crows to get them . . . (*Exits.*)

TELEGIN *plays a polka; everyone listens in silence. A* WORKMAN *enters.*

WORKMAN. Is the doctor here? (*To* ASTROV.) Dr Astrov, we've been sent to fetch you.

ASTROV. Sent from where?

WORKMAN. From the factory.

ASTROV (*irritated*). Thank you so much. Well, I suppose I'd better go . . . (*Looks round for his cap.*) This is a damned nuisance . . .

SONYA. It is annoying, really . . . Come back for dinner, after the factory.

ASTROV. No, it'll be too late by then. No chance . . . (*To the* WORKMAN.) Look, you might bring me a glass of vodka, there's a good chap. (*The* WORKMAN *exits.*) No, no hope, I'm afraid . . . (*Finds his cap.*) In one of Ostrovsky's plays there's a character with a very large moustache, and a very little talent . . . That's like me. Anyway, I'll bid you goodbye . . . (*To* YELENA.) If you'd like to drop in on me sometime, with Sonya here of course, I'd be delighted. I have a small estate, ninety acres or so, but if you're interested, there's a model garden and nursery – you won't find their like for hundreds of miles around. And there's a government plantation alongside . . .

The forester there's quite old, and always ill, so I actually oversee all the work.

YELENA. Yes, you're very keen on trees, so I've been told. It's no doubt of great benefit, but doesn't it interfere with your real work? After all, you are a doctor.

ASTROV. Only God knows what our real work is.

YELENA. And is it interesting?

ASTROV. It is interesting, yes.

VANYA (*ironically*). Oh, very.

YELENA (*to* ASTROV). You're still young – you look about – what? Thirty-six, thirty-seven? It can't be that interesting, surely . . . Nothing but trees and more trees. I should think it was monotonous.

SONYA. No, it's extremely interesting. Dr Astrov plants new forests every year, and they've already sent him a bronze medal and a diploma. He goes to endless trouble to make sure the old forests aren't destroyed. And if you hear what he has to say, you'll agree with him absolutely. He says the forests beautify the earth, that they teach us to appreciate beauty, and instil a true majesty of spirit in us. Forests temper a harsh climate, and in countries with a mild climate, people spend less energy struggling with nature, so man himself is milder and more gentle. People in those countries are beautiful, pliant, easily moved, their speech is elegant, their gestures graceful. The arts and sciences flourish among them, their philosophy isn't gloomy, and their attitudes towards women are courteous and refined . . .

VANYA (*laughing*). Bravo, bravo! That's all very nice, but not convincing . . . (*To* ASTROV.) So, my friend, you won't mind if I carry on burning logs in my stove, and building my barns out of wood.

ASTROV. You can burn peat in your stove, and build your barns out of stone. Anyway, I don't mind people cutting wood from necessity, but why destroy the forests? Our Russian forests are groaning under the axe, millions of trees are perishing, the habitats of animals and birds are being laid waste, rivers are shrinking and drying up, the most wonderful landscapes are disappearing, never to return, all because some lazy individual hasn't the wit to bend down and pick up his firewood from the ground. (*To* YELENA.) Isn't it the truth, dear lady? A man would need to be a mindless savage to burn up such beauty in his stove, to destroy what he cannot create. We've been endowed with reason, and creative power, so we can increase what has been given to us, but up to now we've created nothing, only destroyed. There are fewer and fewer forests, the rivers are running dry, wild life is becoming extinct, the climate's ruined, and with each passing day the earth gets poorer and uglier. (*To* VANYA.) Yes, you're giving me that ironical look, you don't take anything I say seriously, and maybe . . . well, maybe I am a crank, but when I walk past the peasants' woods, which I've saved from being cut down, or when I hear my own young trees rustling, trees I've planted with my own hand, I'm conscious of the fact that the climate is in my control, to some extent, and that if people are happy a thousand years from now, then that will be my doing, to some extent, also. When I plant a birch tree, and see it coming into leaf, and swaying in the wind, my heart fills with pride, and I . . . (*Notices the* WORKMAN, *who has brought him a glass of vodka on a tray.*) Anyway . . . (*Drinks.*) It's time I was off. I suppose it's just one of my eccentricities, in the long run. Well, I bid you goodbye! (*Goes towards the house.*)

SONYA (*takes his arm and walks with him*). When will you come back to see us?

ASTROV. I don't know . . .

SONYA. In a month's time, again?

    ASTROV *and* SONYA *exit to the house;* MARIA VASILIEVNA *and* TELEGIN *remain by the table;* YELENA *and* VANYA *walk towards the veranda.*

YELENA. Ivan Petrovich, you're impossible. Did you really need to annoy your mother, with all that talk about a writing machine? And you were arguing with Alexander at lunch again today. It's so petty!

VANYA. What if I hate the man?

YELENA. You've no reason to hate him, he's no different from anyone else. He's no worse than you.

VANYA. If you could just see your face, the way you move . . . As if everything's too much effort. Sheer indolence!

YELENA. Oh yes, indolent and bored. Everyone decries my husband, they all look at me with such compassion: poor, unhappy creature, she's got an old husband. Well, I know all about that kind of sympathy. It's just what Astrov was saying a moment ago: you destroy the forests without a thought, and soon there'll be nothing left on the earth. And you'd destroy a human being the same way, senselessly, and thanks to you, there'll soon be no fidelity, no integrity, no capacity for self-sacrifice left either! Why is it you can't look at a woman indifferently, unless she's yours? I'll tell you why – that doctor's right – it's because there's a demon of destruction in every one of you. You spare nothing, neither forests, nor birds, nor women, nor one another.

VANYA. I don't care for this line of thought!

A pause.

YELENA. The doctor has a tired, sensitive face. An interesting face. Sonya's obviously attracted to him; she's in love with him, and I can understand her feelings. He's been at the house three times since I've been here, but I'm too shy – I haven't once had a proper talk with him, or been nice to him. He'll think I'm bad-tempered. No doubt that's why we get on so well, Ivan Petrovich – that we're both such tiresome, boring people! Tiresome, yes! Don't look at me like that, please, I don't like it.

VANYA. How else can I look at you, if I love you? You're my happiness, my life, my youth! I know the chances of you returning my love are non-existent, virtually nil, but I don't want anything, just let me look at you, hear your voice . . .

YELENA. Sshh, they might hear you!

They walk towards the house.

VANYA (*following her*). Let me speak about my love, don't drive me away, and that'll be the greatest happiness for me . . .

YELENA. This is agony . . .

They exit into the house. TELEGIN *is strumming on his guitar, playing a polka;* MARIA VASILIEVNA *is making notes on the margins of her pamphlet.*

Curtain.

ACT TWO

*The dining-room of the Serebryakov house. It is night, and
the* WATCHMAN *can be heard tapping in the garden.*
SEREBRYAKOV *is sitting in an armchair in front of the open
window, dozing.* YELENA *is sitting beside him, also dozing.*

SEREBRYAKOV (*waking up*). Who's that? Sonya, is that
  you?

YELENA. It's me.

SEREBRYAKOV. Oh, it's you, Lena . . . This pain, it's
  unbearable.

YELENA. Your rug's fallen on the floor. (*Wraps it around his
  legs.*) I'll close the window, Alexander.

SEREBRYAKOV. No, it's too stuffy. I dozed off just now,
  and dreamt my left leg didn't belong to me. Then I woke
  up with this agonizing pain. No, this isn't gout, it's more
  likely rheumatism. What time is it now?

YELENA. Twenty past twelve.

  A pause.

SEREBRYAKOV. See if you can find Batyushkov in the
  library in the morning. I think we've got him.

YELENA. What?

SEREBRYAKOV. Batyushkov – have a look in the morning.
  We had a copy at one time, as I remember. Why am I
  finding it so hard to breathe?

YELENA. You're tired. This is your second night without
  sleep.

SEREBRYAKOV. They say Turgenev got angina from gout.
  I'm afraid I might do the same. Damnable, disgusting old

age! To hell with it! Since I've grown old, I've become repellent even to myself. Yes, and all of you, no doubt, hate the sight of me.

YELENA. That tone of voice – you talk about your old age as if it was our fault.

SEREBRYAKOV. And you must hate me most of all.

YELENA *gets up and sits down a little way off.*

Well, you're right, of course. I'm not stupid, I do understand. You're a young woman, healthy, attractive, you want to live, and I'm an old man, practically a corpse. Isn't that so? D'you think I don't understand? And of course it's stupid of me to carry on living. Well, just wait a while, I'll set you all free soon enough. I haven't much longer to go.

YELENA. I'm worn out . . . For God's sake, be quiet.

SEREBRYAKOV. Yes, thanks to me, it seems, everybody's exhausted, bored, wasting their youth – I'm the only one who's contented, and enjoying life. Yes, of course.

YELENA. Oh, stop it! You're getting on my nerves.

SEREBRYAKOV. I get on everybody's nerves. Of course I do.

YELENA (*tearfully*). This is intolerable! What do you want from me, tell me!

SEREBRYAKOV. Nothing.

YELENA. Well, be quiet then. Please.

SEREBRYAKOV. You know, it's strange – when Ivan Petrovich starts talking, or his mother, that old fool, that's fine, everyone listens. But I've only to utter one word, and everyone starts feeling miserable. The very sound of my voice disgusts them. Well, supposing I am disgusting, selfish, a tyrant – surely I have a right to be selfish, in my old age? Haven't I earned it? I'm asking you, haven't I the right to a bit of peace, to a little consideration from people?

YELENA. Nobody's disputing your rights.

The window is banging in the wind.

The wind's getting up. I'll close the window. (*Does so.*) It's going to rain in a minute. No-one disputes your rights.

A pause. The WATCHMAN *is heard tapping in the garden, and singing a song.*

SEREBRYAKOV. You devote your entire life to learning, you grow accustomed to your study, to the lecture theatre, to your esteemed colleagues – and suddenly, for no discernible reason, you find yourself buried in this hole, looking at stupid people every day, listening to trivial chit-chat . . . I want to live, I love success, I enjoy being famous, causing a stir, and here – it's like being in exile. To spend every minute yearning for what's past, watching other people succeed, fearing death . . . I can't go on! I haven't the strength! And then they can't forgive me for my old age!

YELENA. Wait a little while, have patience. In five or six years, I'll be old too.

SONYA *enters.*

SONYA. Papa, you told us to send for Dr Astrov, and now he's here you're refusing to see him. That isn't nice. We've put him to a lot of trouble for nothing.

SEREBRYAKOV. What do I want with this Astrov of yours? He knows as much about medicine as I know about astronomy.

SONYA. Look, we can't summon the entire medical faculty to attend to your gout.

SEREBRYAKOV. Well, I'm not going to talk to that crank.

SONYA. Do as you please. (*Sits down.*) I don't care.

SEREBRYAKOV. What time is it now?

YELENA. It's after twelve.

SEREBRYAKOV. It's so stuffy. Sonya, hand me my drops from the table.

SONYA. Right. (*Gives him the drops.*)

SEREBRYAKOV (*irritated*). No, not these! Oh, what's the point of asking for anything!

SONYA. Don't make such a fuss, please. That might work with some people, but not with me, if you don't mind. I don't like it. And I haven't the time, I've an early rise tomorrow, we're cutting the hay.

VANYA *enters in his dressing-gown, holding a candle.*

VANYA. There's a storm on the way.

A flash of lightning.

There you are, you see? *Hélène* and Sonya, go to bed, I'll take over here.

SEREBRYAKOV (*alarmed*). No, no! Don't leave me with him! No! He'll talk me to death!

VANYA. But they need some peace! They haven't slept in two nights.

SEREBRYAKOV. Then let them go to bed, but you go too. Thanks all the same, but please go. For the sake of our former friendship, don't argue, please – we'll talk another time.

VANYA (*with a mocking smile*). Our former friendship . . . Former . . .

SONYA. Uncle Vanya, please . . .

SEREBRYAKOV (*to* YELENA). Don't leave me with him, my dear – he will, he'll talk me to death!

VANYA. This is getting ridiculous.

MARINA *enters with a candle.*

SONYA. You should be in bed, Nanny. It's late.

MARINA. The samovar hasn't been cleared away. I can't very well go to bed.

SEREBRYAKOV. Everybody's awake, everybody's worn out – except me, I'm blissfully happy.

MARINA (*goes up to* SEREBRYAKOV, *then soothingly*). What is it, my dear? Is it hurting again? My leg's hurting something awful too. (*Tucks his rug in.*) It's that old trouble of yours, that's what it is. Vera Petrovna, God rest her, Sonya's mother, she used to be up night after night with you, worried sick. She was so fond of you. (*A pause.*) Old folks are like children, they want people to feel sorry for them, but nobody pities us old folks, no. (*Kisses* SEREBRYAKOV *on the shoulder.*) Come on, my dear, let's go to bed . . . Come on, lovey . . . I'll make you some nice lime-flower tea, and warm your feet . . . And I'll say a prayer for you . . .

SEREBRYAKOV (*moved*). We'll go then, Marina.

MARINA. Yes, my leg's hurting something awful, it is. (*She and* SONYA *lead him out.*) Yes, Vera Petrovna used to be worried sick, crying all the time. You were just a girl then, Sonya love, a silly little thing. Now, off we go, my dear . . .

SEREBRYAKOV, SONYA *and* MARINA *exit.*

YELENA. I'm worn out with him. I can hardly stand.

VANYA. You're worn out with him, I'm worn out with myself. I haven't slept in three nights.

YELENA. There's something seriously amiss in this house. Your mother hates everything except those pamphlets of hers and the Professor; the Professor's constantly irritated, he doesn't trust me, and he's afraid of you. Sonya's annoyed with her father, and annoyed with me − she hasn't spoken to me for two weeks now. You detest my husband, and openly despise your own mother. And I'm upset − I've been on the verge of tears a dozen times already today. No, there's something badly amiss in this house.

VANYA. We can do without the philosophy.

YELENA. You're an educated man, Vanya, a clever man − you surely ought to know that it's not fire and gangs of thieves destroying the world, but hatred, enmity, all these petty squabbles . . . You should be trying to keep the peace, not complaining all the time.

VANYA. Then first make me at peace with myself! Oh, my darling . . . (*Suddenly bends down to kiss her hand.*)

YELENA. Stop it! (*Pulls her hand free.*) Go away!

VANYA. The rain'll be over in a minute, and everything in nature'll be refreshed, breathing easily again. Except me, the storm won't refresh me. Day and night, it's like some sort of hobgoblin, choking me, the thought that my life's wasted, gone beyond recall. I've no past, it's been stupidly squandered on trifles, and my present is so absurd it's terrifying. So there you have it, my life and love: where am I to put them, what's to be done with them? My feelings for you are dying to no purpose, like a ray of sunlight falling into a pit, and I'm dying along with them.

YELENA. When you talk to me about your love, I just go numb, and I don't know what to say. I'm sorry, there's nothing I can tell you. (*Makes to leave.*) Good night.

VANYA (*barring her way*). And if you only knew how much I suffer, knowing that there's another life perishing alongside mine in this house – yours! What are you waiting for? What damned philosophy's holding you back? Think, for God's sake, think!

YELENA (*looks at him intently*). Ivan Petrovich, you're drunk.

VANYA. Possibly. It's possible . . .

YELENA. Where's the doctor?

VANYA. He's in there . . . In my room, he's staying the night. Yes, it's possible. Anything's possible.

YELENA. And you've been drinking today? What on earth for?

VANYA. At least it's some sort of life . . . *Hélène*, don't make me stop.

YELENA. You never used to drink. And you never used to talk so much . . . Go to bed. You're getting on my nerves.

VANYA (*impulsively kissing her hand*). Oh, my darling . . . wonderful . . .

YELENA (*angrily*). Stop it! Leave me alone! This is disgusting. Honestly! (*Exits.*)

VANYA (*alone*). She's gone . . . (*A pause.*) I first met her at my sister's house, ten years ago. She was seventeen, and I was thirty-seven. Why didn't I fall in love with her then, and ask her to marry me? It would've been quite possible. And she would be my wife now . . . Yes . . . We'd both have been wakened by the storm just now; she'd be frightened by the thunder, I'd hold her in my arms and whisper: 'Don't be afraid, I'm here.' Oh, it's a wonderful thought, so beautiful, it actually makes me laugh . . . but, dear God, my mind's in such a muddle . . . Why am I old? Why doesn't she understand me? That empty rhetoric of hers, that facile morality – her silly, half-baked ideas about the destruction of the world – I detest all that. (*A pause.*) Oh, I've been cheated so badly! I worshipped that Professor, that sorry gout-ridden specimen, I worked like a slave for him! Sonya and I squeezed every last drop out of this estate; we sold linseed oil, and peas, and curds, haggling like peasants, skimping on food, saving up every miserable kopeck so we could send him thousands of roubles! I was so proud of him and his learning, I lived and breathed for that man! Everything he wrote, every word he uttered, seemed to me like a work of genius . . . And now? My God . . . Here he is, retired, and the sum total of his life is plain to see. Not one page of his labours will survive him, he's completely unknown, a nonentity! A soap bubble! And I've been cheated . . . I can see it now – stupidly deceived . . .

ASTROV *enters wearing a coat, but no waistcoat or tie; he is slightly drunk. He is followed by* TELEGIN, *with his guitar.*

ASTROV. Play!

TELEGIN. They're all asleep.

ASTROV. Go on, play!

TELEGIN *begins quietly strumming.*

(*To* VANYA.) All alone here? No ladies? (*Stands with his arms akimbo, begins quietly singing.*) 'Go, little hut, go, little stove too – now what will poor master do? . . . ' The storm woke me up. Fair old spot of rain. What time is it?

VANYA. God knows.

ASTROV. I thought I heard Yelena Andreyevna's voice.

VANYA. She was here a moment ago.

ASTROV. A glorious woman. (*Inspects the medicine bottles on the table.*) Medicines. Prescriptions from all over the place . . . Kharkov, Moscow, Tula . . . He's plagued every town in Russia with his gout. Is he ill, or just pretending?

VANYA. He's ill.

A pause.

ASTROV. Why are you so glum today? Feeling sorry for the Professor, is that it?

VANYA. Leave me alone.

ASTROV. Or maybe you're in love with the Professor's wife?

VANYA. She's my friend.

ASTROV. Already?

VANYA. What's that mean – 'already'?

ASTROV. Well, a woman can only become a man's friend in a certain sequence: first, charming acquaintance, then mistress, then friend.

VANYA. That's a rather crude outlook.

ASTROV. Really? Yes . . . I have to admit – I am becoming rather crude. See, I'm even drunk. As a rule, I get this drunk only once a month. When I'm in this state I become arrogant and insolent in the extreme. I don't give a damn about anything. I take on the most difficult operations and do them beautifully; I draw up the most ambitious plans for the future. At times like this I no longer see myself as a crank – I believe I'm of tremendous benefit to mankind – tremendous! At such times I have my own personal philosophical system, and all of you, my friends, appear to me like insects . . . or microbes. (*To* TELEGIN.) Waffles, play!

TELEGIN. Dearest good friend, I'd be happy to, with all my heart, but do remember – people are asleep.

ASTROV. Play, I said! (TELEGIN *begins softly playing.*) I could do with a drink. Come on, I think there's still some cognac left. As soon as it's light we'll go to my place. Roight? I've got a male nurse who never says 'right', but 'roight'. A terrible rogue. All roight, then? (*Catches sight of* SONYA *entering.*) I beg your pardon – I'm not dressed . . . (*Hurriedly exits.* TELEGIN *follows him out.*)

SONYA. Uncle Vanya, you've been drinking with the doctor again. You're a fine pair! He's always like that, but why you? It's not very becoming at your age.

VANYA. Age has nothing to do with it. When people have no real life, they live off illusions. They're better than nothing.

SONYA. The hay's all been cut, and it's raining every day – everything's rotting, and you sit daydreaming. You've completely neglected the estate . . . I've had to work on my own, and I'm absolutely worn out . . . (*Alarmed.*) Uncle, you have tears in your eyes!

VANYA. What tears? Nothing of the kind . . . nonsense . . . The way you looked at me then – just like your mother. Oh, dearest Sonya . . . (*Feverishly kisses her hands and face.*) My sister . . . my darling sister . . . where is she now? If only she knew! Oh, if only she knew!

SONYA. Knew what? Uncle, if she knew what?

VANYA. It's too painful . . . I feel terrible . . . No, it doesn't matter . . . Later . . . It's nothing . . . I'll go . . . (*Exits.*)

SONYA (*knocks at* ASTROV'S *door*). Doctor? You're not asleep, are you? A minute, please.

ASTROV (*behind the door*). Just coming! (*Enters a few moments later. He is now wearing his waistcoat and tie.*) What can I do for you?

SONYA. Doctor, you can drink if you want, if it doesn't bother you, but please don't let my uncle drink. It's not good for him.

ASTROV. Fine. We won't drink any more (*A pause.*) I'm leaving for home now. Signed, sealed and delivered. By the time the horses are ready it'll be daylight.

SONYA. It's still raining. Wait till morning.

ASTROV. The storm's passing us by, we'll just catch the edge of it. I'll go now. And please, don't ask me to attend your father again. I tell him he has gout, he tells me it's rheumatism; I ask him to go to bed, he stays up. And today he wouldn't even speak to me.

SONYA. He's been spoiled. (*Goes over to the sideboard.*) Would you like something to eat?

ASTROV. Yes, why not?

SONYA. I like a snack at night-time. I think there's something in the sideboard. You know, he's supposed to have been a big success with women in his day, and the ladies have spoiled him. Here, have some cheese.

They both stand by the sideboard and eat.

ASTROV. I haven't had a thing to eat today, just drink. Your father's a difficult man. (*Takes a bottle out of the sideboard.*) May I? (*Drinks a glass.*) There's no-one else here, and I can speak frankly. You know, I don't think I could survive a month in this house, I'd simply suffocate in this atmosphere . . . Your father, going on all the time about his gout, and his books, Uncle Vanya, with his depression, that grandmother of yours, and on top of that, your stepmother . . .

SONYA. What about my stepmother?

ASTROV. Everything about a human being should be beautiful – face, clothes, soul, thoughts. And she is beautiful, there's no denying it, but . . . I mean, all she does is eat, sleep, go for walks, enchant us all with her beauty, and that's it. She has no responsibilities, other

people work for her . . . Isn't that the case? And an idle
life can't be virtuous. (*A pause.*) Well, maybe I'm being too
severe. I'm dissatisfied with life, like your Uncle Vanya,
and we're becoming a pair of old grumblers.

SONYA. Are you really not content with life?

ASTROV. I actually love life, but this narrow, provincial
Russian life of ours I simply can't abide, I despise it with
every fibre of my being. And as for my own personal life,
God knows, I can find absolutely nothing good in it. You
know, if you're walking through the forest on a dark
night, and you happen to see a light shining in the
distance, you don't notice your fatigue, or the dark, or the
thorny branches, whipping against your face . . . I work,
as you well know, harder than anyone else in this
province, I suffer the blows of fate incessantly, at times it's
unbearable, but I don't have any light shining in the
distance. I no longer expect anything for myself, I really
don't like people . . . I haven't cared for anybody in
years.

SONYA. Nobody?

ASTROV. No. I feel a certain affection towards your
old nurse, that's all – for old time's sake. The peasants are
all alike, backward, living in squalor, and I can't get along
with our intelligentsia – it's hard work, they wear you out.
The whole lot of them, all our good friends, they're so
shallow, the way they think and feel, they can't see farther
than the end of their noses – to put it bluntly, they're
stupid. And those with a bit more intelligence and
substance to them are hysterical, consumed with analysis
and introspection . . . They do nothing but whine,
indulging their petty hatreds and morbid slanders; they
sidle up to a man and squint at him out of the corner of
their eyes, and deliver their judgment: 'Yes, that one's a
neurotic!' or, 'Oh, he's full of hot air!' And since they
don't know what label to stick on my forehead, they say,
'He's a strange man, very strange.' I love the forest –
that's strange; I don't eat meat, that's strange too. No,
there's no longer any spontaneous, pure, free relationship

with nature, or with other people . . . Absolutely none!
(*He is about to drink.*)

SONYA (*prevents him*). No, please don't . . . don't drink any
more.

ASTROV. Why not?

SONYA. It's just so unlike you. You're so refined, you have
such a gentle voice . . . Besides, more than anyone else I
know, you're a wonderful person. So why do you want to
be like these commonplace people, the kind of men who
drink and play cards? No no, please don't do that. You
always say people don't create, they only destroy what's
been given to them from on high. Well, then, why are
you destroying yourself? Please, please, you mustn't, I
implore you!

ASTROV (*holds out his hand to her*). I won't drink any more.

SONYA. Give me your word.

ASTROV. Word of honour.

SONYA (*warmly squeezes his hand*). Thank you.

ASTROV. Enough! I've sobered up. You can see I'm sober
now, and I'll stay like that till the end of my days. (*Looks
at his watch.*) Anyway, to continue . . . As I was saying, my
time's past, it's too late for me . . . I've grown old, I'm
burned out, I've become coarse and vulgar, my emotions
are dulled, and I don't think I could become attached to
anyone. I don't love anyone, and now I never will. What
still attracts me is beauty. I'm not indifferent to that. And
frankly, if Yelena Andreyevna wanted to, she could turn
my head in a single day . . . However, that's not love,
that's not affection . . . (*Covers his eyes with his hand and
shudders.*)

SONYA. What's the matter?

ASTROV. Nothing . . . Just before Easter, one of my
patients died under the chloroform.

SONYA. It's time you forgot about that. (*A pause.*) Doctor,
tell me something . . . Say I had a girlfriend, or a

younger sister, and you found out that she . . . well, let's say she was in love with you, how would you feel about that?

ASTROV (*shrugs*). I don't know. I'd probably feel nothing at all. I'd let her know I couldn't love her . . . and besides, I've got other things on my mind. Anyway, I'd better go, if I'm going. I'll say goodbye, my dear, or it'll be morning before we're finished. (*Presses her hand.*) I'll go out through the drawing-room, if I may, otherwise I'm afraid your uncle might detain me. (*Exits.*)

SONYA (*alone*). He didn't tell me anything . . . His heart and soul are still hidden from me, yet why do I feel so happy? (*Laughs from sheer joy.*) I said to him: you're so refined, so noble, you have such a gentle voice . . . did that sound out of place? His voice thrills me, it's so caressing . . . I feel it in the air even now. But when I spoke to him about a younger sister, he didn't understand . . . (*Wringing her hands.*) Oh, it's dreadful that I'm so plain! It's terrible! I know I'm not attractive, I know it, I know it . . . Last Sunday, when we were coming out of church, I heard them talking about me, and one woman said: 'She's such a kind girl, so goodhearted, it's just a pity she's so plain . . . ' So plain . . .

YELENA *enters.*

YELENA (*opens the windows*). The storm's over. What lovely fresh air! (*A pause.*) Where's the doctor?

SONYA. He's gone.

A pause.

YELENA. Sophie . . .

SONYA. Yes?

YELENA. How long are you going to stay cross with me? We haven't done each other any harm. Why should we be enemies? Let's call it a day.

SONYA. I've been wanting to . . . (*Embraces her.*) No more anger.

YELENA. Excellent!

They are both very excited.

SONYA. Has papa gone to bed?

YELENA. No, he's sitting in the drawing-room. We don't talk to each other for weeks on end, God knows why . . . (*She notices the sideboard is open.*) What's this?

SONYA. The doctor was having some supper.

YELENA. And there's wine . . . Let's drink to our friendship.

SONYA. Yes, let's.

YELENA. Out of the same glass . . . (*Fills it.*) It's better that way. So . . . we're friends now?

SONYA. Friends. (*They drink, and kiss.*) I've been wanting to make it up with you for ages, but I felt ashamed somehow. (*Begins to cry.*)

YELENA. Heavens, what are you crying for?

SONYA. It's nothing, I can't help it.

YELENA. There, there . . . (*Begins to cry.*) Silly, I'm crying too, now . . . (*A pause.*) You're angry with me because you think I married your father for money. If you believe in oaths, then I'll swear to you I married him for love. I was attracted to him as a famous learned man. It wasn't genuine love, it was artificial, but it seemed real enough to me at the time. I'm not to blame. But from the very day of our wedding you've never stopped punishing me with those clever, suspicious eyes of yours.

SONYA. Anyway, peace, peace! Let's forget all that.

YELENA. You shouldn't look at people like that – it doesn't become you. You should trust people – otherwise life's just impossible.

A pause.

SONYA. Tell me truthfully, as a friend . . . Are you happy?

YELENA. No.

SONYA. I knew that. One more question. Tell me honestly – wouldn't you have liked a young husband?

YELENA. What a child you are still. Of course I would. (*Laughs.*) Well, ask me something else – go on . . .

SONYA. Do you like the doctor?

YELENA. Yes, very much.

SONYA (*laughs*). I look silly, don't I? I mean, he's gone now, but I can still hear his voice and his footsteps, and when I look at the dark window, it's as if I can see his face there. Let me tell you about it . . . But I can't say it out loud, I'm too ashamed. Let's go to my room, we can talk there. Do I seem silly to you? Now, confess . . . Tell me something about him . . .

YELENA. What d'you mean?

SONYA. He's so clever . . . He knows how to do things, he can do anything . . . He heals the sick, and he plants forests . . .

YELENA. It's not a question of medicine or forests . . . My dear, don't you understand? He has genius! And you know what that means? It means boldness, freedom of mind, breadth of vision . . . He plants a little tree, and already he's wondering what will come of it in a thousand years' time, he's already dreaming of the happiness of mankind. People like him are so rare, we must love them . . . Yes, he drinks, he's sometimes rather coarse, but what does that matter? No man of genius in Russia can be entirely without fault. Just imagine the sort of life that doctor leads! Impassable muddy roads, freezing cold, blizzards, enormous distances, an uncouth, primitive people, poverty and disease all around him – I mean, in conditions like that, slaving away day in, day out, it would be hard for any man to keep himself chaste and sober until he was forty . . . (*Kisses her.*) I wish you happiness with all my heart, you deserve it . . . (*Stands up.*) Anyway, I'm a tiresome creature, a person of no importance. In my music, in my husband's house, in all my little romantic affairs – everywhere, in fact, I've never been of any consequence. Actually, Sonya, when you come to think of it, I'm a very, very unfortunate woman. (*She is pacing about the stage in agitation.*) There's no happiness for me on this earth – none! Why are you laughing?

SONYA (*laughs, covering her face*). I'm just so happy . . . so happy!

YELENA. I feel like playing the piano . . . I could play something just now.

SONYA. Do, please. (*Embraces her.*) I can't sleep . . . Play something.

YELENA. In a minute. Your father isn't asleep. Music irritates him when he's sick. Go and ask him. If he doesn't mind, I'll play. On you go.

SONYA. Right. (*Exits.*)

The WATCHMAN *is heard tapping in the garden.*

YELENA. It's been ages since I've played. I'll play and I'll cry . . . cry like a silly girl. (*Calls out of the window.*) Yefim, is that you knocking?

WATCHMAN (*offstage*). It's me!

YELENA. Don't do that, the master's not well.

WATCHMAN. I'm just going! (*Whistles to his dog.*) Come on, Blackie! Good boy! Blackie, come on!

A pause.

SONYA (*returning*). We can't!

Curtain.

ACT THREE

The drawing-room of SEREBRYAKOV's *house. Three doors, at right, left and centre. Afternoon.* VANYA *and* SONYA *are seated, while* YELENA *paces about the stage, deep in thought.*

VANYA. The Herr Professor has graciously expressed the desire that we should all assemble here in this drawing-room today at one o'clock. (*Looks at his watch.*) Quarter to one. He wishes to make some statement to the world.

YELENA. Probably a business matter.

VANYA. He hasn't any sort of business. All he does is write nonsense, grumble, and feel jealous.

SONYA (*reproachfully*). Uncle!

VANYA. All right, all right, I'm sorry. (*Points at* YELENA.) Just look at her. Practically staggering from sheer indolence. Charming. Quite charming.

YELENA. And you keep droning on the whole day, on and on. Don't you ever get fed up? (*Wistfully.*) I'm dying of boredom, I just don't know what to do.

SONYA (*shrugs*). Well, there's plenty to do. If you felt like it . . .

YELENA. Like what, for instance?

SONYA. You could help with running the estate, teach children, or look after the sick. That's plenty, surely? And before you and papa came, Uncle Vanya and I used to go to the market ourselves and sell the flour.

YELENA. I wouldn't know how. And besides, it's not very interesting. It's only in romantic novels that people teach school and nurse the peasants. How am I going to take up teaching and nursing all of a sudden, just out of the blue?

SONYA. Well, that's what I don't understand. How can you help not going out to teach? Anyway, wait a while, and you'll get used to the idea. (*Embraces her.*) Try not to be bored, my dearest. (*Laughs.*) You're bored, you don't know what to do with yourself, but boredom and idleness are infectious. Look – Uncle Vanya does nothing, all he does is follow you around like a shadow, while I've left my work and come running in to have a chat with you. I've grown lazy, I can't help it! Doctor Astrov used to visit us only very rarely, once a month perhaps, and he took some persuading, but now he rides over here every day – he's abandoned his forests and medicine both. You must be a witch.

VANYA. What are you pining away for? (*Animatedly.*) Come on, my dearest, you glorious creature, be sensible! You've got mermaid's blood flowing in your veins, be a mermaid! Let yourself go even just once in your life, fall madly in love with some water-sprite, and plunge headlong into the depths – make the Herr Professor and all of us throw up our hands in horror!

YELENA (*angrily*). Leave me alone! This is so cruel! (*Makes to exit.*)

VANYA (*prevents her*). No, please, please, my darling, forgive me . . . I'm truly sorry. (*Kisses her hand.*) Peace?

YELENA. You'd try the patience of a saint, honestly.

VANYA. As a token of peace and harmony I'll bring you a bouquet of roses; I've had them ready for you since morning . . . Autumn roses – beautiful, melancholy roses . . . (*Exits.*)

SONYA. Autumn roses – beautiful, melancholy roses.

Both women look out of the window.

YELENA. It's September already. How are we going to get through the winter here? (*A pause.*) Where's the doctor?

SONYA. He's in Uncle Vanya's room. Writing something. I'm glad Uncle Vanya's gone out, I need to have a talk with you.

YELENA. What about?

SONYA. What about? (*Lays her head against* YELENA*'s bosom.*)

YELENA. There, there . . . (*Strokes her hair.*) It's all right . . .

SONYA. I'm not attractive.

YELENA. You have beautiful hair.

SONYA. No! (*Turns round to look at herself in the mirror.*) No!
When a woman isn't attractive, they always say: 'You
have beautiful eyes, you have beautiful hair' . . . I've
loved him now for six years, I love him more than my
own mother. I seem to hear him every minute, I can feel
the pressure of his hand, and I watch the door, waiting,
thinking he's just about to enter. And you see how I keep
coming to you, to talk about him. He's here every day
now, but he doesn't look at me, he doesn't see me . . .
It's sheer torture! I've no hope at all, absolutely none! (*In
despair.*) Oh God, give me strength . . . I've been praying
the whole night . . . I often go up to him, start talking to
him, look into his eyes . . . I've no pride left, I can't
control myself . . . I just couldn't help it, yesterday I told
Uncle Vanya I was in love . . . And all the servants know
I love him. Everybody knows.

YELENA. And what about him?

SONYA. He doesn't even notice me.

YELENA (*musing*). He's a strange man . . . I'll tell you what –
why don't I have a word with him? I'll be very careful,
do it in a roundabout way . . . (*A pause.*) I mean, really, to
go all this time without knowing . . . Let me try. (SONYA
nods her consent.) Splendid. He either loves you or he
doesn't – that won't be difficult to find out. Don't be
embarrassed, my darling, and don't worry – I'll question
him very tactfully, he won't even be aware. Yes or no,
that's all we need to know. (*A pause.*) If it's no, then
perhaps he shouldn't come here any more. Right?
(SONYA *nods.*) It'll be easier if you're not seeing him. We
won't put it off, we'll speak to him right now. He was
going to show me some of his charts . . . Go and tell him
I'd like to see him.

SONYA (*greatly agitated*). You'll tell me the truth?

YELENA. Yes, of course. I think the truth, no matter what, can't be more terrible than not knowing. You can trust me, my darling.

SONYA. Yes . . . yes . . . I'll tell him you want to see his charts . . . (*Goes to the door and stops.*) No, it's better not knowing . . . At least there's hope . . .

YELENA. What did you say?

SONYA. Nothing. (*Exits.*)

YELENA (*alone*). There's nothing worse than knowing somebody else's secret, and not being able to help. (*Musing.*) He's not in love with her, that's obvious, but why shouldn't he marry her? She's not attractive, but for a country doctor, someone of his age, she'd make an excellent wife. Intelligent, extremely kind, innocent . . . No, that's not the point . . . (*A pause.*) I understand that poor girl. In the midst of this desperate boredom, surrounded by grey shadows wandering in and out, instead of human beings, listening to vulgar chit-chat from people who know nothing but eating, drinking and sleeping – now and again he appears, so different from the rest, handsome, interesting, attractive, like a bright moon rising in the darkness . . . To fall under the spell of such a man, to forget oneself . . . I think I'm a little in love myself. Yes, I'm bored when he's not here, and just look at me, smiling when I think of him. Uncle Vanya says I have mermaid's blood in my veins. 'Let yourself go even just once in your life' . . . Well? Perhaps that's what I should do . . . Just fly away, free as a bird, away from all of you, away from your sleepy faces, and your talk, just forget you even exist . . . But I'm too cowardly, too timid . . . My conscience would torment me . . . Yet he comes here every day, I can guess why, and I already feel guilty . . . I feel like kneeling before Sonya and begging her forgiveness, crying . . .

ASTROV (*enters carrying a chart*). Good afternoon. (*They shake hands.*) You wanted to see my painting?

YELENA. You promised yesterday you'd show me your work. Have you the time?

ASTROV. But of course! (*Spreads the chart on a card-table and fixes it with drawing-pins.*) Where were you born?

YELENA (*helping him*). In Petersburg.

ASTROV. And where did you study?

YELENA. At the music conservatory.

ASTROV. I don't suppose this'll interest you.

YELENA. Why not? I don't know much about the country, it's true, but I've read a good deal.

ASTROV. I have my own work-table here . . . In Vanya's room. When I'm absolutely worn out, to the point of stupefaction, I drop everything and escape here, amuse myself with this stuff for an hour or two . . . Vanya and Sonya click away at their abacus, doing the accounts, and I sit alongside them at my own table, messing about with my paints – it's warm, and quiet, and the cricket chirps. However, that's a pleasure I allow myself only rarely, once a month . . . (*Pointing to the chart.*) Look at this now. This is a map of our district as it was fifty years ago. The dark and light green represent forest; half of the entire area was covered with woodland. Where the green's cross-hatched with red, that used to be inhabited by elks and wild goats . . . I show both flora and fauna on this. This lake was home to swans, geese, ducks – as the old folks say, a 'power of birds' of all sorts, no end of them: they used to fly in great clouds. Apart from the villages and hamlets, you can see scattered here and there various little settlements – small farms, Old Believers' hermitages, water-mills . . . There were a lot of cattle and horses too. That's shown in blue. In this district, for example, the blue's very heavy; there were droves of horses here, an average of three to every homestead. (*A pause.*) Now let's look lower down. This is how it was twenty-five years ago. Already there's only a third of the total area given over to forest. The wild goats have gone, but there are still some elks. The green and blue colours are paler. And so on, and so forth. Now we turn to the third section, showing the district as it is now. The green appears here and there, but only in patches, not solid; the elks have disappeared, so have the swans, and grouse . . . And there's no trace of the earlier settlements, the farms, hermitages, mills. In general it's a picture of gradual and unmistakable decay, which will quite clearly be complete, in another ten to fifteen years. You may say there are cultural influences at work, that the old way of life must naturally give way to the new. Well, yes, I can understand that, if these devastated forests had been replaced by good roads and railways, if we now had workshops, factories, schools − the people would be better off, healthier, more intelligent, but there's clearly nothing of the kind! We still have the same swamps and mosquitoes, the same trackless waste, the same poverty, typhus, diphtheria, fires . . . What we're dealing with here is a case of degeneration, the outcome of a back-breaking struggle for existence − a degeneration caused by inertia, by ignorance, by a complete lack of self-awareness, as when a sick man, starving, chilled to the bone, in order to save what's left of his life, to protect his children, will instinctively, unconsciously, grab hold of anything that might satisfy his hunger or warm him, and in so doing destroy everything, without a thought for tomorrow . . . We've already destroyed almost everything, and created nothing yet to take its place. (*Coldly.*) I can see by your expression that this doesn't interest you.

YELENA. But I understand so little of these things . . .

ASTROV. There's nothing to understand, you're just not interested.

YELENA. To tell you the truth, my mind was elsewhere. I'm sorry. Actually, I want to put you through a little interrogation, and I'm embarrassed. I don't know how to begin.

ASTROV. An interrogation?

YELENA. Yes, an interrogation, but . . . well, it's quite innocent. Let's sit down. (*They sit.*) It's to do with a certain young person. We'll talk openly, as friends, without beating about the bush. We'll have a little talk, then forget all about it. Yes?

ASTROV. Yes.

YELENA. It concerns my stepdaughter Sonya. Tell me, do you like her?

ASTROV. Yes, I respect her.

YELENA. Do you like her as a woman?

ASTROV (*after a pause*). No.

YELENA. Another few words, and that'll be the end. You haven't noticed anything?

ASTROV. No, nothing.

YELENA (*takes his hand*). You don't love her, I can see it in your eyes . . . She's suffering . . . You must realise that, and . . . stop coming here.

ASTROV (*stands up*). I've outstayed my welcome. Anyway, I've no time . . . (*Shrugs.*) When do I ever have time? (*He is embarrassed.*)

YELENA. Whew, what an unpleasant conversation! I'm all on edge, as if I've been carrying a ton weight around. Well, that's that over, thank God. We'll forget this, as if we'd never mentioned it, and . . . and you can leave now. You're an intelligent man, you do understand . . . (*A pause.*) I feel quite flushed.

ASTROV. If you'd told me this a month or two ago, I might've taken it seriously, but now . . . (*Shrugs.*) Of course, if she's suffering, well . . . Just one thing I don't understand: why did you need to have this interrogation? (*Looks into her eyes, and wags his finger accusingly.*) Oh, you're a crafty one!

YELENA. What's that supposed to mean?

ASTROV (*laughing*). So clever! All right, let's say Sonya is suffering, I can readily accept that, but what's the point of this interrogation of yours? (*Prevents her from speaking, animatedly.*) Oh, please, don't look so surprised, you know perfectly well why I come here every day . . . Why, and on whose account – you know very well indeed. And don't look at me like that, you charming predatory creature – I'm too wise a bird . . .

YELENA (*bewildered*). Predatory? I don't understand.

ASTROV. A beautiful, fluffy little weasel . . . And you need a victim! I've spent an entire month doing nothing, I've dropped everything to chase after you – and that pleases you enormously, oh yes! Well, what now? I'm conquered, you knew that even without an interrogation. (*Folds his arms and hangs his head.*) I submit. Here I am, devour me!

YELENA. You've gone mad!

ASTROV (*laughs sardonically*). You're shy . . .

YELENA. Oh, I'm not as bad as you think, I'm not so low! I swear to you! (*Makes to exit.*)

ASTROV (*barring her way*). I'm leaving today, I won't be back again, but . . . (*Takes her by the hand, and looks round.*) Where shall we meet? Tell me, quickly – where? Someone might come in – tell me, quickly. (*Passionately.*) You're so wonderful, glorious . . . Just one kiss . . . Let me kiss your beautiful, fragrant hair . . .

YELENA. I swear to you . . .

ASTROV (*prevents her from speaking*). Why swear anything? There's no need to swear. No need for words . . . oh, you're so beautiful! Such lovely hands! (*Kisses her hands.*)

YELENA. No, please, stop it . . . go away . . . (*Withdraws her hands.*) You're forgetting yourself.

ASTROV. Then tell me, tell me! Where shall we meet tomorrow? (*Puts his arms round her waist.*) It's inevitable, don't you see? We must meet. (*He kisses her. At that same moment* VANYA *enters with a bouquet of roses and stops in the doorway.*)

YELENA (*not seeing* VANYA). Have pity on me, please . . . leave me alone . . . (*Lays her head on* ASTROV's *chest.*) No! (*Tries to go.*)

ASTROV (*holding her by the waist*). Come to the plantation tomorrow . . . at two o'clock . . . Yes? Yes? You'll come?

YELENA (*catching sight of* VANYA). Let me go! (*Acutely embarrassed, goes over to the window.*) This is terrible.

VANYA (*lays the bouquet down on a chair; nervously wipes his face and neck with his handkerchief*). It's all right . . . Yes . . . It's all right . . .

ASTROV (*unabashed*). The weather's not bad today, my dear Ivan Petrovich. Overcast in the morning, looked like rain, but now it's sunny. One must say, autumn's turned out splendidly . . . and the winter crops are coming along. (*Rolls up his chart.*) Only thing is – the days are getting shorter . . . (*Exits.*)

YELENA (*quickly goes up to* VANYA). You must try, you must use all your influence to see that my husband and I leave here this very day! Do you hear? This very day!

VANYA (*mopping his brow*). Eh? Oh, yes . . . fine . . . I saw everything, *Hélène*, everything . . .

YELENA (*agitatedly*). Do you hear? I've got to get away from this place today!

Enter SEREBRYAKOV, SONYA, TELEGIN, *and* MARINA.

TELEGIN. I'm not feeling too well myself, Your Excellency. That's two days now I've been poorly. Something up with my head . . .

SEREBRYAKOV. Where is everybody? I don't like this house, it's a perfect labyrinth. Twenty-six enormous rooms, people wander off in all directions, and you can never find anybody. (*Rings.*) Ask Maria Vasilievna and Yelena to come in.

YELENA. I am here.

SEREBRYAKOV. Please sit down, my friends.

SONYA (*goes up to* YELENA, *impatiently*). What did he say?

YELENA. Later.

SONYA. You're trembling. Are you upset? (*Peers intently into her face.*) I understand . . . He said he wouldn't be coming here any more . . . yes? (*A pause.*) Tell me: yes?

YELENA *nods.*

SEREBRYAKOV. One can put up with ill-health, all things considered, but what I really cannot endure is this routine of country life. I feel as if I'd dropped off the earth onto some other planet. Do sit down, friends, please. Sonya! (SONYA *doesn't hear him; she is standing with her head bowed, dejectedly.*) Sonya! (*A pause.*) She doesn't hear me. (*To* MARINA.) You too, Nanny, sit down. (MARINA *sits down and begins knitting a stocking.*) Now, friends, please, lend me your ears, as the saying goes. (*Laughs.*)

VANYA (*agitatedly*). I don't think I'm needed here. May I leave?

SEREBRYAKOV. No, you're needed here more than anybody.

VANYA. What is it you require of me?

SEREBRYAKOV. Require of you . . . Vanya, why are you so angry? (*A pause.*) If I've done anything to offend you, please forgive me.

VANYA. Don't take that tone with me. Let's get down to business . . . What is it you want?

MARIA VASILIEVNA *enters.*

SEREBRYAKOV. Ah, here's *maman*. Now, my friends, I shall begin. (*A pause.*) I have invited you here, ladies and gentlemen, in order to inform you that a government inspector is coming to visit us. However, joking aside, this is a serious matter. I've called you together, my friends, to ask your help and advice, and knowing how obliging you are, I hope I shall receive it. I am a scholar, a man of letters, and I've always been a stranger to the world of business. I can't get by without the guidance of experienced people, so I'm asking you, Ivan Petrovich, and you, Mr Telegin, and you, *maman* . . . The fact is, *manet omnes una nox* – in other words, we are all in God's hands. I am old, and ill, and I think it's time I settled matters relating to my property, insofar as they concern my family. My life's over, I'm not thinking about myself, but I have a young wife, and an unmarried daughter. (*A pause.*) I can't go on living in the country, it's impossible. We're just not made for country life. However, living in town, on the income we receive from this estate, is also impossible. If we were to sell the forest, say, that would be an extreme measure, and one we couldn't resort to every year. We need to find some means of guaranteeing a permanent, more or less fixed income. Well, I've thought of just such a means, and I should like to submit it for your consideration. Leaving out the details, I'll describe it in rough outline. Our estate yields a profit on average of no more than two percent. I propose to sell it. If we invest the proceeds in interest-bearing bonds, we should make between four and five percent, and I think there'll even be a few thousand surplus, which will enable us to buy a small villa in Finland.

VANYA. Hold on . . . I think my ears must be deceiving me. Say that again.

SEREBRYAKOV. Invest the money in interest-bearing bonds, and with the surplus, whatever's left over, buy a villa in Finland.

VANYA. No, not Finland . . . You said something else.

SEREBRYAKOV. I propose to sell the estate.

VANYA. That's it. You'll sell the estate – that's wonderful, that's rich . . . And what do you plan to do with me, and my old mother, and Sonya here?

SEREBRYAKOV. We can discuss all that in due course. We can't do everything at once.

VANYA. No, wait. Obviously, up until now, I've been completely devoid of common sense. Up until now, I've been stupid enough to believe that this estate belonged to Sonya. My late father bought this estate as a dowry for my sister. And up until now, I've been so naive as to think – not interpreting the law like a Turk, that is – that the estate passed from my sister to Sonya.

SEREBRYAKOV. That's right, the estate does belong to Sonya. Who's disputing it? Without Sonya's consent, I can't decide to sell it. Besides, what I'm proposing to do is for Sonya's benefit.

VANYA. This is incomprehensible, utterly incomprehensible! Either I've gone out of my mind, or . . . or . . .

MARIA. *Jean*, don't contradict *Alexandre*! Believe me, he knows better than we do, what's right and what's wrong.

VANYA. No, give me some water. (*Has a drink of water.*) Say what you like! Say whatever you like!

SEREBRYAKOV. I don't understand why you're getting so worked up. I'm not saying my plan is ideal. And if everyone finds it inappropriate, well, I won't insist on it.

A pause.

TELEGIN (*embarrassed*). Your Excellency, I cherish a feeling not only of reverence towards scholarship, but of kinship too. My brother Grigory's wife's brother – perhaps you know him – Konstantin Trofimovich Lakedemonov, was an M.A. . . .

VANYA. Hold on, Waffles, we're talking business . . . Just wait . . . later . . . (*To* SEREBRYAKOV.) Here, ask him. The estate was bought from his uncle.

SEREBRYAKOV. Indeed, and why should I ask him? What's the point?

VANYA. This estate was originally bought for ninety-five thousand roubles. My father could pay only seventy, so there was a debt left of twenty-five thousand. Now listen to me . . . The estate would never have been bought, if

I hadn't given up my share of the inheritance in favour of my sister, whom I loved dearly. What's more, I worked like an ox for ten years, and paid off the entire debt . . .

SEREBRYAKOV. I wish I'd never started this conversation.

VANYA. This estate is clear of debt, and in good order, solely because of my personal efforts. And now that I've grown old, I'm to be flung out on my ear!

SEREBRYAKOV. I don't understand what you're driving at!

VANYA. I've managed this estate for twenty-five years, I've worked, I've sent you money, like the most conscientious steward you could have, and all that time you've never once thanked me. All that time – both when I was young, and now – I've been drawing a salary of five hundred roubles a year from you – a mere pittance! Not once did it ever occur to you to increase it by so much as a rouble!

SEREBRYAKOV. Ivan Petrovich, how was I to know? I've no head for business, I don't understand these things. You could have increased it yourself, as much as you wanted.

VANYA. Why didn't I steal? Why don't you all despise me for not stealing? It would've been simple justice, and I wouldn't be a beggar now!

MARIA (sternly). Jean!

TELEGIN (upset). Vanya, dear friend, don't . . . don't . . . I'm trembling . . . Why spoil our good relations? (Kisses him.) Please don't . . .

VANYA. For twenty-five years I've been stuck with my mother here, buried like a mole within these four walls . . . All our thoughts and feelings belonged to you alone. Our days were spent talking about you, about your work, we were so proud of you, we used to bless your very name. And we wasted our nights reading books and journals for which I now have the utmost contempt!

TELEGIN. Vanya, don't, please . . . I can't bear it . . .

SEREBRYAKOV (angrily). I don't understand – what is it you want?

VANYA. To us, you were a being of a higher order, we knew all your articles by heart . . . But now I've had my eyes opened! I see it all! You write about art, but you haven't the first idea about art! All your works, those works I used to love, aren't worth a damn! You've hoodwinked us all!

SEREBRYAKOV. Friends! Stop him, for God's sake! I'm leaving!

YELENA. Ivan Petrovich, I insist you stop talking now! Do you understand?

VANYA. I won't, I won't shut up! (*Barring* SEREBRYAKOV's *way.*) Wait, I haven't finished. You've ruined my life! I haven't lived, I've never lived! Thanks to you I've destroyed, I've annihilated the best years of my life! You're my worst enemy!

TELEGIN. I can't bear it . . . I can't . . . I'm leaving . . . (*Exits in great distress.*)

SEREBRYAKOV. What is it you want of me? What right have you to speak to me in that fashion? You nonentity! If the estate's yours, then take it, I don't need it!

YELENA. I'm getting out of this hell, this very instant! (*Shrieks.*) I can't stand it any longer!

VANYA. My life's ruined! I have talent, intelligence, courage . . . If I'd had a normal life, I might've been a Schopenhauer, a Dostoevsky . . . Oh, I'm raving! I'm going out of my mind . . . Mother, I'm in despair! Mother!

MARIA (*sternly*). Do as *Alexandre* says!

SONYA (*kneels before* MARINA *and huddles close to her*). Nanny! Nanny!

VANYA. Mother! What am I going to do? No, don't tell me, there's no need! I know what to do myself! (*To* SEREBRYAKOV.) You're going to remember me! (*Exits by the middle door.*)

MARIA *follows him out.*

SEREBRYAKOV. What's this all about, friends, eh? Get that madman away from me! I can't stay under the same roof as him! He's in there, (*Points to the middle door.*) living almost next door to me . . . Either he moves to the village, or into the lodge, or else I move out of here, but I can't stay in the same house, I can't . . .

YELENA (*to* SEREBRYAKOV). We're leaving here today! We need to make arrangements right now.

SEREBRYAKOV. Absolute nonentity!

SONYA (*on her knees, turns to* SEREBRYAKOV, *agitated and tearful*). Papa, have pity on him, you must! Uncle Vanya and I are so unhappy! (*Trying to restrain her despair.*) Have pity on us, please. Remember when you were younger, how Uncle Vanya and Grandma used to sit up at nights translating books for you, and copying out your papers . . . night after night. Uncle Vanya and I worked incessantly, frightened to spend even a kopeck on ourselves, we sent everything to you . . . We truly earned our daily bread. I'm saying it all wrong, it's all wrong, but you've got to understand us, papa. You must have pity!

YELENA (*upset*). *Alexandre*, for God's sake, talk to him . . . please!

SEREBRYAKOV. All right, I'll have a word with him . . . I'm not accusing him of anything, I'm not angry, but I think you'll agree he's behaving rather strangely, to say the least. Anyway, I'll go and see him. (*Exits by the middle door.*)

YELENA. Be gentle with him, try to calm him down . . . (*Follows him out.*)

SONYA (*clinging tightly to* MARINA). Oh, Nanny, Nanny!

MARINA. It's all right, child. The geese'll cackle a bit, then they'll stop . . . They'll cackle, then stop . . .

SONYA. Nanny!

MARINA (*stroking her hair*). You're trembling, it's as if you were out in the frost. There, there, little orphan, God is merciful. Some of that nice lime-flower tea, or raspberry, and it'll soon pass . . . Don't get upset, my little orphan. (*Looks at the middle door, then vehemently.*) What a racket they're making, the silly geese! Go on, clear off!

A shot is heard offstage, followed by a scream from YELENA. SONYA *shudders.*

Oh, my God, you . . .

SEREBRYAKOV (*runs in, reeling in alarm*). Stop him! Stop him! He's gone mad!

YELENA *and* VANYA *struggle in the doorway.*

YELENA (*trying to take the revolver away from him*). Give it to me! Give it to me, I tell you!

VANYA. Let me go, *Hélène!* Let me go! (*Breaks free, runs in and looks round for* SEREBRYAKOV.) Where is he? Ah, there he is! (*Fires at him.*) Bang! (*A pause.*) Missed? Missed again?! (*Furiously.*) Damn! Damn! Damn it to hell!

He throws the revolver to the floor, and sinks onto a chair exhausted. SEREBRYAKOV *is stunned.* YELENA *leans against the wall, almost fainting.*

YELENA. Take me away from here! Take me away, kill me . . . I can't stay here, I can't!

VANYA. Oh, what have I done? What have I done?

SONYA. Nanny, oh, Nanny!

Curtain.

ACT FOUR

VANYA*'s room, which serves as his bedroom, and also the estate
office. A large table by the window, with account books and various
papers, a desk, cupboards, scales. A smaller table for* ASTROV; *on it
are his drawing materials and paints, and a portfolio. A bird-cage with
a starling in it. There is a map of Africa on the wall, obviously of no
use to anyone. An enormous divan, upholstered in oil-cloth. To the left,
a door, leading to another room; to the right, a door into the hall, with
a mat placed in front of it, so the peasants won't muddy the floor. It is
an autumn evening, very still.* TELEGIN *and* MARINA *are sitting
facing one another, winding wool.*

TELEGIN. You'd better hurry, Marina my dear, they'll soon
be calling us to say goodbye. They've already ordered the
horses.

MARINA (*trying to wind faster*). There's not much left.

TELEGIN. They're going to Kharkov. That's where they'll
be living.

MARINA. And a good thing too.

TELEGIN. They've had a bit of a fright. Yelena Andreyevna
keeps saying, 'I won't stay here another hour . . . we must
get away, must get away . . . We can stay in Kharkov
for a while,' she says, 'have a look round, and then
send for our things . . . ' They're travelling light. Well,
Marina, it seems they weren't meant to live here. Not
their destiny . . . the workings of fate.

MARINA. And a good thing too. All that row this morning,
shooting – it's a disgrace!

TELEGIN. Indeed, a subject worthy of the brush of
Aivazovsky.

MARINA. I could've done without seeing that. (*A pause.*) Well, we'll go back to the old ways now. Tea by eight o'clock in the morning, dinner at twelve, and we'll sit down to supper in the evening: everything in its place, the way other folk live . . . like Christians. (*With a sigh.*) It's ages since I've tasted noodles, old sinner that I am.

TELEGIN. Yes, it's been quite a while since they've made noodles. You know, this morning, Marina, I was walking through the village, and a shopkeeper shouted after me: 'Hey, you – sponger! Living off other people!' That was really hurtful.

MARINA. Take no notice, my dear. We're all spongers, we all live off God. You and Sonya, and Ivan Petrovich – none of us sits idle, we all work hard! All of us . . . Where's Sonya?

TELEGIN. In the garden. She's going round with the doctor, looking for Ivan Petrovich. They're afraid he might do himself an injury.

MARINA. And where's the revolver?

TELEGIN (*in a whisper*). I hid it in the cellar!

MARINA (*with a smile*). What a carry-on!

VANYA *and* ASTROV *enter from outside.*

VANYA. Leave me alone. (*To* MARINA *and* TELEGIN.) Go away, please, leave me alone, even for just one hour! I can't stand being watched.

TELEGIN. At once, Vanya. (*Exits on tiptoe.*)

MARINA. Silly goose – honk-honk-honk! (*Gathers up her wool and exits.*)

VANYA. Leave me alone!

ASTROV. With the greatest of pleasure. I should have left here long ago, but I'm telling you again, I'm not leaving until you return what you took from me.

VANYA. I didn't take anything from you.

ASTROV. I'm serious – don't keep me waiting. I should have gone ages ago.

VANYA. I've taken nothing from you.

They both sit down.

ASTROV. Really? Well, I'll wait a little longer, and I'm sorry, but after that I'll have to use force. We'll tie you up and search you. I'm absolutely serious.

VANYA. As you please. (*A pause.*) Dear God, to have made such a fool of myself! Firing twice, and missing both times! I'll never forgive myself.

ASTROV. If you really felt like shooting, you'd have done better to put a bullet into your own head.

VANYA (*shrugs*). It's strange. I attempt to commit murder, but they don't arrest me, they don't charge me – that means they think I'm insane. (*A bitter laugh.*) Yes, I'm insane, but people who hide their lack of talent, their stupidity, their sheer heartlessness, under the guise of professor, learned sage – they're not insane! And people who marry old men, and then deceive them right under everyone's nose, they're not insane, no! I saw you, I saw you with your arms around her!

ASTROV. That's right, sir, I did have my arms round her, and this is for you. (*Thumbs his nose at him.*)

VANYA (*looking at the door*). The earth's insane, that it doesn't swallow you up!

ASTROV. Well, that's just silly.

VANYA. So what? I'm insane, I'm not responsible. I have the right to say silly things.

ASTROV. That's an old trick. You're not insane, you're just a crank. A buffoon. There was a time when I regarded every crank as sick, or abnormal, but I'm now of the opinion that that's the normal condition of mankind – to be a crank. And you're perfectly normal.

VANYA (*covers his face with his hands*). So ashamed! If you knew how ashamed I was! There's no pain on earth like it, this acute sense of shame! (*Wretchedly.*) It's unbearable! (*Leans over the table.*) What am I going to do? What am I going to do?

ASTROV. Nothing.

VANYA. Give me something! Oh, my God . . . I'm forty-seven years old. If I live to be sixty, that leaves me another thirteen years. Such a long time! How am I to get through those thirteen years? What am I going to do, how am I going to fill them? Try to understand . . . (*Convulsively squeezes* ASTROV's *hand.*) Don't you see? Oh, if only you could live out the rest of your life in some new way! To wake up some clear, calm morning, and feel you were starting life afresh, that all your past was forgotten, dispersed into the air, like smoke. (*Weeps.*) To start a new life . . . Tell me how to begin . . . where to begin . . .

ASTROV (*irritated*). Oh, don't be absurd! What kind of new life can there be? Our situation's hopeless – yours and mine!

VANYA. It is?

ASTROV. I'm convinced of it.

VANYA. Give me something, please . . . (*Pointing to his heart.*) I've a burning pain, here.

ASTROV (*shouts angrily*). Oh, stop it! (*Then softening.*) Look, the people who come after us, in a hundred or two hundred years' time, and who will despise us for having lived such stupid, insipid lives – maybe they'll find some way to be happy, but as for us . . . well, there's only one hope for you and me, and that's the hope that when we're at rest in our graves, we'll be attended by visions, perhaps even pleasant ones. (*Sighs.*) Yes, my friend. In this entire district there have been only two decent, cultured men – you and I. But after some ten years of this contemptible provincial life we've been dragged under; its putrid miasma has poisoned our blood, and we've become philistines, the same as everybody else. (*Suddenly animated.*) But don't think you can talk me round. Give me back what you took from me.

VANYA. I didn't take anything from you.

ASTROV. You took a bottle of morphine out of my medicine bag. (*A pause.*) Listen, if you're determined to end it all, then go into the woods and shoot yourself. Give me back the morphine, otherwise there'll be all sorts of gossip and conjecture – people will think I gave it to you . . . Bad enough that I'll have to perform a post-mortem on you. D'you think that's funny?

SONYA *enters.*

VANYA. Leave me alone!

ASTROV. Sonya, your uncle has removed a bottle of morphine from my bag and he won't give it back. Tell him it's not . . . well, it's not very clever. And I don't have time for this. I've got to go.

SONYA. Uncle Vanya, did you take the morphine?

A pause.

ASTROV. He did. I'm certain of it.

SONYA. Give it back. Why do you want to frighten us? (*Tenderly.*) Give it back, Uncle Vanya. I dare say I'm as unhappy as you, but I'm not going to despair. I can bear it, and I'll go on bearing it, until my life comes to an end . . . You can bear it too. (*A pause.*) Give it back. (*Kisses his hands.*) Dear, kind, darling Uncle, give it back! (*Weeps.*) You're a good man, have pity on us and give it back. You can bear it, Uncle, you must!

VANYA (*takes a bottle out of his desk and hands it to* ASTROV). Here, take it! (*To* SONYA.) We need to get back to work quickly, do something quickly, otherwise I can't . . . I can't . . .

SONYA. Yes, yes, work. As soon as we see them off, we'll get down to work . . . (*Begins nervously sorting out papers on the table.*) We've let everything go.

ASTROV (*puts the bottle into his bag and fastens the straps*). So, I can be on my way now.

YELENA (*enters*). Ivan Petrovich, are you here? We're leaving
now . . . Go and see *Alexandre*, he wants to say something
to you.

SONYA. Go on, Uncle Vanya. (*Takes* VANYA's *arm.*) Let's
go. You and Papa must make it up. That's essential.

SONYA *and* VANYA *exit.*

YELENA. I'm going now. (*Gives* ASTROV *her hand.*)
Goodbye.

ASTROV. Already?

YELENA. The carriage is waiting.

ASTROV. Goodbye.

YELENA. You promised me today you'd be leaving here.

ASTROV. I remember. I'm just going. (*A pause.*) Were you
frightened? (*Takes her hand.*) Is it really so dreadful?

YELENA. Yes.

ASTROV. If only you'd stay! Well? Tomorrow, at the
plantation . . .

YELENA. No . . . It's all settled . . . That's why I have the
courage to look at you now, because our departure's been
arranged . . . I've just one thing to ask of you: please
don't think badly of me. I'd like you to respect me.

ASTROV. Oh! (*With a gesture of impatience.*) Stay, please, I beg
you. You must realise, you have absolutely nothing to do,
no sort of purpose in life, nothing to occupy your mind,
and sooner or later, you will give way to your feelings – it's
inevitable. And it's better if that happens not in Kharkov,
or somewhere in Kursk, but here, in the lap of nature. At
least it's poetic, it's even beautiful in autumn . . . And
there's the plantation, half-ruined country houses in the
style of Turgenev . . .

YELENA. You're very funny . . . I'm angry with you, and
yet . . . I'll remember you with pleasure. You're an
interesting, original man. We won't ever see each other
again, so why try to hide it? I was even a little in love

with you. Anyway, let's shake hands and part as friends. Don't think ill of me.

ASTROV (*shakes hands*). Yes, you'd better go . . . (*Musing.*) You seem a good, kindhearted person, but there's something strange about your whole being. You arrive here with your husband, and all of us who had been working, running around trying to create something, were obliged to drop our work, and occupy ourselves the entire summer with nothing but you, and your husband's gout. The two of you have infected us all with your indolence. I've been infatuated with you, and I haven't done a stroke for a whole month – meanwhile people have been falling ill, the peasants have been grazing their cattle amongst my young trees . . . So really, wherever you set foot, you and your husband, you bring ruin . . . I'm joking, of course, but I'm quite convinced that if you were to stay, the devastation would be enormous. I'd be destroyed, and you wouldn't get off too lightly either. Anyway, off you go. *Finita la commedia!*

YELENA (*takes a pencil from his table and quickly pockets it*). I'm taking this pencil to remember you by.

ASTROV. It's strange, somehow . . . To have known each other, and then suddenly, for some reason . . . never to see each other again. That's the way of the world . . . While there's no-one here, before Uncle Vanya comes in with a bouquet, let me . . . let me kiss you . . . Goodbye . . . Yes? (*Kisses her on the cheek.*) Now . . . that's fine.

YELENA. I wish you all the very best. (*Looks round.*) Oh, who cares! For once in my life! (*Impulsively embraces him, then both almost immediately withdraw.*) I must go.

ASTROV. Do, go quickly. If the carriage is ready, you'd better leave.

YELENA. I think someone's coming. (*Both listen.*)

ASTROV. *Finita!*

Enter SEREBRYAKOV, VANYA, MARIA VASILIEVNA *with a book*, TELEGIN *and* SONYA.

SEREBRYAKOV (*to* VANYA). Let bygones be bygones.
After what has happened in these past few hours, I've
lived through and thought so much that I believe I could
write an entire treatise, for the benefit of posterity, on
how to live one's life. I readily accept your apologies,
and I ask you to forgive me too. Goodbye! (*Kisses* VANYA
three times.)

VANYA. You'll receive exactly the same amount as before.
Everything will be as it was.

SEREBRYAKOV (*kisses* MARIA VASILIEVNA's *hand*).
Maman . . .

MARIA (*kissing him*). *Alexandre*, have another photograph
taken and send it to me, please. You know how dear you
are to me.

TELEGIN. Goodbye, Your Excellency! Don't forget us!

SEREBRYAKOV (*kisses* SONYA). Goodbye . . . Goodbye,
everyone! (*Offering his hand to* ASTROV.) Thank you for
the pleasure of your company. I respect your way of
thinking, your enthusiasm, your passion, but if you'll
permit an old man to add just one observation to his
farewell remarks: you need to do some real work, my
friends, real work! (*Bows to the company.*) All the very best!
(*Exits, followed by* MARIA VASILIEVNA *and* SONYA.)

VANYA (*fervently kisses* YELENA's *hand*). Goodbye . . . Forgive
me . . . We'll never see each other again.

YELENA (*moved*). Goodbye, my dearest. (*Kisses him on the
forehead and exits.*)

ASTROV (*to* TELEGIN). Waffles, you might tell them to
bring my horses round at the same time.

TELEGIN. At your service, dear friend. (*Exits.*)

Only ASTROV and VANYA remain.

ASTROV (*gathers up his paints from the table and puts them into
his suitcase*). Aren't you going to see them off?

VANYA. Let them go. I . . . I can't. I'm too depressed. I need to get busy with something quickly . . . Work, work! (*Rummages among the papers on the table.*)

A pause. The sound of harness bells.

ASTROV. They've gone. The Professor's glad, that's certain. He wouldn't come back here for love nor money.

MARINA (*enters*). They've gone. (*Sits down in an armchair and begins knitting a stocking.*)

SONYA (*enters*). They've gone. (*Wipes her eyes.*) God grant them a safe journey. (*To* VANYA.) Now, Uncle Vanya, let's get busy.

VANYA. Work, work . . .

SONYA. We haven't sat together at this table for ages and ages. (*Lights the lamp on the table.*) I don't think there's any ink . . . (*Takes the inkwell to the cupboard and fills it.*) Just the same, I'm sad they've gone.

MARIA (*slowly enters*). They've gone! (*Sits down and immerses herself in her reading.*)

SONYA (*sits at the table and begins leafing through the accounts book*). Let's write out the invoices first, Uncle Vanya. We've let things go terribly. Someone sent in for his bill again today. You make it out. While you're doing one, I'll do the next.

VANYA (*writing*). 'Invoice to . . . Mister . . . '

Both write in silence.

MARINA (*yawns*). Well, I'm ready for bye-byes . . .

ASTROV. It's so quiet. Pens scratching, a cricket chirping . . . So warm, and cosy . . . I don't feel like leaving. (*The sound of harness bells.*) They're bringing round the horses . . . I suppose all that remains is to say goodbye to you, my dear friends, to say goodbye to this table of mine – then I'm off! (*Puts his charts into his portfolio.*)

MARINA. Why are you in such a hurry? You should stay.

ASTROV. I can't.

VANYA (*writing*). 'Leaving a debit of two roubles, seventy-five kopecks . . . '

A WORKMAN *enters.*

WORKMAN. The horses are ready, Doctor.

ASTROV. Yes, I heard. (*Hands him his medical bag, his suitcase and portfolio.*) Here, take these. Mind you don't bend the portfolio.

WORKMAN. Yes, Doctor. (*Exits.*)

ASTROV. Well, now . . . (*Makes to say goodbye.*)

SONYA. When shall we see you again?

ASTROV. Next summer, at the earliest, I expect. Not in the winter, at any rate . . . Of course, if anything happens, do let me know, and I'll come. (*Shakes hands.*) Thank you for all your hospitality, your kindness . . . for everything, in fact. (*Goes up to* MARINA *and kisses her on the forehead.*) Goodbye, old woman . . .

MARINA. You're leaving without any tea?

ASTROV. I don't want any, Nanny.

MARINA. You'll have a drop of vodka, maybe?

ASTROV (*undecided*). Hm . . . maybe . . . (MARINA *exits. A pause.*) One of my horses has gone lame for some reason. I noticed it yesterday, when Petrushka was taking it to water.

VANYA. You'd better have him re-shod.

ASTROV. Yes, I'll have to stop at the smith's in Rozhdestvennoye. Can't be helped. (*Goes up to the map of Africa on the wall and looks at it.*) I suppose it'll be scorching hot down there in Africa now − terrific!

VANYA. Yes, probably.

MARINA *returns carrying a tray with a glass of vodka and a piece of bread.*

MARINA. Here you are. (ASTROV *drinks the vodka.*) Your good health, my dear. (*Makes a low bow.*) You ought to have a bit of bread.

ASTROV. No, this'll do . . . Anyway, all the very best! (*To* MARINA.) Don't bother to see me out, Nanny, there's no need.

He exits. SONYA *follows with a candle to see him off.* MARINA *sits back down in her armchair.*

VANYA (*writing*). 'February second, linseed oil, twenty pounds . . . February sixteenth, more linseed oil, twenty pounds . . . Buckwheat . . . '

A pause. The sound of harness bells.

MARINA. He's gone.

A pause. SONYA *re-enters and puts the candle back on the table.*

SONYA. He's gone . . .

VANYA (*counts on the abacus, then makes a note*). 'Total . . . fifteen . . . twenty-five . . .

SONYA *sits down and begins writing.*

MARINA (*yawns*). Oh, Lord have mercy on us . . .

TELEGIN *enters on tiptoe, sits down by the door, and begins quietly tuning his guitar.*

VANYA (*to* SONYA, *passing his hand over her hair*). Oh, my child, I'm so depressed. If you only knew how depressed I am.

SONYA. What can we do? We must go on living. (*A pause.*) And we shall live, Uncle Vanya. We'll live through a long, long succession of days and endless nights; we'll patiently bear whatever trials fate has in store for us; we'll work for others, now and in our old age, without ever knowing rest, and when our time comes, we'll die without a struggle, and beyond the grave we'll say that we have suffered, we've wept, we've had a hard life, and God will look kindly on us, and you and I, Uncle, dear Uncle, will see before us a life that is bright and beautiful, and fine.

And we'll rejoice, and look back on our present troubles with tenderness, with a smile – and we shall rest. I believe that, Uncle, I believe that fervently, passionately . . .

She kneels down before him and lays her head on his hands. She sounds worn out.

We shall rest! (TELEGIN *quietly plays his guitar.*) We shall rest! We'll hear the angels, we'll see the heavens sparkling like diamonds, we'll see all earthly evil, all our sufferings washed away by a mercy that will flood the entire world, and our life will become as peaceful, gentle and sweet as a caress. I believe it, I believe it . . . (*Wipes away his tears with her handkerchief.*) Poor, poor Uncle Vanya, you're crying . . . (*Tearfully.*) You've known no joy in your life, but wait, Uncle Vanya, wait . . . We shall rest . . . (*Embraces him.*) We shall rest!

The WATCHMAN *taps.* TELEGIN *softly strums his guitar;* MARIA VASILIEVNA *makes notes in the margins of her pamphlet;* MARINA *knits her stocking.*

We shall rest!

The curtain falls slowly.

THREE SISTERS

Dramatis Personae

PROZOROV, Andrei Sergeyevich

NATALYA IVANOVNA, *his fiancée, later his wife*

OLGA

MASHA } *his sisters*

IRINA

KULYGIN, Fyodor Ilyich, *a high school teacher,
Masha's husband*

VERSHININ, Aleksandr Ignatyevich, *Lieut. Colonel,
battery commander*

TUZENBAKH, Nikolai Lvovich, *Baron, Lieutenant*

SOLIONY, Vasily Vasilyevich, *Staff Captain*

CHEBUTYKIN, Ivan Romanovich, *military doctor*

FEDOTIK, Aleksei Petrovich, *Second Lieutenant*

RODE, Vladimir Karlovich, *Second Lieutenant*

FERAPONT, *the local council watchman, an old man*

ANFISA, *nurse, an old woman of eighty*

The action takes place in a provincial town.

For a Guide to Pronunciation of Names, see page 279.

ACT ONE

The PROZOROVS' *house. A drawing-room with pillars, behind which can be seen a large ballroom. It is mid-day, bright and sunny. In the ballroom, the table is being set for lunch.* OLGA *is wearing the blue uniform dress of a teacher at the girls' high school, and while she stands and moves around, she corrects exercise books;* MASHA, *in a black dress, sits with her hat in her lap, reading a book.* IRINA, *dressed in white, stands deep in thought.*

OLGA. Father died exactly a year ago, this very day. On your name-day, Irina, the fifth of May. It was very cold then – snowing. I thought I'd never get over it, and you had fainted, lying as if you were dead. And here we are, a year's gone by, and we can talk about it quite calmly. You're wearing white again, looking radiant . . .

A clock strikes twelve.

The clock struck then too.

A pause.

And I remember, when they carried father out, the band was playing, and they fired a salute at the graveside. He was a general, a brigade commander, yet so few people came to the funeral. Still, it was raining. Heavy rain, and sleet.

IRINA. Why bring it all back?

In the ballroom, beyond the pillars, BARON TUZENBAKH, CHEBUTYKIN *and* SOLIONY *appear at the table.*

OLGA. It's warm today, we can even have the windows open, and the birch-trees still aren't out. Father got his brigade, and we left Moscow eleven years ago, yet I can remember so well, how everything's already in flower in Moscow by this time, the beginning of May, how warm it

is, everything bathed in sunlight. Yes, eleven years have
passed, and I remember it all, as if we'd left only
yesterday. Oh, dear God – I woke up this morning, saw
the light streaming in, the spring sunshine, and felt such
joy welling up in my heart, such an intense longing to go
home.

CHEBUTYKIN. Oh, forget it!

TUZENBAKH. It's nonsense, of course.

MASHA, *absorbed in her book, begins softly whistling.*

OLGA. Masha, stop whistling. How can you?

A pause.

Yes, I daresay it's because I'm at school all day, and then
in the evening I have to give lessons, but my head aches
the whole time, and I've already started to think like
an old woman. To tell you the truth, these past four years
I've been teaching at the high school, it's as if all my
strength and youth have been ebbing away, drop by drop.
The only thing that grows and gets stronger, is the one
dream I have . . .

IRINA. To go to Moscow! To sell this house, leave it all
behind, and head for Moscow . . .

OLGA. Oh, yes! To Moscow, as soon as possible!

CHEBUTYKIN *and* TUZENBAKH *laugh.*

IRINA. Our brother'll no doubt be a professor – in any case
he won't go on living here. There's only one snag, and
that's poor Masha.

OLGA. Masha can come to Moscow for the whole summer,
every year.

MASHA *is still softly whistling.*

IRINA. God willing, it'll all work out. (*Looking out of the
window.*) What a beautiful day it is. I don't know why, I
just feel so light-hearted! This morning I remembered it
was my name-day, and I suddenly felt so happy. I
remembered when I was little, and Mama was still alive.

Oh, and such wonderful thoughts came into my mind, such feelings!

OLGA. You're looking radiant today, even more beautiful than usual. And Masha's beautiful too. Andrei could be quite handsome, except he's got so stout, and it doesn't suit him. And I've grown old and terribly thin, I suppose from losing my temper with the girls at school. Still, I have a day off today, I'm at home, my headache's gone, and I feel younger than I did yesterday. Twenty-eight, that's all I am . . . Everything's fine, it's God's will, but even so – I think I'd have done better if I'd got married and stayed home all day.

A pause.

Yes, I'd have loved my husband.

TUZENBAKH (*to* SOLIONY). Honestly, you talk such nonsense, I'm fed up listening to you. (*Entering the drawing-room.*) By the way, I forgot to mention. You'll be having a visit today from our new battery commander, Vershinin. (*He sits down at the piano.*)

OLGA. Really? That'll be nice.

IRINA. Is he old?

TUZENBAKH. No, not particularly. He's about forty, forty-five at most. (*He begins to play, softly.*) He's a decent chap, by all accounts. He's no fool, that's for sure. Talks too much, though.

IRINA. Is he an interesting person?

TUZENBAKH. Yes, I suppose so. He's got a wife, mind you, and a mother-in-law and two little girls. Married for the second time, no less. Pays calls on everybody, tells them he's got a wife and two little girls. He'll say it here too. His wife's a bit cracked, wears her hair in a long braid, like a schoolgirl, talks all sorts of pretentious rot, philosophy and so on. Keeps trying to commit suicide, obviously to spite him. I'd have cleared off long ago, but he sticks it out, just complains.

SOLIONY (*entering from the dining room, with* CHEBUTYKIN).
Now, with one hand, I can lift fifty pounds – but with
two, a hundred and eighty, possibly two hundred. And
from that I conclude that two men aren't just twice as
strong as one, but three times, or even more . . .

CHEBUTYKIN (*reading a newspaper as he enters*). For falling
hair . . . nine grammes of naphthalene in a half-bottle of
alcohol . . . to be dissolved, and applied daily . . . (*He
writes in a notebook.*) Better jot that down! (*To* SOLIONY.)
So anyway, as I was telling you, you put a cork into a
little bottle, and pass a glass tube through it . . . Then
you take just a pinch of common-or-garden alum . . .

IRINA. Ivan Romanych, dearest Ivan Romanych!

CHEBUTYKIN. My dear, sweet child, what is it?

IRINA. Tell me, why am I so happy today? It's as if I'm
sailing, with a wide deep sky above me and great white
birds flying past. Why is that? Tell me, why?

CHEBUTYKIN (*kisses both her hands, tenderly*). My little white
bird . . .

IRINA. When I woke up this morning, I got up and washed,
and it was as if everything in this life had suddenly
become clear to me, and I knew how I ought to live.
Dear Ivan Romanych, I know everything now. A man
must labour, he should work in the sweat of his brow, no
matter who he is, and that's the only thing that gives
meaning and purpose to his life, the source of all his
happiness and joy. Oh, it must be wonderful to be a
workman, and get up when it's still barely light, to break
stones on the road, or a shepherd, or a teacher, teaching
children, or an engine-driver on the railway . . . Dear
God, better to be a dumb ox, or a horse, if only to work
– anything but a girl who gets up at twelve o'clock, takes
her coffee in bed, then spends two hours dressing! That's
awful! It's like having a terrible thirst in a heatwave, that's
how much I long to work. And if I don't get up early,
and really work, well then, Ivan Romanych, you can just
refuse to be my friend.

CHEBUTYKIN (*tenderly*). That's exactly what I'll do.

OLGA. Father trained us to get up at seven. Nowadays Irina wakes at seven, and then lies thinking until at least nine o'clock. And with such a serious face! (*Laughs.*)

IRINA. You're so used to seeing me as a little girl − you think it's strange if I look serious. But I'm twenty!

TUZENBAKH. This longing for work − dear God, it's all so familiar! I've never done a stroke of work in my life. I was born in St Petersburg, a cold, listless town, to a family that'd never known either work, or want. I remember I used to come home from the cadet corps, and a manservant had to pull off my boots; I'd be acting the goat, while my mother looked on admiringly; she just couldn't believe other people saw me in a different light. No, they shielded me from work. But they only just managed it, yes indeed! The time has come, the storm clouds are massing for all of us, a fierce, cleansing wind's blowing up, it's coming, it's not far away, and it's going to sweep the idleness right out of our society, all the apathy, and prejudice against work, the rotten boredom. I shall work, yes, and in twenty-five or thirty years' time, everybody'll work. Every one of us!

CHEBUTYKIN. Well, I shan't work.

TUZENBAKH. You don't count.

SOLIONY. In twenty-five years' time you won't even be alive, thank God. In another couple of years you'll die of a stroke. Either that or I'll lose my temper and plant a bullet in your brain, my angel. (*He takes a little bottle of scent from his pocket and sprinkles some on his chest and hands.*)

CHEBUTYKIN (*laughs*). Well, I've never done a thing, I must say. Since I left university, I haven't so much as lifted a finger, haven't read a single book, nothing but newspapers . . . (*He takes another newspaper out of his pocket.*) Look, see . . . I know from the papers that there was somebody called Dobrolyubov, but what he wrote about, I haven't a clue. God knows . . .

Someone knocks up from downstairs.

Ah! They're calling me down, someone's come to see me. I'll be back in a minute . . . wait there . . . (*He hurriedly exits, stroking his beard.*)

IRINA. He's up to something.

TUZENBAKH. Yes. He's gone off with such a pompous look on his face, he's obviously about to bring in your present.

IRINA. Oh, I hate that!

OLGA. Yes, it's awful. He's always doing something silly.

MASHA. 'By a curving shore stands a green oak tree, Hung with a golden chain . . . Hung with a golden chain . . . '

She rises, and begins to hum softly.

OLGA. You're not very cheerful today, Masha.

MASHA, *still humming, puts on her hat.*

Where are you going?

MASHA. Home.

IRINA. Surely not?

TUZENBAKH. What, leaving on a name-day?

MASHA. It's all right. I'll come back this evening. Goodbye, my dear . . . (*Embraces* IRINA.) Once again, I wish you health and happiness . . . You know, in the old days, when father was alive, and it was someone's name-day, we'd have as many as thirty or forty officers arriving, and the noise . . . Today we can barely scrape up two people, and it's so quiet, it's like a desert. I'll go now. I'm in a foul mood today, I feel depressed – you don't want to listen to me. (*Laughs tearfully.*) We'll have a talk later, but I'll say goodbye now, my dear, I must go.

IRINA (*displeased*). Well, really . . .

OLGA (*in tears*). I understand you, Masha.

SOLIONY. Yes, when a man has a serious talk, it's either philosophy, or sophistry; but when a woman, or two women start talking – well, I couldn't care two hoots.

MASHA. What do you mean by that, you horrible, frightful man?

SOLIONY. Nothing. 'Before he had time to gasp, the bear had him in its grasp . . . '

A pause.

MASHA (*to* OLGA, *angrily*). Stop howling!

ANFISA *and* FERAPONT *enter, carrying a cake.*

ANFISA. In here, old man. Go on, your feet are clean enough. (*To* IRINA.) It's from the council, from Protopopov . . . he's sent a cake.

IRINA. Thank you. Tell him thanks very much.

She accepts the cake.

FERAPONT. What's that?

IRINA (*louder*). Tell him thank you!

OLGA. Nanny, give him some of the cake. Ferapont, off you go, they'll give you some cake.

FERAPONT. What?

ANFISA. Come on, old man. Ferapont, this way . . . (*Exits with* FERAPONT.)

MASHA. I can't stand that Protopopov, that Mikhail Potapych or Ivanych or whatever his name is. You shouldn't invite him.

IRINA. I haven't invited him.

MASHA. Just as well.

Enter CHEBUTYKIN, *and behind him a soldier carrying a silver samovar; cries of astonishment and dismay.*

OLGA (*covering her face with her hands*). A samovar! This is terrible! (*Exits to the ballroom, by the table.*)

IRINA. Dearest Ivan Romanych, what are you doing!

TUZENBAKH (*laughs*). I told you!

MASHA. Ivan Romanych, you've absolutely no shame!

CHEBUTYKIN. My darling girls, my sweet girls, you're all
I have, you're the dearest thing on earth to me. I'll be
sixty soon, I'm an old man, a lonely, useless old man.
There's nothing any good about me, except the love I have
for you, and if it wasn't for you, well, I'd have been dead
long ago . . . (*To* IRINA.) My sweet, darling child, I've
known you since the day you were born . . . I've carried
you in my arms . . . I loved your poor mother . . .

IRINA. But why give me such expensive presents?

CHEBUTYKIN (*through tears, angrily*). Expensive presents?
Get away with you . . . (*To his batman.*) Take the samovar
in there . . . (*Mimicking* IRINA.) Expensive presents . . .

The batman removes the samovar into the ballroom.

ANFISA (*passing through the drawing room*). Oh, my dears,
there's a stranger arrived, a colonel! He's already taken his
coat off, my dears, and he's coming in. Now, Irina, love,
you be nice to him, won't you, and polite . . . (*Exits.*) And
it's long past lunch-time . . . Heavens!

TUZENBAKH. That'll be Vershinin.

VERSHININ *enters.*

Lieutenant-Colonel Vershinin!

VERSHININ (*to* MASHA *and* IRINA). Allow me to
introduce myself – Vershinin. I'm so pleased to be here –
at last. My, how you've grown!

IRINA. Please sit down. You're very welcome.

VERSHININ (*delightedly*). I'm so glad, I really am! But surely
there should be three sisters. Three little girls, I
remember. I don't remember your faces, but I certainly
recall your father, Colonel Prozorov, having three little
girls, I remember seeing them for sure. My, doesn't time
fly! Yes, time flies all right!

TUZENBAKH. Aleksandr Ignatyevich is from Moscow.

IRINA. From Moscow? You're from Moscow?

VERSHININ. Yes, I am. Your late father was battery commander there, and I was an officer in the same brigade. (*To* MASHA.) You know, I believe I do remember you, slightly.

MASHA. Well, I don't remember you!

IRINA. Olya! Olya! (*Calls into the ballroom.*) Olya, do come!

OLGA *emerges into the drawing-room.*

Lieutenant-Colonel Vershinin is from Moscow, would you believe.

VERSHININ. You must be the older sister, Olga Serge-yevna . . . And you're Mariya . . . And you're Irina – the youngest . . .

OLGA. You're from Moscow?

VERSHININ. Yes. I studied in Moscow, entered the service in Moscow – served there a long time, until I eventually got this battery – transferred here, as you see. I don't remember you in detail, only that you were three sisters. Your father's stayed in my memory, though. I need only close my eyes and I can see him, as large as life. I used to visit you in Moscow.

OLGA. I thought I could remember everybody, but now . . .

VERSHININ. I'm Aleksandr Ignatyevich . . .

IRINA. Aleksandr Ignatyevich, and you're from Moscow . . . That really is amazing!

OLGA. We'll be moving there, you see.

IRINA. Yes, we should be there by autumn, we think. It's our home town, we were born there . . . On Old Basmanny Street . . .

They both laugh delightedly.

MASHA. They've spotted a fellow-Muscovite. (*Animatedly.*) Ah, now I remember! Olya, you remember all the talk

about the 'lovesick Major' . . . You were a lieutenant
then, and you were in love with somebody or other, and
they all used to tease you, calling you a major for some
reason . . .

VERSHININ (*laughs*). That's right, that's right . . . 'The
lovesick Major', it's true . . .

MASHA. You only had a moustache then . . . Oh, and
you've got so much older! (*Tearfully*.) You've grown so old!

VERSHININ. Yes, when they called me the lovesick Major,
I was still young, and in love. And now I'm not.

OLGA. But you haven't a single grey hair. You've grown
older, yes, but you're not old.

VERSHININ. Well, I don't know, I've turned forty-two.
Have you been away from Moscow long?

IRINA. Eleven years. Masha, you're crying, what's wrong?
Don't be silly . . . (*Tearfully*.) Now I'll start crying . . .

MASHA. I'm all right. Where did you stay in Moscow?

VERSHININ. On Old Basmanny Street.

OLGA. Why, so did we . . .

VERSHININ. At one time I stayed in Nemetsky Street, and
I used to walk from Nemetsky Street to the Krasny
Barracks. There's a gloomy-looking bridge on the way,
with the water roaring underneath it. You could feel quite
depressed, if you were on your own.

A pause.

Still, the river here's so wide, so majestic! A superb river!

OLGA. Yes, but it's cold. It's cold here, and the mosquitoes . . .

VERSHININ. Nonsense! It's fine and healthy, a good
Russian climate. The forest, the river . . . you've got
birch-trees too. The gentle, modest birch, I love it above
all other trees. It's a good life here. The only odd thing is
the railway station, fifteen miles away . . . And nobody
seems to know why.

SOLIONY. Well, I know why.

Everyone turns to look at him.

It's because if the station were nearer, then it wouldn't be so far, but since it's far, that means it isn't near.

An awkward silence.

TUZENBAKH. You're a great joker, Soliony.

OLGA. Now I've remembered you too. I do remember.

VERSHININ. I knew your dear mother.

CHEBUTYKIN. She was a fine woman, may God rest her soul.

IRINA. Mama was buried in Moscow.

OLGA. In the Novo-Devichy cemetery . . .

MASHA. Would you believe, I'm already beginning to forget her face? We won't be remembered either. We'll be forgotten.

VERSHININ. Forgotten, yes. That's our fate, and there's nothing we can do about it. What seems so important or significant to us, what we take so seriously, well, in time it'll all be forgotten, or else seem trivial.

A pause.

And the strange thing is, we can have absolutely no idea what people will come to value, or think important, and what they'll find pathetic or ludicrous. I mean, didn't the discoveries of Copernicus, or Columbus, say, seem pointless and stupid at first, while the most arrant non-sense, scribbled down by some crank, passed for truth? It could even be that this life of ours, which we take so much for granted, will come to be seen as bizarre and uncomfortable, mindless, and none too clean, maybe even sinful . . .

TUZENBAKH. Who knows? It's also possible that our life will be highly thought of, and people will look back on it with respect. We don't have torture nowadays, or executions, or invasions, though there's still a great deal of suffering!

SOLIONY (*in a squeaky voice*). Cheep! Cheep! Cheep! . . . Just give the Baron the floor, and he's as happy as a sandboy!

TUZENBAKH. Soliony, I wish you'd leave me in peace . . . (*Sits apart.*) It's very boring, if you must know.

SOLIONY. Cheep! Cheep! Cheep!

TUZENBAKH (*to* VERSHININ). Yes, the suffering we see around us today – and there's so much of it – even so, it indicates a certain rise in moral standards, which our society has already achieved . . .

VERSHININ. Yes, of course.

CHEBUTYKIN. Baron, you've just said that people'll look up to us, but we're pretty small all the same . . . (*Stands up.*) Look how small I am, for instance. You've obviously got to say my life has some sort of value and meaning, just to console me.

In the adjoining room, a violin is being played.

MASHA. That's Andrei, our brother.

IRINA. He's the brains in our family. He really ought to be a professor. Papa was a soldier, but his son's chosen an academic career.

MASHA. At Papa's wish.

OLGA. We've been teasing him today. We think he's a little in love.

IRINA. With a young lady locally. She'll be here today, very possibly.

MASHA. Ugh! The way she dresses! Not just unattractive and unfashionable – it's absolutely pitiful. Some sort of bizarre, garish yellow skirt, with a silly fringe and a red blouse. And her cheeks shining, absolutely scrubbed! No, Andrei isn't in love, I won't hear of it – he's got more taste, he's simply teasing us, playing the fool. I heard yesterday she was going to marry Protopopov, the chairman of our local council. And a good thing, too. (*Calling through the side door.*) Andrei, come here! Just for a minute, dear!

ANDREI *enters.*

OLGA. This is my brother, Andrei Sergeyich.

VERSHININ. Vershinin.

ANDREI. Prozorov. (*Wipes the perspiration from his brow.*) So, you're our new battery commander?

OLGA. Just imagine, Aleksandr Ignatych is from Moscow.

ANDREI. Really? Well, I congratulate you, my dear sisters won't give you any peace now.

VERSHININ. Oh, I've already managed to bore your sisters.

IRINA. Look at the little picture frame Andrei gave me today! (*Shows him the frame.*) He made it himself.

VERSHININ (*inspects the frame, uncertain what to say*). Yes, it's . . . it's very . . .

IRINA. And that little frame over the piano, he made that too.

ANDREI w*aves his hand dismissively and moves apart.*

OLGA. He's our intellectual as well, and he plays the violin – he makes all sorts of little things out of wood. Really, he's a jack of all trades. Andrei, don't go! Oh, that's his way, he's always running off. Andrei, come back!

MASHA *and* IRINA *take hold of his arms and lead him back, laughing.*

MASHA. Come on, come on.

ANDREI. Let me go, please.

MASHA. You're so funny! They used to call Aleksandr Ignatyevich the lovesick Major, and it didn't upset him.

VERSHININ. Not in the least!

MASHA. And I'm going to call you . . . the lovesick fiddler!

IRINA. Or the lovesick professor!

OLGA. He's in love! Andryusha's in love!

IRINA (*clapping her hands*). Bravo! Bravo! Andryusha's in love!

CHEBUTYKIN *approaches* ANDREI *from behind and seizes him with both arms around his waist.*

CHEBUTYKIN. 'For love alone did Nature bring us forth upon this Earth!' (*Laughs, still holding his newspaper.*)

ANDREI. Enough, enough! (*Mopping his brow.*) I haven't slept all night, and I'm not exactly at my best, as they say. I read till four o'clock, then went to bed, but it wasn't any use. I kept thinking, about this and that, but the dawn comes up early here, and next thing the sun's creeping into my bedroom. While I'm here I want to spend the summer translating a little book from English.

VERSHININ. You read English?

ANDREI. Oh yes, our father, God bless him, burdened us with an education. It's a ludicrous idea, I know, but I must confess I've started to put on weight since his death, and I've got quite stout in a year, as you see, as if my body's been relieved of its burden. Thanks to father, my sisters and I know French, German and English, and Irina also knows Italian. But at what cost!

MASHA. In this town, knowing three languages is an unnecessary luxury. No, not even a luxury – a useless appendage, like a sixth finger. Superfluous knowledge.

VERSHININ. I don't believe it! (*Laughs.*) Superfluous? I don't think there's a town anywhere – there can't be – that's so dismal and boring that it has no use for an intelligent, well-educated person. Let's say that among a population of a hundred thousand in this town, backward and ignorant, agreed – let's say there are only three like yourselves. It stands to reason you can't win over the benighted masses all around you; in the course of your life, little by little, you'll be forced to submit, lose yourself

in the crowd, the hundred thousand. Life'll swallow you
up, but you won't disappear all the same, you won't cease
to have some influence; after you've gone, there'll be
others like you, perhaps six, then twelve, and so on, until
finally people like you will be in the majority. In two or
three hundred years' time, life on this earth will be
unimaginably beautiful, astonishing. Man needs such a
life, and even if it isn't here yet, he's still got to have a
presentiment of it, to wait, and dream, and prepare for it,
and that's why he has to see more, know more, than his
father and grandfather did. (*Laughs.*) And you're talking
about superfluous knowledge!

MASHA (*takes off her hat*). I'll stay for lunch.

IRINA (*with a sigh*). We really ought to have noted all that
down . . .

ANDREI *has slipped out, unnoticed.*

TUZENBAKH. What you're saying is that after many years,
life on earth'll be beautiful and astonishing. That's true.
But in order to be a part of it now, remote as we may be,
we must prepare ourselves for it, we must work . . .

VERSHININ (*rises*). Yes. Still, what a lot of flowers you have!
(*Looking round.*) And such a splendid house. I envy you! I've
knocked around all my life in poky rooms, with two chairs
and a sofa, and stoves forever belching smoke. Yes, there's
been a distinct shortage of flowers like this in my life!
(*Rubs his hands together.*) Ah, well, never mind, eh?

TUZENBAKH. Yes, we must work. No doubt you're
thinking, well, that's just a German getting emotional. But
I'm Russian, my word of honour – I don't even speak
German. My father's Orthodox . . .

A pause.

VERSHININ (*pacing about the stage*). You know, I often think:
what if we could start life over again, knowing what we
do now? If this one life, which we've lived out, could've
been a rough draft, as they say, and the next one, the fair

copy! Well, first and foremost, my guess is we'd try not to repeat ourselves. At the very least we'd create a different set of circumstances for ourselves, a house like this, say, with flowers, flooded with light . . . I have a wife, and two little girls, and on top of that, my lady wife doesn't keep well, and so forth. But if I could begin life over again, I wouldn't get married . . . No, indeed!

KULYGIN *enters, in his uniform frock coat.*

KULYGIN (*goes up to* IRINA). My dear sister, allow me to congratulate you on your saint's day, and to wish you, most sincerely, from the bottom of my heart, good health, and everything a young woman of your age could hope for. And also to make you a present of this little book. (*Hands her the book.*) It's the history of our school during the last fifty years, written by myself. It's a trifling thing, written to pass the time, but do read it all the same. Good morning, ladies and gentlemen! (*To* VERSHININ.) I'm Kulygin, teacher at the local high school, and court counsellor. (*To* IRINA.) You'll find the names in there of everyone who passed through our school in the last fifty years. *Feci quod potui, faciant meliora potentes.* (*He kisses* MASHA.)

IRINA. But you already gave me this book, at Easter.

KULYGIN (*laughs*). No, it's not possible! Well, in that case give it back to me – or better still, give it to the Colonel. Please take it, Colonel. You can read it sometime when you've nothing better to do.

VERSHININ. Thank you. (*Makes ready to leave.*) Well, I'm extremely pleased to have made your acquaintance . . .

OLGA. You're leaving? Surely not!

IRINA. Stay and have lunch with us. Please.

OLGA. Yes, please stay.

VERSHININ (*bows*). I seem to have intruded on a name day party. Forgive me, I didn't know, and I haven't congratulated you . . . (*Exits with* OLGA *to the ballroom.*)

KULYGIN. Ladies and gentlemen, today is Sunday, a day of rest, and rest we shall. We shall amuse ourselves, each one as befits his age and condition. These carpets'll have to be taken up for the summer, and put away until winter . . . they'll need some Persian powder, or naphthalene . . . Yes, the Romans were healthy, because they knew how to work, and how to rest, they had *mens sana in corpore sano*. Their lives had a distinct form. As our headmaster says, the most important thing about any sort of life is its form . . . Anything that loses its form is finished – and it's exactly the same with our everyday lives. (*He clasps* MASHA *around the waist, laughing.*) Masha loves me. My wife loves me. Yes, and the curtains should be put away along with the carpets . . . Today I'm happy, I'm in excellent high spirits. Masha, we have to be at the headmaster's today at four o'clock. He's organised a little outing for the teachers and their families.

MASHA. I'm not going.

KULYGIN (*pained*). But, Masha dear, why not?

MASHA. We'll talk about it later . . . (*Crossly.*) Oh, all right, I'll go. Just leave me alone, please. (*She moves apart.*)

KULYGIN. And afterwards we're to spend the evening at the headmaster's house. You know, in spite of ill health, that man does his level best to be sociable. A first-rate individual, quite brilliant – a truly magnificent man. After the staff meeting yesterday, he said to me, 'I'm tired, Fyodor! I'm so tired!' (*Looks at the wall-clock, then at his watch.*) Your clock's seven minutes fast. 'Yes,' he says, 'I'm tired.'

A violin is being played offstage.

OLGA. Gentlemen, please sit down to lunch! It's a pie!

KULYGIN. Ah, my dear Olga, dear kind Olga! I had to work all day yesterday, from morning till eleven o'clock at night, I'm tired, and today I feel so happy. (*Exits to the table in the ballroom.*) My dearest Olga!

CHEBUTYKIN (*puts his newspaper into his pocket, and strokes his beard*). A pie? Wonderful!

MASHA (*to* CHEBUTYKIN, *severely*). Just see you don't drink today. Do you hear? Drinking's bad for you.

CHEBUTYKIN. Oh, stuff – I've got over all that. It's two years since I last hit the bottle. (*Testily.*) Anyway, what difference does it make?

MASHA. You'd better not, all the same. Don't you dare drink! (*Angrily, but taking care her husband doesn't hear.*) Damn! Another whole evening, bored stiff at the headmaster's!

TUZENBAKH. If I were you, I wouldn't go . . . Simple as that.

CHEBUTYKIN. Don't go, my dear.

MASHA. Oh yes, don't go . . . This damnable life, I can't bear it . . . (*Exits to the ballroom.*)

CHEBUTYKIN (*exits behind her*). Well, well . . .

SOLIONY (*as he crosses to the ballroom*). Cheep! Cheep! Cheep!

TUZENBAKH. That's enough, Soliony. Give it a rest.

SOLIONY. Cheep! Cheep! Cheep!

KULYGIN (*cheerfully*). Your good health, Colonel! Yes, I'm a schoolmaster, one of the family here, Masha's husband. She's a good woman, a very kind woman . . .

VERSHININ. I think I'll have some of this dark vodka . . . (*Drinks.*) Your good health! (*To* OLGA.) I feel really at home here! . . .

IRINA *and* TUZENBAKH *remain alone in the drawing room.*

IRINA. Masha's in a bad mood today. She got married at eighteen, when she thought he was the cleverest of men. Now, she doesn't. He's the kindest, but not the cleverest.

OLGA (*impatiently*). Andrei, what's keeping you!

ANDREI (*offstage*). I'm coming! (*He enters and comes to the table.*)

TUZENBAKH. What're you thinking?

IRINA. Oh, nothing . . . You know, I don't like that Soliony of yours, he frightens me. He says such stupid things.

TUZENBAKH. He's a strange man. I feel sorry for him. He annoys me, but more often I pity him. I think he's shy . . . When it's just the two of us, he's quite witty and charming, but in company he can be extremely rude, a real bully. No, don't go, let them get settled first. I want to stay here with you a minute. What're you thinking about?

A pause.

You're twenty, Irina, and I'm not yet thirty. And we've so many years left ahead of us, a long, long line of days, filled with my love for you . . .

IRINA. Nikolai, please don't speak to me about love.

TUZENBAKH (*not listening*). I have a desperate thirst for life, for the struggle, for work, and this thirst in my soul has merged with my love for you, Irina. It's as if by design – you're beautiful, and that's why I find life so beautiful. Tell me what you're thinking.

IRINA. You say life is beautiful. Well, yes, but supposing it only seems that way? Life hasn't been beautiful for us yet, us three sisters. It's trampled us down, like weeds . . . My eyes are filling up. I mustn't cry . . . (*Hurriedly dries her eyes, smiles.*) We must work, work! That's why we're so depressed, and have such a gloomy outlook on life – it's because we know nothing of work. We've come from people who despised work . . .

NATALYA IVANOVNA *enters, dressed in a pink frock with a green belt.*

NATASHA. They're sitting down to lunch already . . . I'm late . . . (*Glances in passing at the mirror, composes herself.*) My hair's not too bad, I think. (*Catching sight of* IRINA.) Irina Sergeyevna, my dear, congratulations! (*Gives her a firm, prolonged kiss.*) You've got so many guests, I'm really embarrassed . . . Good morning, Baron!

OLGA (*entering the drawing room*). And Natasha's here now, too! How are you, my dear!

They embrace.

NATASHA. And it's Irina's name-day, congratulations! You've got such a crowd of people, I feel terribly awkward . . .

OLGA. Don't be silly, we're all family here. (*Sotto voce, alarmed.*) You're wearing a green belt. My dear, that's all wrong!

NATASHA. Is it bad luck?

OLGA. No, no, it just doesn't match . . . it's a bit odd . . .

NATASHA (*a catch in her voice*). D'you think so? Actually, it's not green, it's more sort of neutral. (*She follows* OLGA *into the ballroom.*)

They sit down to lunch in the ballroom; the drawing room is now completely deserted.

KULYGIN. I wish you a handsome young man, Irina. It's time you were getting married.

CHEBUTYKIN. And I wish you a fine young man too, Natasha!

KULYGIN. Natasha already has a young man in mind.

MASHA. Well, I shall down a little glass of wine! Yes, why not, let's eat, drink and be damned!

KULYGIN. That's a C-minus for conduct, Masha.

VERSHININ. This is a fine liqueur. What's it made from?

SOLIONY. From cockroaches.

IRINA (*close to tears*). Ugh! That's really disgusting! . . .

OLGA. For supper we're having roast turkey, and apple pie. Thank goodness I've got the whole day at home, the evening too . . . Do come this evening, gentlemen . . .

VERSHININ. Am I allowed to come too?

IRINA. By all means.

NATASHA. They don't stand on ceremony here.

CHEBUTYKIN. 'For love alone did Nature bring us forth upon this Earth . . . ' (*Laughs.*)

ANDREI (*annoyed*). Oh, stop it, all of you! Don't you ever get tired?

FEDOTIK *and* RODE *enter carrying a large basket of flowers.*

FEDOTIK. But they're already at lunch.

RODE (*loudly, with a guttural accent*). They're at lunch? Yes, so they are . . .

FEDOTIK. Hold on a minute! (*He takes a photograph.*) One! And again, wait a second . . . (*He takes another photograph.*) Two! Now we're ready!

They carry the basket into the ballroom, where they are noisily welcomed.

RODE (*shouts*). Congratulations, all the very best! The weather's wonderful today, an absolute marvel. I've been out walking with the high school boys all morning. I teach them gymnastics.

FEDOTIK. You can move now, Irina, it's all right! (*Taking a photograph.*) You look quite special today. (*Produces a spinning-top from his pocket.*) Look what I have besides – a top . . . it makes an amazing sound . . .

IRINA. What a lovely thing!

MASHA. 'By a curving shore stands a green oak tree, hung with a chain of gold . . . ' 'Hung with a chain of gold . . . ' (*Tearfully.*) Why do I keep saying that? That line's been going through my head since morning . . .

KULYGIN. Thirteen at table!

RODE (*shouts*). Gentlemen, gentlemen, you surely don't attach any significance to superstitions?

Laughter.

KULYGIN. Thirteen at table, that means there's somebody in love. It's not you by any chance, Ivan Romanych?

Laughter.

CHEBUTYKIN. No, I'm just an old sinner, but Natasha's blushing, and I can't for the life of me think why!

Hearty laughter. NATASHA *rushes out of the ballroom into the drawing room, pursued by* ANDREI.

ANDREI. Don't worry, don't take any notice of them! Wait, don't go, please . . .

NATASHA. I'm so ashamed . . . I don't know what's the matter with me, and they're making a fool of me. I shouldn't have left the table, it's bad manners, but I can't help it . . . I just can't . . .

Covers her face with her hands.

ANDREI. Oh, my dear love, please don't be upset. They're only joking, honestly, they're harmless. Dearest, darling Natasha, they're good people, kindhearted, and they love us both. Come over to the window, where they can't see us . . . (*He looks around.*)

NATASHA. I'm just not used to company! . . .

ANDREI. Oh, you're so young, so beautiful, so wonderful! My dear, sweet Natasha, you mustn't get upset . . . Believe me, please, trust me . . . I'm so happy, my heart's filled with love and joy . . . No, no, they can't see us, they can't! I don't know why I've fallen in love with you, or when it happened – oh, I don't know anything. My dearest, good, pure Natasha, be my wife! I love you, I love you as I've never loved anyone . . .

They kiss.

Two officers enter, and catching sight of the embracing couple, pause in astonishment.

Curtain.

ACT TWO

The stage is set as in Act One. It is eight o'clock in the evening. Offstage, an accordion is being played outside, faintly audible. The room is unlit. NATASHA enters in her dressing-gown, holding a candle. She crosses the stage and pauses at the door leading to ANDREI's room.

NATASHA. Andrei, what are you doing? You're reading? Oh, it doesn't matter, I was just wondering . . . (*She moves on, opens another door, looks in, then closes it.*) No lights left on . . .

ANDREI (*emerging with a book in his hand*). What is it, Natasha?

NATASHA. I'm checking to see if there's a light on . . . It's carnival time, the servants are getting careless, you have to keep an eye on them constantly, to make sure nothing's wrong. I walked through the dining room at midnight last night, and there was a candle left burning. And I still haven't found out who lit it. (*She sets down the candle.*) What time is it?

ANDREI (*looks at his watch*). Quarter past eight.

NATASHA. And Olga and Irina still aren't in. They haven't come home. They're kept busy the whole time, poor things. Olga at her staff meeting, Irina at her telegraph office . . . (*Sighs.*) I said that to your sister this morning, 'You must look after yourself, Irina darling,' I said. But she doesn't listen. Quarter past eight, did you say? You know, I'm afraid our little Bobik isn't at all well. Why is he so cold? He had a fever yesterday, and today he's freezing . . . I'm really worried about him!

ANDREI. He's fine, Natasha. The boy's fine.

NATASHA. Still, we'd better see he's eating properly. I'm worried. And there's supposed to be carnival people arriving at ten o'clock, I'd rather they didn't come, Andryusha.

ANDREI. Well, I don't know . . . After all, we did invite them.

NATASHA. You know, that darling little boy woke up this morning and looked at me, and he suddenly smiled – yes, he recognised me. 'Hello, Bobik!' I said, 'Hello, my darling!' And he laughed, yes. Children know everything that's going on, they understand perfectly. Anyway, Andryusha, I'll tell them not to let the musicians in.

ANDREI (*indecisively*). Well, that's surely up to my sisters. I mean, it's their house . . .

NATASHA. Yes, of course, I'll tell them too. They're so kind . . . (*Makes to leave.*) I've ordered sour milk for supper. The doctor says you're to have nothing but sour milk, otherwise you'll never lose weight. (*Pauses.*) Bobik gets a chill so easily. I'm worried in case it's too cold for him in there. We ought to put him in another room, at least until the warm weather. Irina's room, for instance – that's just perfect for a baby: it's dry, and it gets the sun all day. She'll have to be told, and she can move in with Olga meantime . . . She's not at home during the day anyway, she's only here at nights . . .

A pause.

Andryusha, love, you're not answering.

ANDREI. I'm thinking . . . Anyway, I've nothing to say . . .

NATASHA. Well . . . There was something I meant to tell you . . . Oh yes, Ferapont's come from the council, he wants to see you.

ANDREI (*yawns*). Send him in.

NATASHA *exits.* ANDREI, *stooping over the candle she has left behind, goes on reading his book.* FERAPONT *enters; he is wearing an old shabby overcoat, with the collar turned up, and a scarf round his ears.*

Well, hello, old chap – what is it?

FERAPONT. The Chairman's sent you a book, and papers of some sort. I've got them here . . . (*Hands over a book, and a package.*)

ANDREI. Thank you. That's fine. Why didn't you come earlier? It's gone eight o'clock.

FERAPONT. What?

ANDREI (*louder*). I said, you're late, it's eight o'clock already.

FERAPONT. That's true. It was still light when I came to see you, but they wouldn't let me in, no. The master's busy, they said. Well, never mind. If you're busy, you're busy, I'm in no hurry. (*He thinks* ANDREI *has asked him something.*) What?

ANDREI. Nothing. (*Inspects the book.*) Tomorrow's Friday, there's no meeting, but I'll go in anyway . . . it'll give me something to do. I'm bored stiff at home . . .

A pause.

Yes, my dear old chap, it's odd how things change, how life plays tricks on us. Out of sheer boredom today, nothing better to do, I picked up this book – my old university lectures, and I thought it was so funny . . . Good God, I'm the secretary to the district council, under chairman Protopopov – I'm secretary, and the most I can aspire to is to become a member! Yes, me – a member of the district council . . . and there I am dreaming every night that I'm a professor at Moscow University, a famous scholar, the pride of all Russia!

FERAPONT. I dunno . . . I don't hear too well . . .

ANDREI. Well, if you *could* hear, I doubt if I'd be talking like this. I've got to talk to somebody, but my wife doesn't understand me, and for some reason or other I'm afraid of my sisters. I'm afraid they'll laugh at me, or make me feel ashamed . . . I don't drink, I don't like taverns, but oh, my dear old chap, what wouldn't I give to be sitting right now in Moscow at Tyestov's, or the Grand Hotel!

FERAPONT. A builder at the council was saying just the other day that some merchants in Moscow were eating pancakes; and one of them, who'd eaten forty of the things, dropped down dead. Maybe it wasn't forty, maybe it was fifty. I don't rightly recall.

ANDREI. Yes, you can sit in Moscow, in an enormous restaurant dining-room, you don't know anybody, nobody knows you, and yet you don't feel like a stranger. But in this place, you know everybody, everybody knows you, but you're an outsider, a total stranger . . . Alone, and alien . . .

FERAPONT. What?

A pause.

That same builder was saying – maybe he was making it up – he said there was a rope stretched right across Moscow, from one end to the other.

ANDREI. What for?

FERAPONT. I dunno. That's what the builder said.

ANDREI. That's rubbish. (*Returns to his book.*) Have you ever been in Moscow?

FERAPONT (*after a pause*). I haven't. It's not been God's will.

A pause.

Shall I go?

ANDREI. You can go now. Take care, old chap.

FERAPONT *exits.*

Take care. (*Reading.*) You can come back tomorrow morning, collect these papers . . . Off you go . . .

A pause.

He's gone.

The door-bell rings.

Yes, more work . . . (*Stretches, and makes his way slowly off to his own room.*)

The old nurse is heard singing offstage, rocking the baby to sleep.
MASHA *and* VERSHININ *enter. While they converse, a maid*
lights the oil-lamp and candles.

MASHA. I don't know.

A pause.

I don't know. Habit counts for a great deal, of course,
what you're accustomed to. After father's death, for
example, we just couldn't get used to the fact that we
didn't have orderlies any longer. But quite apart from
habit, I think I'm justified in saying this. Maybe it isn't
the same in other places, but in this town the most
decent, the most honourable and well-bred people are the
military.

VERSHININ. I'm really thirsty. I wouldn't mind some tea.

MASHA (*glancing at her watch*). They'll be bringing it soon.
Yes, I got married when I was eighteen – I was in awe of
my husband, because he was a teacher, and I'd only just
left school. He was terribly learned, clever and important,
so I thought. And now I don't, sad to say.

VERSHININ. Yes . . . I see.

MASHA. I'm not talking about my husband, I've got used to
him, but among civilians in general there are so many
boorish people, no manners, badly brought up. It upsets
me, rudeness really offends me – when people show a lack
of sensitivity, or kindness, or common courtesy, I feel pain.
When I'm with the teachers, for instance, my husband's
colleagues, I really suffer.

VERSHININ. Yes . . . Even so, I think the military and
civilians are pretty much of a muchness, in this town at
any rate. No difference! If you listen to any educated
person hereabouts, soldier or civilian, they're fed up with
their wives, they're fed up with their house or their land,
they're sick to death of their horses . . . I mean, why is it
that Russians, who lay claim to the most exalted ideas,
have such low expectations of life? Why is that?

MASHA. Why?

VERSHININ. Why is your average Russian sick to death of his wife and children? And why are his wife and children sick of him?

MASHA. You're not at your best today.

VERSHININ. It's possible. I haven't eaten today, I've had nothing since morning. My daughter's a bit off-colour, and whenever my little girls are ill I get terribly worried, I get conscience-stricken about the sort of mother they have. Oh, you should have seen her today! Talk about pettyminded! We started shouting at each other at seven in the morning, and at nine I slammed the door and left.

A pause.

I never talk about these things, and it's strange I should be telling you. (*He kisses her hand.*) Don't be angry with me. Apart from you, I have nobody, no-one at all . . .

A pause.

MASHA. The stove's making such a noise. The chimney howled like that just before Father died. Exactly like that.

VERSHININ. You're not superstitious?

MASHA. Yes.

VERSHININ. That's odd. (*He kisses her hand.*) What a magnificent, wonderful creature you are. Truly magnificent, and wonderful! It's dark in here, yet I can still see your eyes shining.

MASHA (*sits down on another chair*). It's lighter over here . . .

VERSHININ. I love you, I love you . . . I love your eyes, your every movement, I dream about them . . . A magnificent, wonderful woman!

MASHA (*softly laughing*). When you speak to me like that, I laugh, I don't know why, even though I'm terrified. Please, don't say it again . . . (*Barely audible.*) No, go on, say it, I don't mind . . . (*Covers her face with her hands.*) It doesn't matter. There's someone coming, change the subject . . .

IRINA *and* TUZENBAKH *enter through the ballroom.*

TUZENBAKH. Yes, I have a triple-barrelled name – Baron Tuzenbakh-Krone-Altschauer, but I'm Russian, and Orthodox, the same as you. There's hardly any of the German left in me, unless you count my dogged persistence, the way I keep pestering you, walking you home every evening.

IRINA. Oh, I'm worn out!

TUZENBAKH. And I'll turn up at the telegraph office every day and walk you home, I'll do that for ten, twenty years, until you chase me away . . . (*Catches sight of* MASHA *and* VERSHININ, *delightedly.*) Oh, it's you! Hello!

IRINA. Home at last! (*To* MASHA.) You know, a woman came in just now, she was sending a telegram to her brother in Saratov, to let him know her son had died, and she couldn't for the life of her remember his address. And she sent it off like that, without an address, just Saratov. She was crying, and I was rude to her for no good reason. 'I haven't got all day,' I said. It was really stupid of me. Are we having the musicians tonight?

MASHA. Yes.

IRINA (*sits in the armchair*). I need a rest. I'm exhausted.

TUZENBAKH (*smiling*). Every time you come in from work you look such a pathetic little thing . . .

A pause.

IRINA. I'm tired. No, I don't like that telegraph office, I really don't.

MASHA. You've got thinner . . . (*Whistles.*) And younger-looking, quite boyish about the face . . .

TUZENBAKH. That's her hair-style.

IRINA. I'll have to find another job, this isn't for me. Whatever I wanted so much, and dreamed about, this definitely isn't it. There's no poetry in the work, it's mindless . . .

A knocking on the floor.

That's the Doctor knocking. (*To* TUZENBAKH.) Be a dear and answer him . . . I can't . . . I'm too tired . . .

TUZENBAKH *knocks on the floor.*

He'll be up any minute. We'll have to do something about this. He was with Andrei at the club yesterday, losing money again. Andrei lost two hundred roubles, apparently.

MASHA (*indifferently*). There's nothing we can do about that.

IRINA. He lost money a fortnight ago, and in December, too. I wish he'd lose everything, then perhaps we'd be able to get away from this town. Dear God in Heaven, I dream about Moscow every night, it's as if I'm going crazy. (*Laughs.*) We'll be moving there in June, and between now and June there's still . . . February, March, April . . . May . . . almost six months!

MASHA. Let's just hope Natasha doesn't find out about the money he's lost.

IRINA. I don't think she cares.

CHEBUTYKIN *has just got up out of bed, an after-dinner nap, and he now enters the ballroom, stroking his beard, sits down at the table and takes a newspaper out of his pocket.*

MASHA. Here he is now . . . Has he paid his rent?

IRINA (*laughs*). No. Not a penny for the past eight months. It's obviously slipped his mind.

MASHA (*laughs*). And sitting there, so self-importantly!

They all laugh. A pause.

IRINA. You're very quiet, Colonel?

VERSHININ. Yes, I don't know why. I'd like some tea. My kingdom for a glass of tea! I've had nothing to eat since morning . . .

CHEBUTYKIN. Irina Sergeyevna . . .

IRINA. Yes, what is it?

CHEBUTYKIN. Come here, please. *Venez ici!*

IRINA *goes to him and sits down at the table.*

I need your help.

IRINA *begins setting out the cards for a game of patience.*

VERSHININ. Oh well, if they won't give us any tea, then at least we can have a discussion.

TUZENBAKH. Yes, let's – what about?

VERSHININ. What about? Well, let's imagine, for example, what life'll be like after we're gone, say in two, or three hundred years' time.

TUZENBAKH. Really? Well, people'll fly around in balloons, there'll be a new fashion in men's jackets, they'll possibly discover some sixth sense, and develop it, but basically life'll remain the same – difficult, full of mystery, and happy. Yes, in a thousand years' time people'll still be sighing: 'God, what a life!' – and they'll be just as afraid of death, just as unwilling to die, as they are now.

VERSHININ *(after some thought)*. I'm not sure, but it seems to me that everything in life changes, little by little, it must do, and it's already happening, before our very eyes. In two or three hundred years' time, or a thousand, say – it doesn't matter how long – a new, happy life will dawn. Of course, we shan't be a part of that life, but we're living and working towards it now, suffering, indeed, to create it, and that's the whole point of our existence, that's our happiness, if you like.

MASHA *laughs softly.*

TUZENBAKH. What is it?

MASHA. Oh, nothing. I've been laughing the whole day.

VERSHININ. Well, I went to the same cadet school as you, I didn't go on to the Academy. I read a great deal, but I've no idea how to choose books, and possibly I don't read the things I should, but the longer I live, the more I want to know. My hair's turning grey, I'm practically an old man, and yet I understand so little – so very little. Nevertheless, I think I know what's genuinely important – yes, that I do know. I just wish I could prove to you that there's no such thing as happiness, there simply can't be, for us . . . All we can do is keep working, but as for happiness – well, that's reserved for our remote descendants.

A pause.

Not for me, no, but at least posterity, my children's children.

FEDOTIK *and* RODE *appear in the ballroom; they sit down and begin quietly singing, to a guitar accompaniment.*

TUZENBAKH. So, according to you, we can't even imagine happiness. But what if I'm happy now?

VERSHININ. You aren't.

TUZENBAKH (*throws up his hands, laughing*). Well, obviously we don't understand each other. So, how am I to convince you?

MASHA *laughs softly.*

(*Wags his finger at her.*) Go ahead and laugh. (*To* VERSHININ.) Yes, whether it's two, or three hundred years, or even a million years from now, life'll be the same as it's always been; it doesn't change, it remains constant, following its own laws, which don't concern us, or at least we can never know. Take migrating birds, for instance, like cranes – they keep on flying, and no matter what kind of thoughts, great or small, should pass through their heads, they'll fly on and on just the same, without knowing why or where to. They fly, and they'll keep flying, supposing all manner of thinkers were to spring up amongst them. They can think all they want, as long as they keep flying . . .

VERSHININ. And what about meaning?

TUZENBAKH. Meaning? . . . Look, it's snowing. What does that mean?

A pause.

MASHA. I think people should believe in something, or seek after truth, otherwise their lives are empty, just empty . . . To live, without knowing why cranes fly, or why children are born, or why there are stars in the sky . . . I mean, you either know why you're alive, or else it's all just nonsense, absolutely pointless . . .

A pause.

VERSHININ. Still, it's a shame we're no longer young.

MASHA. As Gogol says, 'Life's a bore, my friends!'

TUZENBAKH. Yes, and I say it's hard work arguing with you, my friends! I give up . . .

CHEBUTYKIN (*reading from his newspaper*). Balzac got married in Berdichev.

IRINA *begins softly singing.*

I really must make a note of that. (*Notes it down.*) Balzac was married in Berdichev . . . (*Goes on reading his newspaper.*)

IRINA (*laying out a game of patience, abstractedly*). Balzac was married in Berdichev . . .

TUZENBAKH. Anyway, the die is cast. You know I'm leaving the service, Mariya Sergeyevna?

MASHA. So I've heard. I can't see anything good about that. I don't like civilians.

TUZENBAKH. Well, it can't be helped . . . (*Stands up.*) I'm not good-looking, what sort of officer do I make? Anyway, it doesn't matter . . . I'm going to work. Just as long as I can work even one day in my life, come home at night and collapse onto the bed exhausted, fall asleep on the spot. (*Exiting to the ballroom.*) Yes, working people sleep soundly, I should imagine.

FEDOTIK (*to* IRINA). Look, I bought you some coloured pencils in a shop on Moscow Street. And you can have this penknife . . .

IRINA. You've got so used to treating me like a child, but I'm a grown woman . . . (*Accepts the pencils and penknife, delightedly.*) Oh, these are lovely!

FEDOTIK. I bought myself a knife, too . . . see, have a look. There's one blade, there's another, this one's for cleaning out your ears, and this one's for your fingernails . . .

RODE (*loudly*). Doctor, how old are you?

CHEBUTYKIN. Me? Thirty-two.

Laughter.

FEDOTIK. Here, I'll show you a different kind of patience . . . (*Sets out the cards for patience.*)

The samovar is brought in. ANFISA attends to the samovar, and after a while NATASHA enters and also busies herself at the table. SOLIONY then arrives, greets everyone and sits down at the table.

VERSHININ. Just listen to that wind!

MASHA. Yes. I'm sick of winter. I've already forgotten what summer's like.

IRINA. This patience is coming out, I can see it. We'll be going to Moscow.

FEDOTIK. No, it isn't. Look, the eight's covering the two of spades. (*Laughs.*) That means you won't be going to Moscow.

CHEBUTYKIN (*reading from his newspaper*). Tsitsikar . . . There's a smallpox epidemic in Tsitsikar . . .

ANFISA (*goes up to MASHA*). Masha, come and have some tea, my dear. (*To VERSHININ.*) And you too, Your Honour – I beg your pardon, sir, I've forgotten your name . . .

MASHA. Bring it here, Nanny. I'm not coming over there.

IRINA. Nanny!

ANFISA. I'm coming, I'm coming.

NATASHA (*to* SOLIONY). You
understand. 'Hello, Bobik,' I say
he looks up at me in that special
that's just a mother talking, but it
He really is an extraordinary child.

SOLIONY. Yes, well, if that child was n
in a pan and eat him. (*Walks off, glass i.
drawing-room and sits in a corner.*)

NATASHA (*covering her face with her hands*). Oh,   ue,
ignorant man!

MASHA. Some people don't even notice whether it's winter
or summer. They're lucky. If I were in Moscow, I don't
think I'd care twopence about the weather.

VERSHININ. I was reading a diary recently, written by
some French government Minister in prison. He was
jailed in connection with that business in Panama. He
goes into absolute raptures about the birds he can see
from his cell-window, which he'd never even noticed when
he was a Minister. And of course now he's been released,
he doesn't notice the birds any more. You won't notice
Moscow either, once you're living there. No, there's no
happiness for us, and never can be – it's just wishful
thinking.

TUZENBAKH (*picks up a box from the table*). Where've all the
sweets gone?

IRINA. Soliony's eaten them.

TUZENBAKH. All of them?

ANFISA (*serving the tea*). There's a message for you, sir.

VERSHININ. For me? (*Takes the note.*) It's from my daughter.
(*Reads it.*) Ah, I see . . . I'm sorry, Masha, I've got to
leave. I won't take any tea. (*Stands up, agitated.*) The same
old story . . .

MASHA. What's wrong? If it isn't a secret?

VERSHININ (*in a low voice*). My wife's taken poison again.
I must go. I'll try and slip out unnoticed. This is all

pleasant. (*Kisses* MASHA's *hand.*) Oh, my
darling, glorious Masha . . . I'll go out this way . . .
(*Exits.*)

ANFISA. Where's he gone? I've just brought his tea . . .
Well, there's a fine thing.

MASHA (*flaring up*). Oh, get away! Stop pestering me, leave
me in peace . . . (*She takes her cup to the table.*) You're
getting on my nerves, you silly old woman!

ANFISA. Why are you so angry? Masha, my dear . . .

ANDREI *calls, offstage: 'Anfisa!'*

(*Mimicking.*) Anfisa! And he's just sitting there . . . (*Exits.*)

MASHA (*at the table in the ballroom, angrily*). Move over, let me
sit down! (*Muddles up the cards on the table.*) You've got cards
spread out everywhere. Drink your tea!

IRINA. You're in a foul mood, Masha.

MASHA. Yes, well, if I'm in a foul mood, don't speak to me.
Don't come near me!

CHEBUTYKIN (*laughing*). Keep off, don't touch!

MASHA. And you're sixty years of age, jabbering on like a
schoolboy, a lot of damned nonsense!

NATASHA (*sighs*). Masha, my dear . . . You shouldn't use
such expressions, you really shouldn't . . . I mean, with
your good looks you could be quite enchanting, honestly,
even in the very best society, if it weren't for your
language. *Je vous prie pardonnez-moi, Marie, mais vous avez des
manières un peu grossières.*

TUZENBAKH (*trying not to laugh*). Pass me that . . . pass
me . . . I think that's the brandy . . .

NATASHA. *Il paraît que mon Bobik déjà ne dort pas*, he's
wakened up. I don't think he's well today. I'll take a look
at him, excuse me . . . (*Exits.*)

IRINA. So, where's the Colonel gone?

MASHA. Home. His wife's up to her tricks again.

TUZENBAKH (*goes up to* SOLIONY, *taking the decanter of brandy*). You're always on your own, deep in thought – and nobody knows what about, eh? Well, come on, let's be friends. Let's have some brandy.

They drink.

I'll most likely have to play the piano the whole night, all kinds of silly nonsense . . . well, that's life.

SOLIONY. Why shouldn't we be friends? I've no quarrel with you.

TUZENBAKH. No, but you always make me feel as if something's happened between us. You're a strange man, you must admit.

SOLIONY (*declaiming*). 'I am strange, yet who is not! Be not angry, Aleko!'

TUZENBAKH. What's Aleko got to do with it?

A pause.

SOLIONY. When I'm alone with someone, it's fine, I'm just like anybody else, but in company I get depressed, and withdrawn . . . I say all kinds of stupid things. Still, I'm as decent and honourable as the next man, a great deal more so, indeed. And I can prove it.

TUZENBAKH. You know, I often get angry with you, you're forever picking on me in front of people. All the same I can't help liking you. Well, so be it, I'm getting drunk tonight. Cheers!

SOLIONY. Cheers.

They drink.

I've nothing against you personally, Baron. It's just my temperament, like Lermontov's. (*Quietly.*) I even look a bit like Lermontov . . . so I've been told . . . (*He takes a bottle of scent from his pocket and pours it over his hands.*)

TUZENBAKH. Well, I shall be leaving the service. Enough!

I've been thinking about it for five years, and I've finally made up my mind. I intend to work!

SOLIONY (*declaiming*). 'Be not angry, Aleko . . . Forget, forget thy dreams . . . '

While they are talking, ANDREI *enters quietly with a book, and sits down by a candle.*

TUZENBAKH. Yes, I'm going to work . . .

CHEBUTYKIN (*entering the drawing-room with* IRINA). And the food they served up was genuine Caucasian, too: onion soup, then *chekhartmà* for the meat course . . .

SOLIONY. *Cheremshà* isn't a meat dish at all, it's a vegetable, like our onion.

CHEBUTYKIN. No, no, my dear chap – *chekhartmà* isn't an onion, it's roast mutton.

SOLIONY. And I say *cheremshà* is an onion.

CHEBUTYKIN. *Chekhartmà* is mutton, I tell you.

SOLIONY. And I'm telling you – *cheremshà* is an onion!

CHEBUTYKIN. Why am I arguing with you? You've never even been to the Caucasus, you've never eaten *chekhartmà*.

SOLIONY. I've never eaten it because I can't stand it. It smells like garlic.

ANDREI (*pleading*). Gentlemen, please! Stop it!

TUZENBAKH. When are the carnival people coming?

IRINA. They said they'd be here by nine. Any minute now.

TUZENBAKH *hugs* ANDREI, *and begins singing a comic song.* ANDREI *joins in, then he and* CHEBUTYKIN *sing and dance together, to everyone's amusement.*

TUZENBAKH (*kisses* ANDREI). Damn it, let's have a drink, Andryusha, let's drink to friendship. I'm coming with you, old chap, to Moscow, to the university.

SOLIONY. Which one? There are two universities in Moscow.

ANDREI. There's only one university in Moscow.

SOLIONY. And I say there are two.

ANDREI. Why not three? The more the merrier.

SOLIONY. There are two universities in Moscow!

Murmurs of disagreement, and hissing.

There are two universities in Moscow, the old one and the new one. But if you don't care to listen to me, if my conversation annoys you, I won't speak at all. I can always go into the other room . . . (*Exits by one of the doors.*)

TUZENBAKH. Bravo, bravo! (*Laughs.*) Ladies and gentlemen, let the dancing begin, I shall sit down to play! That Soliony's so funny . . . (*Sits at the piano, begins playing a waltz.*)

MASHA (*waltzing by herself, sings*). 'The Baron's drunk, the Baron's drunk, the Baron's drunk . . . !'

Enter NATASHA.

NATASHA (*to* CHEBUTYKIN). Ivan Romanych! (*Says something to* CHEBUTYKIN, *then quietly exits.*)

CHEBUTYKIN *taps* TUZENBAKH *on the shoulder and whispers something to him.*

IRINA. What's the matter?

CHEBUTYKIN. It's time we were going. Good night, all.

TUZENBAKH. Good night. Time to go.

IRINA. What do you mean? What about the musicians?

ANDREI (*embarrassed*). There won't be any. The thing is, my dear – you see, Natasha says Bobik's not too well, and because of that . . . Oh, I don't know – frankly, I don't care either way.

IRINA (*shrugs*). Bobik's not well . . .

MASHA. Oh, to hell with it! We're being thrown out, it seems, we've got to go. (*To* IRINA.) It's not Bobik that's sick, it's her . . . Up here! (*Taps her forehead.*) Stupid woman!

ANDREI *exits right, to his own room.* CHEBUTYKIN *follows him out, the others say goodbye.*

FEDOTIK. What a shame! I'd been looking forward to spending the evening here, but if the child's sick, well, of course . . . I'll bring him a toy tomorrow . . .

RODE (*loudly*). And I had a nap after lunch today specially, I thought I'd be dancing the whole night. I mean, it's only just nine o'clock!

MASHA. Let's go outside, we can talk there. We'll decide what to do.

Cries of 'Goodbye!', 'All the best!', etc. TUZENBAKH's *merry laughter is heard, as everyone leaves.* ANFISA *and the* MAID *then clear the table, extinguish the lights, the old nurse singing as she does so.* ANDREI, *in his hat and coat, quietly enters with* CHEBUTYKIN.

CHEBUTYKIN. No, I never got round to marrying, life flashed past me like lightning. Besides, I was madly in love with your dear mother, and she was already married . . .

ANDREI. People shouldn't marry. They shouldn't, it's too boring.

CHEBUTYKIN. Ah yes, but what about loneliness? You can dress it up any way you like, my dear chap, but loneliness is a terrible thing . . . Although when all's said and done . . . well, does it really matter?

ANDREI. Let's be on our way.

CHEBUTYKIN. What's the hurry? We've plenty of time.

ANDREI. I don't want my wife stopping us.

CHEBUTYKIN. Ah, I see.

ANDREI. I won't play cards tonight, I'll just sit and watch. I'm not feeling too well . . . What should I do about shortness of breath, d'you think?

CHEBUTYKIN. Why ask me? I can't remember, dear boy, haven't a clue!

The doorbell rings, then again. Voices are heard, laughter.

ANDREI. We'll go out through the kitchen. (*They exit.*)

IRINA (*enters*). Who is it?

ANFISA (*in a whisper*). It's the people from the carnival. (*Another ring.*)

IRINA. Nanny, tell them there's no-one home. Say we're sorry.

ANFISA *exits.* IRINA *paces about the room, deep in thought, clearly upset.* SOLIONY *enters.*

SOLIONY (*puzzled*). There's no-one here . . . Where's everyone gone?

IRINA. They've gone home.

SOLIONY. That's strange. And you're here alone?

IRINA. Yes.

A pause.

Goodnight.

SOLIONY. I behaved a little indiscreetly just now, a little tactlessly. But you're not like the others. You're high above them, you're pure, you can see the truth . . . You're the only one who understands me. I love you, with a deep, everlasting . . .

IRINA. Goodnight! Please leave.

SOLIONY. I can't live without you. (*Following her.*) You're my soul's delight, my happiness! (*Through tears.*) Your wonderful, dazzling, astonishing eyes, like no other woman's I've ever seen . . .

IRINA (*coldly*). Captain Soliony, stop it.

SOLIONY. This is the first time I've spoken of my love for you, and it's as if I were on another planet, not on this earth. (*Rubs his forehead.*) Well, all right, it doesn't matter. Obviously I can't force you to love me . . . But I won't tolerate a successful rival . . . I won't . . . I swear to you, by all that's holy, I'll kill any rival . . . Oh, you wonderful creature . . .

NATASHA *crosses the room with a candle.*

NATASHA (*looks into one room, then another, and walks past the door leading to her husband's room*). Andrei'll be in there. Reading, I suppose. Oh, I beg your pardon, Captain, I didn't know you were here, I'm not properly dressed . . .

SOLIONY. It's all the same to me. Goodnight. (*Exits.*)

NATASHA. Oh, my poor dear girl, you look so tired! (*Kisses IRINA.*) You really should go to bed earlier.

IRINA. Is Bobik asleep?

NATASHA. Yes, he's sleeping. But he's a little restless. Oh, by the way, my dear, I've been meaning to have a word with you, but either you're out at work, or I've been too busy . . . I think the nursery's really too cold and damp for Bobik. But your room's just perfect for a child. Be an absolute dear and move in with Olga for a bit.

IRINA (*uncomprehending*). Move where?

The sound of a troika, with bells jingling, drawing up outside.

NATASHA. You and Olya can share for a while, and Bobik can have your room. He's such a sweet little thing, I was just saying to him today, 'You're my little Bobik. You're all mine!' And he looked up at me with his darling little eyes.

The door-bell rings.

That must be Olga. She's very late.

The MAID *approaches* NATASHA *and whispers something in her ear.*

NATASHA. Protopopov? What a strange man. Protopopov's just arrived, and he wants to take me for a ride in his troika. (*Laughs.*) Really, men are so funny! . . .

The door-bell rings again.

That's someone else at the door. I think I will go for a spin, just a quarter of an hour or so . . . (*To the* MAID.) Tell him I'll be down directly.

The door-bell rings again.

That's the bell again, it must be Olga . . . (*Exits.*)

The MAID *hurries out.* IRINA *remains seated, deep in thought.* KULYGIN *and* OLGA *enter, followed by* VERSHININ.

KULYGIN. Well, there's a thing. And they said there was going to be a party.

VERSHININ. That's odd – I left a short while ago, about half an hour, and they were expecting the carnival people . . .

IRINA. They've all gone.

KULYGIN. Has Masha left too? Where did she go? And why's Protopopov waiting outside with his troika? Who's he waiting for?

IRINA. Please, don't ask questions . . . I'm too tired.

KULYGIN. Oh, well, if you're in a mood . . .

OLGA. The staff meeting's only just finished, and I'm worn out. Our headmistress is off sick, and I have to take her place. I've got a splitting headache. (*Sits down.*) Andrei lost two hundred roubles at cards last night . . . The whole town's talking about it . . .

KULYGIN. Yes, I felt tired at the meeting, too.

VERSHININ. My wife took it into her head to give me a fright just now – tried to poison herself. Still, it's all over now, I can relax . . . I suppose we ought to leave. Anyway, my very best wishes. Come along, my dear chap, let's go on somewhere – I can't stay at home, I simply can't. Let's go.

KULYGIN. No, I'm too tired. Count me out. (*Rises.*) I'm exhausted. Has my wife gone home?

IRINA. I think so.

KULYGIN (*kisses* IRINA's *hand*). Well, goodnight. We've got all tomorrow and the next day off. Goodnight, everyone! (*Makes to exit.*) I'd love some tea. I was rather hoping to spend the evening in congenial company, too − *o, fallacem hominum spem!* Accusative case of exclamation . . .

VERSHININ. Well, it looks as if I'm on my own. (*Exits with* KULYGIN, *whistling.*)

OLGA. My head's aching, it really is . . . Andrei's lost again . . . the whole town's talking . . . I'm going to lie down. (*Makes to exit.*) I have the day off tomorrow . . . Thank God for that! Free tomorrow and the next day . . . My head's absolutely splitting . . . (*Exits.*)

IRINA (*left alone*). They've all gone. There's no-one left.

Someone is playing a concertina outside. ANFISA *is heard singing.*

NATASHA *passes through the ballroom wearing a fur coat and hat, followed by the* MAID.

NATASHA. I'll be back in about half an hour. I'm just going for a little drive. (*Exits.*)

IRINA (*with intense longing*). To Moscow! Moscow! Moscow!

Curtain.

ACT THREE

OLGA *and* IRINA's *room. To left and right are beds, behind screens. It is past two o'clock in the morning, and an alarm can be heard in the distance, sounding for a fire which started some time before. It is is obvious that no-one in the house has yet been to bed.* MASHA *is lying on the divan, wearing a black dress as usual.* OLGA *and* ANFISA *enter.*

ANFISA. They're sitting at the bottom of the stairs now . . . 'Why don't you go upstairs,' I says, 'You can't sit there.' And they're crying, 'We don't know where our Papa is,' they say, 'Please God he hasn't died in the fire.' That's what's on their minds! And there's more people out in the yard . . . still in their night things.

OLGA (*taking some dresses out of a cupboard*). Here, take this grey dress . . . And this one . . . And this cardigan, too . . . And here, Nanny, take this skirt . . . Oh God, this is a dreadful business – Kirsanov Street's burnt to the ground, it seems . . . And take this . . . And this . . . (*Flinging a dress into her arms.*) The Vershinins got a terrible fright, the poor things . . . Their house only just escaped. They can spend the night here, we can't let them go home . . . And poor Fedotik's lost everything, completely burned out . . .

ANFISA. Olya dear, if you would call Ferapont – I can't manage all these . . .

OLGA (*rings the bell*). I don't think they can hear . . . (*Calls through the door.*) Will someone come up here, please!

The open door reveals a window, glowing red from the fire; a fire engine is heard passing the house.

This is terrible, terrible. And so exhausting . . .

FERAPONT *enters.*

Take these downstairs, please . . . Give them to the
Kolotilin girls, they're waiting in the hall . . . Give them
this, too.

FERAPONT. Right, ma'am. Yes, there was a fire in Moscow
too, in 1812. By God, the Frenchies didn't half get a
fright!

OLGA. Now go on, quickly.

FERAPONT. Yes, ma'am. (*Exits.*)

OLGA. Nanny dear, just give everything away. We don't
need it, give it all away, Nanny . . . I'm so tired, I can
scarcely stand . . . We can't let the Vershinins go home . . .
The girls can sleep in the drawing-room, and we can put
the Colonel downstairs with the Baron . . . Fedotik can
move in with the Baron, too, or go into the ballroom . . .
The Doctor's drunk – it's as if he did it on purpose – he's
terribly drunk, we can't put anyone in with him. And put
Vershinin's wife into the drawing-room as well.

ANFISA (*exhausted*). Olya, dearest – please don't send me
away! Don't send me away!

OLGA. Nanny, don't talk nonsense. Nobody's sending you
anywhere.

ANFISA (*lays her head on* OLGA's *bosom*). Oh, my dearest,
darling Olya, I do my work, I work hard . . . But I'm
getting feeble, and they'll tell me to go. 'Clear off!' they'll
say. But where can I go? Where? I'm over eighty –
coming up for eighty-two . . .

OLGA. Nanny, sit down . . . You're worn out, you poor
dear . . . (*Makes* ANFISA *sit.*) Have a rest, you've gone
quite pale.

NATASHA *enters*.

NATASHA. They're talking about setting up a fund to help
the fire victims – a splendid idea, don't you think? We've
got to do what we can for the poor, the rich have an
obligation. Bobik and little Sophie are tucked away in
bed, fast asleep, as if nothing's happened. We've got

people all over the place, the house is full of them.
There's a 'flu epidemic in the town, I'm frightened in case
the children catch it . . .

OLGA (*not listening to her*). You can't see the fire from this
room, it's quiet here . . .

NATASHA. Yes . . . I must look a mess. (*In front of the mirror.*)
They tell me I've put on weight . . . it's not true.
Absolutely not. And Masha's asleep, she's worn out, the
poor thing . . . (*To* ANFISA, *coldly.*) How dare you sit
down in my presence! Stand up! Get out of here!

ANFISA *exits. A pause.*

I really can't imagine why you keep that old creature on.

OLGA (*bemused*). I'm sorry, I don't understand . . .

NATASHA. She's no use here. She's a peasant, she ought to
be living in the country . . . She's completely spoilt. I
must have order in the home! There's no room for
hangers-on. (*Strokes* OLGA's *cheek.*) Poor thing, you're tired.
Our headmistress is tired! Yes, when my little Sophie
grows up and goes to school, I shall be afraid of you.

OLGA. I don't want to be headmistress.

NATASHA. But they're going to appoint you, Olya dear. It's
already decided.

OLGA. I'll refuse. I can't do it . . . I haven't the strength . . .
(*She takes a drink of water.*) You know, you were so rude to
Nanny just now . . . I'm sorry, but I just can't bear it . . .
I felt quite faint . . .

NATASHA (*agitatedly*). I'm sorry, Olya, I'm sorry – I didn't
mean to upset you.

MASHA *rises from the divan, picks up a pillow, and exits angrily.*

OLGA. You must understand, my dear . . . perhaps it's our
strange upbringing, but I really can't abide that. That
sort of behaviour depresses me, it makes me ill. I just feel
drained . . .

NATASHA. I'm sorry, I'm sorry . . . (*Embraces her.*)

OLGA. Any form of rudeness, even the slightest thing, a harsh word . . . it upsets me.

NATASHA. Well, I often speak out of turn, that's true, but you must admit, my dear, she ought to be living in the country.

OLGA. But she's been with us for thirty years.

NATASHA. Yes, but she can't work any longer! Look, either I don't understand you, or you simply don't want to understand me. She's not fit for work, she does nothing but sit around and sleep.

OLGA. Well, let her sit!

NATASHA (*amazed*). What do you mean, let her sit? I mean, she's a servant, for Heaven's sake. (*Tearfully.*) I just don't understand you, Olya. I have a nanny, a wet-nurse, we have a maid, a cook . . . what do we want with this old woman? What use is she?

In the distance, the fire alarm sounds.

OLGA. I think I've aged ten years tonight.

NATASHA. We'll have to come to some arrangement, Olga. You're out at school, and I'm at home − you have your schoolwork, and I have this house to run. And if I've got something to say about the servants, then I know what I'm talking about. I know whereof I speak . . . So I want that thieving old hag out of here by tomorrow! (*Stamping her foot.*) The old witch! And don't dare cross me! Just don't dare! (*Recovering her composure.*) The truth is, Olga, unless you move downstairs, we're going to be quarrelling all the time. It's terrible.

KULYGIN *enters.*

KULYGIN. Where's Masha? It's time we went home. The fire seems to be dying down. (*Stretches.*) There's only one part of town burnt, although with that wind, it looked at first as if the whole lot would go up. (*Sits down.*) Oh, I'm so tired. Dearest Olga . . . You know, I often think, if it

hadn't been for Masha, I should've married you. You're
so kind. Yes, I'm exhausted. (*Listens.*)

OLGA. What is it?

KULYGIN. The Doctor's been hitting the bottle, he's drunk
as a lord. You'd think he'd done it on purpose! (*Stands up.*)
This is him now, I think. Isn't it? Yes, here he comes . . .
(*Laughs.*) The old rogue . . . I'm going to hide from
him . . . (*Goes over to the cupboard and stands in the corner.*)
He's such a rascal.

OLGA. He hasn't touched a drop in two years, and now he
suddenly has to get drunk . . . (*She goes with* NATASHA *to
the far end of the room.*)

CHEBUTYKIN *enters, and crosses the room without staggering,
as if he were sober. He stops, looks round, then goes to the wash-
basin and washes his hands.*

CHEBUTYKIN (*gloomily*). To hell with the lot of them . . .
damn them . . . They think because I'm a doctor I can
cure all their ailments, but I know absolutely nothing, I've
forgotten all I ever knew, I don't remember a thing, not a
damn thing.

OLGA *and* NATASHA *make their exit, unnoticed by*
CHEBUTYKIN.

To hell with them! Last Wednesday I was attending a
woman in Zasyp Street – she died, and it was my fault
she died. Yes . . . Maybe I knew a few things twenty-five
years ago, but now I can't remember a thing. Not a
thing. Maybe I'm not even human, I'm just pretending
I've got arms, and legs . . . and a head. Maybe I don't
exist, yes, maybe I only imagine I walk, eat, and sleep . . .
(*Starts crying.*) Oh, if only I didn't exist! (*Stops crying, then
morosely.*) Dear God . . . There was some talk at the club
a couple of days ago . . . Shakespeare, Voltaire, and so
on . . . I've never read them, not a word, but I tried to
look as if I had. And the others were doing the same. It's
contemptible. Degrading. And I got to thinking about that
woman I'd killed on Wednesday . . . and it all came back

to me, and I felt so vile, so downright rotten . . . I had to
go and get a drink . . .

IRINA, VERSHININ *and* TUZENBAKH *enter.*
TUZENBAKH *is wearing a fashionable new civilian suit.*

IRINA. We can sit down here. Nobody'll come in.

VERSHININ. Well, if it hadn't been for the military, the
whole town would've gone up in flames. They did
splendidly! (*Rubs his hands in satisfaction.*) They're a fine
bunch, salt of the earth!

KULYGIN (*goes up to them.*) What time is it, anyone?

TUZENBAKH. It's after three already. It's getting light.

IRINA. They're all sitting in the ballroom, no-one wants to
leave. And that Soliony of yours is there, too. (*To*
CHEBUTYKIN.) You ought to go back to bed, Doctor.

CHEBUTYKIN. I'm fine, ma'am . . . Thank you, ma'am . . .
(*Stroking his beard.*)

KULYGIN (*laughs*). You've had one too many, Ivan
Romanych! (*Slaps him on the back.*) Bravo! *In vino veritas*, as
the Romans used to say.

TUZENBAKH. People keep asking me to organise a
concert, in aid of the fire victims.

IRINA. Yes, but who'll play . . .

TUZENBAKH. We could do it, if we really wanted. There's
Masha, for instance. She plays the piano beautifully . . .

KULYGIN. She does indeed!

IRINA. She's forgotten how. She hasn't played in three
years . . . maybe four.

TUZENBAKH. There's absolutely nobody in this town who
appreciates music, not a soul. However, I do, and I tell
you this – Masha is a superb pianist, practically a genius.

KULYGIN. You're quite right, Baron. And I love Masha so
much. She's a wonderful woman.

TUZENBAKH. To be able to play so gloriously, and to know at the same time that nobody, absolutely nobody appreciates it!

KULYGIN (*sighs*). Yes, indeed . . . But would it be proper for Masha to take part in a concert?

A pause.

I mean, I know nothing about such matters. It may be perfectly fine. Our headmaster is a good man, I must say, a thoroughly decent man, extremely clever, but he does have certain views . . . Of course, it's not his concern, but I'll mention it to him all the same, if you don't mind . . .

CHEBUTYKIN *has picked up a china clock and is inspecting it.*

VERSHININ. I got absolutely filthy at the fire, you wouldn't believe it.

A pause.

Incidentally, I heard yesterday they're thinking of transferring our brigade to some outpost or other. Poland, they're saying, or possibly Siberia.

TUZENBAKH. Yes, that's what I heard. Well, well – this town'll be deserted then.

IRINA. And we're leaving too!

CHEBUTYKIN (*drops the clock, which smashes on the floor*). Smithereens!

A pause. Everyone is upset and embarrassed.

KULYGIN (*starts picking up the pieces*). Oh, Ivan Romanych, Ivan Romanych – breaking such a valuable object, really! I shall give you a C-minus for conduct.

IRINA. That was our mother's clock.

CHEBUTYKIN. Maybe . . . Well, what if it was? Maybe I didn't break it, maybe it just looks as if I did. Maybe we don't even exist, and only imagine we do. I don't know anything, nobody knows a damn thing. (*At the door.*) What are you staring at? Natasha's having an affair with

Protopopov, and you can't see it . . . You're all sitting
here, seeing nothing, and Natasha's having an affair
with Protopopov . . . (*Sings.*) 'Oh, lady, please accept this
fruit . . . ' (*Exits.*)

VERSHININ. Yes . . . (*Laughs.*) It's a strange world we live
in.

A pause.

You know, when the fire broke out, I rushed home, and
when I got there I could see our house was still intact,
and out of danger, but my two little girls were standing at
the door, in nothing but their nightgowns, their mother
wasn't with them, there were people dashing around
everywhere, horses and dogs, and I can't describe the
alarm and terror, the pathetic look on those little faces.
My heart almost stopped at the sight of them. Dear God,
I thought, what have those little girls still to suffer in the
course of a long life? I snatched them up and started
running, and all the time I kept thinking – what more will
they have to suffer in this world?

The fire alarm sounds. A pause.

Then I arrive here, and their mother's shouting and
screaming.

MASHA *enters, carrying her pillow, and sits on the divan.*

Yes, when my little girls were standing at the door in their
nightgowns, and the whole street was glowing red with
fire, there was a hellish uproar, and it came into my mind
that things like this used to happen many years ago, when
some enemy would suddenly invade us, looting and
burning . . . But when you come right down to it, there's
a world of difference between then and now. And given a
little more time, say, two or three hundred years, people
will look back on us with the same horror and scorn, our
present-day life will seem hard and awkward, it'll seem
very uncomfortable and bizarre. Oh yes, what a life that's
going to be! (*Laughs.*) I'm sorry, I'm getting carried away
again. But don't stop me, please – I desperately want to
talk, it's the kind of mood I'm in . . .

A pause.

It looks as if everyone's asleep. Anyway, as I was saying: life will be wonderful! We can only imagine what it'll be like . . . I mean, there are only the three of you in this town now, but in future generations there'll be more, many, many more, and the time's coming when everything will change, people will live as you'd like them to, you'll grow old eventually, and there'll be other people born, even better than you . . . (*Laughs.*) Oh yes, I'm in a really good mood today. I have the most damnable desire to live! . . . (*Sings.*) 'To Love all ages humbly bow, her promptings do each heart endow . . . ' (*Laughs.*)

MASHA. Tram-tam-tam . . .

VERSHININ. Tam-tam . . .

MASHA. Tra-ra-ra?

VERSHININ. Tra-ta-ta. (*Laughs.*)

FEDOTIK *enters.*

FEDOTIK (*dancing*). It's all gone! All gone! Burnt to the ground!

Laughter.

IRINA. What's funny about that? Is everything burnt?

FEDOTIK (*laughs*). Yes, gone up in smoke, everything. Not a thing left. My guitar, my camera, all my letters, all gone . . . I was going to give you a little notebook, that's burnt too.

SOLIONY *enters.*

IRINA. No, please, Captain Soliony, please go away. You can't come in here.

SOLIONY. So why can the Baron come in, and I can't?

VERSHININ. Actually, we ought to be leaving. How's the fire?

SOLIONY. It's dying down, they say. No, it's positively peculiar – the Baron's allowed in here, and I'm not. (*Takes out a bottle of scent and sprinkles himself with it.*)

VERSHININ. Tram-tam-tam?

MASHA. Tram-tam.

VERSHININ (*laughs, then to* SOLIONY). Let's go into the ballroom.

SOLIONY. All right. But we shan't forget this. (*Looking pointedly at* TUZENBAKH.) 'This moral I might make more clear, but that would vex the geese, I fear . . . ' Cheep! Cheep! Cheep! (*Exits with* VERSHININ *and* FEDOTIK.)

IRINA. That Soliony's smoked the place out . . . (*Bewildered.*) The Baron's asleep. Baron, wake up!

TUZENBAKH (*coming to*). Oh, I'm so tired still . . . Yes, the brick-works . . . No, I'm not talking in my sleep, I'll be starting work soon, in a brick-works, it's all arranged. (*To* IRINA, *tenderly.*) You're so pale and lovely, quite enchanting . . . It's as if your face lights up the night air, like a moonbeam . . . You're so sad, dissatisfied with life . . . Oh, come with me, Irina, we'll go away and work together! . . .

MASHA. Baron, please leave.

TUZENBAKH (*laughing*). You're here? I didn't see you. (*Kisses* IRINA'*s hand*) . . . Goodbye, I'm going . . . You know, I look at you now, and it all comes back to me, a long time ago on your name-day, how bright and cheerful you were then, talking about the joys of work . . . And what a happy life I could see ahead of me . . . But where is it? (*He kisses her hand.*) There are tears in your eyes. You should go to bed, it's getting light already . . . almost morning . . . Oh, if only I could give my life for you, Irina!

MASHA. Baron, please go. For heaven's sake . . .

TUZENBAKH. I'm going, I'm going . . . (*Exits.*)

MASHA (*lies down*). Fyodor? Are you asleep?

KULYGIN. Pardon?

MASHA. You ought to go home.

KULYGIN. Darling Masha, my dear, sweet Masha . . .

IRINA. She's exhausted. Let her rest, Fedya.

KULYGIN. I'm just going . . . My wife's so good and
kind . . . I love you, my one and only . . .

MASHA (*irritated*). *Amo, amas, amat, amamus, amatis, amant . . .*

KULYGIN (*laughs*). Really, an amazing woman! Yes, we got
married seven years ago, and it seems like only yesterday.
That's the truth. I say again, you're an amazing woman,
Masha. And I'm so very, very happy!

MASHA. And I'm so very, very bored! . . . (*Sits up.*) You
know, I can't get it out of my head . . . It's simply
disgraceful. It's preying on my mind, I can't keep silent.
I'm talking about Andrei . . . He's mortgaged this house
to the bank, and his wife's pocketed the money. I mean,
the house isn't just his, it belongs to all four of us! He
surely knows that, if he's got any decency.

KULYGIN. Masha, why bring this up now? What does it
matter? Andrei owes everybody money, Heaven help him.

MASHA. It's a disgrace, even so. (*Lies down again.*)

KULYGIN. Masha, it's not as if we're poor. I have my
work, I teach at the school, and give private lessons . . .
I'm an honest, simple man . . . *Omnia mea mecum porto*, as
they say.

MASHA. I don't need anything, it's just so unfair, it makes
me angry.

A pause.

Fyodor, go home, please.

KULYGIN (*embraces her*). You're tired. Have a little rest for a
half-hour or so, and I'll wait downstairs. Try and sleep . . .
(*Exits.*) I'm so very, very happy . . .

IRINA. It's true enough, our Andrei's become so mean-
minded – the spirit's gone right out of him, he's grown so

old with that woman. He had his sights set on a
professorship at one time, and there he was yesterday,
bragging because at long last they'd made him a member
of the district council! He's a member of the council, and
the chairman's Protopopov . . . The whole town's talking
about it, laughing behind his back – he's the only one
who doesn't know . . . Yes, and when everybody rushes
out to help with the fire, he sits in his room, not the least
bit concerned. Playing his fiddle. (*Agitated.*) It's terrible,
terrible! (*Begins to cry.*) I can't stand it, I can't take any
more of this! . . . I can't, I can't . . .

OLGA *enters, to tidy up her dressing-table.* IRINA *is sobbing
loudly.*

Oh, throw me out, put me out of here, I can't stand it
any more!

OLGA (*alarmed*). What's the matter, what is it? Irina, dearest!

IRINA (*sobbing*). Where has it all gone? Where? Where is it?
Oh God in Heaven! I've forgotten everything, everything . . . It's all gone right out of my head . . . I can't
remember the Italian for 'window', or 'ceiling' . . . I'm
forgetting more and more each day, life's passing me by,
and it'll never return, we'll never get to Moscow, we'll
never leave here, I know we won't . . .

OLGA. Oh, my poor darling . . .

IRINA (*trying to control herself*). Oh, I'm just so miserable . . .
I can't work, I won't work, I've had enough of it! First
I worked in the telegraph office, now I have a job with
the town council, and I despise everything they give me to
do . . . I'm twenty-four already, I've been working for
ages, my brain's dried up, I've become thin, and old, and
ugly – there's no satisfaction in any of it, absolutely none,
and time's passing, and I feel as if I'm moving further and
further away from a genuine, beautiful life, and heading
into some kind of abyss. I'm in despair, I don't know why
I'm still alive, why I haven't killed myself before now.
I don't understand it . . .

OLGA. Don't cry, darling, don't cry . . . It hurts me . . .

IRINA. I won't, I won't cry . . . Enough . . . Look, I've
    stopped crying . . . It's over . . .

OLGA. Oh, my dear, I'm speaking to you now as a sister, as
    a friend . . . If you want my advice, you should marry the
    Baron.

    IRINA *quietly weeps*.

    After all, you respect him, you think highly of him . . .
    True, he's not good-looking, but he's a decent man, clean-
    living . . . I mean, women don't marry for love, they do it
    out of duty. At least, that's what I think, and I'd marry
    without love. I'd marry anyone that asked me, as long as
    he was a decent person. I'd even marry an old man . . .

IRINA. I kept waiting, waiting for us to move to Moscow,
    and I'd meet my true love there. I've dreamt about
    him, loved him . . . But it's turned out to be nonsense,
    all of it . . .

OLGA (*hugs her sister*). Oh, my dear, darling sister, I understand
    everything. When the Baron left the service, and came to
    see us in his civilian clothes, he looked so awful that I
    actually started to cry . . . And he asked me, 'Why are
    you crying?' What could I tell him? But if it's God's will
    that he should marry you, I'd be very happy. That'd be
    quite different.

    NATASHA *crosses the stage from right to left in silence, holding a
    candle.*

MASHA (*sits up*). The way she's going around, you'd think it
    was her that started the fire.

OLGA. And you're silly, Masha. You're the silliest person in
    this family. If you'll forgive my saying.

    A pause.

MASHA. I've a confession to make, my dear sisters.
    Something on my conscience. I'm going to confess to you,
    and to no-one else, ever . . . I'll tell you now. (*Quietly.*) It's
    my secret, but you ought to know . . . I can't keep it any
    longer . . .

A pause.

I'm in love . . . I'm in love with that man . . . You saw him just now . . . Oh, why not come out with it? I'm in love with Vershinin . . .

OLGA (*goes behind her screen*). That's enough, I'm not listening to you anyway!

MASHA. I can't help it! (*Clutching her head.*) At first I thought he was strange, then I felt sorry for him . . . eventually I fell in love with him . . . I fell in love with his voice, the things he said, his unhappy life, his two little girls . . .

OLGA (*from behind the screen*). I don't care, I can't hear you. You can say whatever stupid things you like, I'm not listening.

MASHA. Oh, Olga, it's you that's stupid. I'm in love, it's fate. It's my destiny . . . And he loves me . . . It's frightening, isn't it? Is it wrong? (*Takes* IRINA *by the hand, draws her close.*) Oh, my dear Irina, how are we going to survive? What's to become of us? . . . You know, when you read a love story you think, well, this is all old-hat, everybody knows this. But when you fall in love yourself, it's obvious that nobody knows anything, we each have to work it out on our own. Oh, my dearest sisters . . . I've confessed to you, now I'll keep silent . . . I'll be like Gogol's madman . . . The rest is silence . . .

ANDREI *enters, followed by* FERAPONT.

ANDREI (*testily*). What is it you want? I can't understand you.

FERAPONT (*at the door, impatiently*). Master Andrei, I've told you half a dozen times.

ANDREI. In the first place, I'm not Master Andrei to you, but Your Honour!

FERAPONT. Your Honour, the firemen want permission to drive through the orchard to the river. Otherwise they've got to go all the way round, and that's a terrible job.

ANDREI. All right. Tell them it's all right.

FERAPONT *exits.*

Honestly, they get on my nerves. Where's Olga?

OLGA *emerges from behind the screen.*

I came to ask you for the cupboard key, I seem to have lost mine. That little key you have.

OLGA *silently hands him the key.* IRINA *goes behind her own screen. A pause.*

What a huge fire! It's dying down now. Damn it, that Ferapont really annoyed me, I came out with something stupid . . . Your Honour, indeed!

A pause.

Why don't you say something, Olya?

A pause.

Look, it's time we put a stop to all this nonsense, all this sulking for no reason. You're here, Masha's here, Irina, well, that's just fine – we can get to the bottom of it now, once and for all. Exactly what is it you have against me? Come on, tell me.

OLGA. Leave it, Andryusha. We'll talk about it tomorrow. (*Upset.*) What a dreadful night it's been!

ANDREI (*rather embarrassed*). Don't get upset. I'm asking you perfectly calmly: what have you got against me? Come right out with it.

VERSHININ *is heard offstage: 'Tram-tam-tam!'*

MASHA (*stands up, then loudly*). Tra-ta-ta! (*To* OLGA.) Goodbye, Olga, and God bless you. (*Goes behind the screen, kisses* IRINA.) Sleep well . . . Goodbye, Andrei. Just leave them, they're exhausted . . . you can have it out with them tomorrow. (*Exits.*)

OLGA. Yes, Andrei, let's put it off till tomorrow . . . (*She goes behind her screen.*) It's time we were in bed.

ANDREI. I'll say my piece and then I'll go. Directly . . . In the first place, you've got something against my wife Natasha, and I've been aware of that since the day of our wedding. Natasha's a fine, honest woman, upright and honourable − that's my opinion. I love and respect my wife, do you understand? I respect her, and I insist that other people respect her too. I'll say it again, she's a decent, honest woman, and all your complaints about her, I'm sorry to say, are nothing but sheer bloody-mindedness.

A pause.

And secondly, it's as if you're annoyed at me for not being a professor, for not being an academic. But I serve on the district council, I'm a member of the executive, and in my view that's just as exalted and sacred an office as any academic post. I'm a member of the district council, yes, and proud of it, if you must know . . .

A pause.

Thirdly . . . I've something more to say . . . I mortgaged the house without asking your permission . . . Well, that was wrong of me, and I'm asking you to forgive me . . . I was driven to it by debt . . . thirty-five thousand . . . I've stopped gambling, gave it up ages ago. The only thing I can say in my own defence is that you girls have an annuity, and I've never had anything . . . no income, I mean . . .

A pause.

KULYGIN (*at the door*). Isn't Masha here? (*Anxiously.*) Where can she be? That's odd . . . (*Exits.*)

ANDREI. They're not listening. Natasha's a first-class, honest person. (*Paces up and down in silence a few moments, then stops.*) When I got married, I thought we'd be so happy . . . all of us . . . But oh, my God . . . (*Begins to cry.*) Oh, my dear sisters, my good, kind sisters, don't listen to me, don't believe a word of it . . . (*Exits.*)

KULYGIN (*appearing anxiously at the door*). Where's Masha? She's still not here? Most peculiar . . . (*Exits.*)

The fire alarm is heard. The stage seems deserted.

IRINA (*from behind her screen*). Olya! Who's that knocking on the floor?

OLGA. It's the Doctor. He's drunk.

IRINA. What a dreadful night!

A pause. She looks out from behind her screen.

Olya! Have you heard? The brigade's to be transferred, somewhere far away.

OLGA. It's just a rumour.

IRINA. We'll be left on our own, then . . . oh, Olya!

OLGA. What is it now?

IRINA. Listen, my dearest — I respect the Baron, I think highly of him, he's a fine man, and I shall marry him, yes, just as long as we go to Moscow! Oh, please, please, let's go to Moscow! There's nowhere in the world like Moscow! We've got to go, Olya, we must!

Curtain.

ACT FOUR

The old garden of the PROZOROV *house. A long avenue of fir-trees, leading to a river, with a wooded opposite bank. To the right is the verandah of the house, and a table with bottles and glasses – they have obviously been drinking champagne. It is mid-day. Now and again people stroll through the garden on their way from the street to the river. Five or six soldiers march quickly past.* CHEBUTYKIN *is sitting in an armchair, in a benign frame of mind, a mood which does not leave him throughout the entire act. He is waiting to be summoned somewhere, wearing his army cap, and carrying a walking-stick.* IRINA *and* KULYGIN, *the latter with a medal hung round his neck, and his moustaches now shaved off, are standing on the terrace with* TUZENBAKH, *bidding farewell to* FEDOTIK *and* RODE, *who are coming down the steps, dressed in their parade uniforms.*

TUZENBAKH (*embraces* FEDOTIK). You're a good chap, Fedotik, we've got on well together. (*Embraces* RODE.) And you too, Rodé . . . Goodbye, my dear friend!

IRINA. *Au revoir*!

FEDOTIK. No, not *au revoir*, it's goodbye, I'm afraid – we'll never see each other again.

KULYGIN. Who knows? (*Wipes his eyes, smiling.*) Look at this, I'm crying too!

IRINA. We'll meet again some day.

FEDOTIK. What, in ten or fifteen years, say? We'll barely recognise each other by then, we'll shake hands very coldly . . . (*Takes a photograph.*) Now, hold still . . . One last time.

RODE (*embraces* TUZENBAKH). We shan't ever meet again . . . (*Kisses* IRINA's *hand.*) Thank you for all you've done for us. Thank you.

FEDOTIK (*irritated*). Oh, do stand still!

TUZENBAKH. If it's God's will, we'll meet again. But you will write to us, though. Be sure and write.

RODE (*looking round at the garden*). Farewell, trees! (*Shouts.*) Coo-eee! Coo-eee!

A pause.

Farewell, echo!

KULYGIN. With any luck, you'll get married there in Poland . . . And your Polish wife'll fling her arms round you and say, 'Kohane! My darleeng!' (*Laughs.*)

FEDOTIK (*glances at his watch*). We've less than an hour left. Soliony's the only one in our unit going by barge, the rest of us are with the infantry. There's three battery divisions moving out today, another three tomorrow – peace and quiet'll descend upon the town.

TUZENBAKH. And deadly boredom.

RODE. So where's Mariya Sergeyevna?

KULYGIN. Masha's in the garden.

FEDOTIK. We must say goodbye to her.

RODE. Goodbye. I'd better go, before I start crying . . . (*Quickly embraces* TUZENBAKH *and* KULYGIN, *and kisses* IRINA'*s hand.*) We've had such good times here . . .

FEDOTIK (*to* KULYGIN). This is for you, a keepsake . . . a notebook and pencil. We'll walk down this way to the river . . .

They move off, turning to look back now and again.

RODE (*shouts*). Coo-eee! Coo-eee!

KULYGIN (*shouts*). Goodbye!

FEDOTIK *and* RODE *encounter* MASHA *in the background, and make their goodbyes to her. She exits along with them.*

IRINA. They've gone. (*She sits down on the bottom step of the verandah.*)

CHEBUTYKIN. They forgot to say goodbye to me.

IRINA. And what about you?

CHEBUTYKIN. I forgot as well. Anyway, I'll be seeing them again soon, I'm leaving tomorrow. Yes . . . Just one more day. And in a year from now when they retire me, I'll come back here and live out my life near you . . . Just one short year to go until my pension . . . (*He puts one newspaper in his pocket, takes out another.*) I'll come back here to you, and turn over a new leaf . . . I'll be so quiet, and well . . . well-behaved, and respectable . . .

IRINA. You really ought to turn over a new leaf, my dear. You really should try.

CHEBUTYKIN. Yes. I know. (*Sings quietly.*) Ta-ra-ra boom-dee-ay, ta-ra-ra boom-dee-ay . . .

KULYGIN. You're incorrigible, Doctor. Quite incorrigible!

CHEBUTYKIN. Yes, I should've come to you for lessons. You'd have straightened me out.

IRINA. Fyodor's shaved off his moustaches. I can't look at him!

KULYGIN. What's the matter?

CHEBUTYKIN. I wish I could say what your phizzog looks like now, but I can't.

KULYGIN. Oh, come on, it's the done thing nowadays, the *modus vivendi*. Our headmaster's shaved off his whiskers, and since I've been made deputy, I've shaved mine off too. Nobody likes it, but I don't care. I'm happy. With or without whiskers, I'm a happy man. (*Sits down.*)

At the bottom of the garden ANDREI is pushing a pram with a sleeping baby in it.

IRINA. Doctor, dear Ivan Romanych, I'm terribly worried. You were in town yesterday, on the boulevard – tell me what happened there?

CHEBUTYKIN. What happened? Nothing. Nothing important. (*Reads his newspaper.*) What's it matter anyway?

KULYGIN. According to the story, Soliony and the Baron bumped into each other on the boulevard outside the theatre . . .

TUZENBAKH. Oh, stop, that's enough. Honestly! (*Waves his hand dismissively and goes into the house.*)

KULYGIN. Yes, outside the theatre . . . Soliony started picking on the Baron, and he lost his temper and insulted Soliony . . .

CHEBUTYKIN. I don't know – it's all bunkum.

KULYGIN. I heard about a teacher in a seminary once, who wrote 'bunkum' on a student's essay, and he thought it was a Latin word! (*Laughs.*) That's really funny. Yes, it seems Soliony's in love with Irina, and he's conceived the most terrible spite against the Baron . . . Well, that's understandable. Irina's a very pretty girl. And she's so like Masha, always deep in thought. You've a gentler nature, though, Irina. Of course, Masha has a very nice nature too. Yes, I do love Masha.

From the far end of the garden, offstage, someone is calling: 'Coo-eee! Coo-eee!'

IRINA (*gives a start*). Everything seems to frighten me today.

A pause.

Well, I've got everything packed, and I'll send off my luggage after lunch. The Baron and I are getting married tomorrow, and we'll leave for the brick-works tomorrow afternoon. I'll be teaching at the school the very next day, beginning a new life, with God's help! You know, when I passed the exam to be a teacher, I actually cried for joy, I was so happy . . .

A pause.

The cart'll be here soon for my things.

KULYGIN. Well, that's as maybe, but it somehow doesn't seem serious. A lot of ideas, yes, but not much serious thought. Still, I wish you well, from the bottom of my heart.

CHEBUTYKIN (*deeply moved*). My dear, darling girl . . . My sweet child . . . You're going so far away, we'll never catch you up . . . And I'm left behind, like some migrating bird that's grown too old to fly. But fly away, my darlings, fly away, and God be with you!

A pause.

You know, Kulygin, you shouldn't have shaved off your moustache.

KULYGIN. Oh, that's enough from you. (*Sighs.*) Yes, the soldiers are leaving today, and soon everything'll be back to normal. You know, people can say what they like, Masha's a fine, honest woman. I love her very much, and I'm thankful the way things have turned out. People have such different fates . . . There's a man called Kozyrev who works in the excise office. He was at school with me, but they expelled him from the fifth form because he couldn't make head or tail of *ut consecutivum*. He's desperately poor now, and sick, and whenever I meet him, I say, 'Hello, *ut consecutivum!*' 'Yes,' he says, '*Consecutivum*, that's it exactly!' and then he starts coughing . . . Whereas I've been lucky all my life, I'm a happy man, I've even been awarded the Order of St Stanislaus, Second Class, and now I'm teaching others that same *ut consecutivum*. Of course, I'm a clever man, cleverer than most, but that's no guarantee of happiness . . .

Inside the house, someone is playing 'The Maiden's Prayer'.

IRINA. And tomorrow evening I'll no longer have to listen to that 'Maiden's Prayer', or run into Protopopov . . .

A pause.

You know Protopopov's sitting in the drawing-room; he's here again today.

KULYGIN. Hasn't our headmistress arrived yet?

IRINA. No. They've gone to fetch her. Oh, if you only knew how hard it's been, living here alone, without Olya . . . She stays at the school now, she's headmistress, she's busy the whole day, but I'm on my own, bored stiff, with

nothing to do, and that hateful room I have to live in . . .
Anyway, I've made up my mind: if it's not God's will I
should go to Moscow, then so be it. It's fate. There's
nothing I can do about it . . . It's in God's hands, and
that's the truth. The Baron's proposed to me . . . Well,
why not? I've thought it over and decided to accept him.
He's a fine man, an extraordinarily fine man . . . And it's
as if my heart's suddenly sprouted wings, I feel bright and
cheerful, and I'm longing to get to work again . . . Only
something happened yesterday, there's some sort of
mystery, and it's preying on my mind . . .

CHEBUTYKIN. Bunkum.

NATASHA (*through the window*). It's our headmistress!

KULYGIN. Our headmistress has arrived. Let's go inside.

Goes into the house with IRINA.

CHEBUTYKIN (*reading his newspaper, quietly singing*). Ta-ra-ra
boom-dee-ay . . . ta-ra-ra boom-dee-ay . . .

MASHA *goes up to him.* ANDREI *is still wheeling the pram in
the background.*

MASHA. Sitting all by himself, not a care in the world.

CHEBUTYKIN. What of it?

MASHA. Nothing . . . (*Sits down.*)

A pause.

Were you in love with my mother?

CHEBUTYKIN. Very much.

MASHA. And did she love you?

CHEBUTYKIN (*after a pause*). I don't remember.

MASHA. Is my man here? That's what our cook, Martha,
used to call her policeman – my man. Is my man here?

CHEBUTYKIN. Not yet.

MASHA. You know, when you have to snatch your
happiness in little bits, and then you lose it, as I'm doing,

you become gradually coarser, you become a shrew . . .
(*Points to her bosom.*) I'm seething inside, in here . . .
(*Looking at her brother* ANDREI, *pushing the pram.*) Look at
our dear brother, Andrei . . . All our hopes lie in ruins.
Like a great bell. It took thousands of people to raise it, at
the expense of vast amounts of money and labour, then it
suddenly fell down and shattered. Just like that, without
rhyme or reason. That was Andrei . . .

ANDREI. Just when are we going to have some peace in
this house? It's so noisy.

CHEBUTYKIN. Soon enough. (*Looks at his watch.*) This is an
old-fashioned watch, it chimes the hour . . . (*He winds it
up, and it chimes.*) The first, second and fifth battalions are
leaving at one o'clock sharp . . .

A pause.

And I go tomorrow.

ANDREI. For good?

CHEBUTYKIN. I don't know. I might come back next year.
Although, God knows, it hardly matters . . .

In the distance, someone is playing a harp and violin.

ANDREI. The town'll be deserted. Snuffed out like a candle.

A pause.

Something happened outside the theatre last night.
They're all talking about it.

CHEBUTYKIN. It was nothing. Foolishness. Soliony started
picking on the Baron, the Baron flared up and insulted
him. In the end, Soliony had to challenge him to a duel.
(*Looks at his watch.*) It's just about time now . . . Half-past
twelve in the Crown forest. You can see it from here, the
other side of the river . . . Bang-bang! (*Laughs.*) Soliony
fancies himself as Lermontov, even writes poetry . . .
Joking aside, this'll be his third duel.

MASHA. Whose?

CHEBUTYKIN. Soliony's.

MASHA. And what about the Baron?

CHEBUTYKIN. What about the Baron?

A pause.

MASHA. I don't know, my head's in a whirl . . . But I don't think it should be allowed. He might wound the Baron, or even kill him.

CHEBUTYKIN. The Baron's a fine chap, but what's one Baron more or less – it hardly matters, does it? Let them fight! Who cares?

Beyond the garden, someone shouts: 'Coo-eee! Coo-eee!'

Oh, let him wait. That's Skvortsov shouting, one of the seconds. He's down there in the boat.

A pause.

ANDREI. Well, I think fighting a duel, or being present at one, even as a doctor, is downright immoral.

CHEBUTYKIN. No, it just seems that way. We're not here, there's nothing here, we don't exist. We only seem to exist. And what difference does it make anyway?

MASHA. That's how they go on the whole day, talk, talk, talk . . . (*Makes to exit.*) You live in a climate where it snows at the drop of a hat, and on top of it all, these stupid conversations . . . (*Stops.*) I'm not going into the house, I can't go in there. Tell me when Vershinin arrives . . . (*Walks off down the avenue.*) The birds are already migrating . . . (*Looks up at the sky.*) Swans, or geese . . . Lucky creatures . . . (*Exits.*)

ANDREI. This house'll be empty soon. The officers are leaving, you're leaving, my sister's getting married . . . I'll be left on my own.

CHEBUTYKIN. What about your wife?

FERAPONT *enters with some papers.*

ANDREI. My wife's my wife. Oh, she's an honest, decent woman, good-natured, I suppose, but there's something about her that reduces her to the level of some small, blind, furry animal. At any rate, she's not human. I'm telling you this as a friend, the only person I can open my heart to. I love Natasha, I do, but at times she seems so incredibly vulgar, and then I'm confused. I just can't understand why I love her, or at any rate *did* love her . . .

CHEBUTYKIN (*stands up*). Listen, my friend, I'm leaving tomorrow. We may never see each other again, so here's my advice to you. Put on your hat, take up your stick, and walk away . . . walk away, and keep walking, without so much as a backward glance. The further the better.

In the background, SOLIONY *goes past with two officers. He catches sight of* CHEBUTYKIN *and turns towards him. The officers continue on.*

SOLIONY. Time we were going, Doctor. It's already half-past. (*Greets* ANDREI.)

CHEBUTYKIN. I'm coming, I'm coming. I'm fed up with all of you. (*To* ANDREI.) Andrei, dear chap, if anyone's looking for me, tell them I'll be back presently . . . (*Sighs.*) Oh, dear . . .

SOLIONY. 'Before he had time to gasp, the bear had him in its grasp!' (*Walks along with* CHEBUTYKIN.) What are you moaning about, old man?

CHEBUTYKIN. What d'you mean?

SOLIONY. How's your health?

CHEBUTYKIN (*testily*). I'm fit as a fiddle.

SOLIONY. Don't upset yourself, old man. I shall indulge myself a little. I'll just wing him, like a woodcock. (*Takes out his scent-bottle and sprinkles some on his hands.*) I've used up a whole bottle of this today, and my hands still stink. They smell like a corpse.

A pause.

Anyway . . . Do you remember the lines? 'But he, rebellious, seeks the storm, as if in storms lay peace . . . '

CHEBUTYKIN. Yes. 'Before he had time to gasp, the bear had him in its grasp . . . ' (*Exits with* SOLIONY.)

Shouts are heard again: 'Coo-eee! Coo-eee!' ANDREI *and* FERAPONT *enter.*

FERAPONT. There's papers to be signed, sir . . .

ANDREI. Leave me alone! Go away, for Heaven's sake! (*Exits with the pram.*)

FERAPONT. I mean, that's what papers are for, for signing . . . (*Walks off into the background.*)

IRINA *enters with* TUZENBAKH, *wearing a straw hat.* KULYGIN *crosses the stage, calling, 'Coo-eee, Masha! Coo-eee!'*

TUZENBAKH. I think he's the only person in town who's glad the army's leaving.

IRINA. That's understandable.

A pause.

The town'll be empty now.

TUZENBAKH (*glancing at his watch*). Listen, darling, I'll be back in a minute . . .

IRINA. Where are you going?

TUZENBAKH. I've got to go into town . . . to see off my comrades.

IRINA. That's not true . . . Nikolai, why are you so distracted today?

A pause.

What happened outside the theatre?

TUZENBAKH (*with a gesture of impatience*). I'll be back within the hour, by your side, Irina. (*Kisses her hand.*) My dearest darling . . . (*Gazing into her eyes.*) You know, five years have gone by, since I fell in love with you, and I still can't get used to it. You grow more beautiful every day. That wonderful, fascinating hair. Those beautiful eyes. And tomorrow I'll take you away, and we'll work, we'll be rich, all my dreams will come true. And you'll be happy, Irina. There's only one thing, just one: you don't love me.

IRINA. There's nothing I can do about that. I'll be your wife, I'll be faithful and obedient, but I don't love you. I can't help it. (*Weeps.*) I've never loved anyone. Oh, I used to dream about love, I dreamt about love all the time, day and night, but it's as if my heart were a valuable grand piano, which someone's locked up, and they've lost the key. (*A pause.*) You look worried.

TUZENBAKH. I didn't sleep last night. Not that there's anything to fear in my life, nothing I'm worried about, but that lost key tears me apart, it won't let me sleep . . . Speak to me, Irina.

A pause.

Say something . . .

IRINA. What? What can I say? Everything around us is so mysterious, the old trees stand silently . . . (*She lays her head on his breast.*)

TUZENBAKH. Speak to me, say anything . . .

IRINA. What can I say?

TUZENBAKH. Anything.

IRINA. Don't, please!

A pause.

TUZENBAKH. You know, it's strange how the silliest things in life can suddenly seem so important, for no particular reason. You laugh at them the same as always, you can see them for the trivial things they are, but you carry on regardless, as if you hadn't the power to stop. Well, let's not talk about that. I feel quite elated. It's as if I'm seeing these fir-trees, and maples and birches, for the very first time, as if everything's watching me, and just waiting. How beautiful the trees are, and how beautiful the life around them should be!

A shout is heard: 'Coo-eee! Coo-eee!'

It's time I was going . . . Look, that tree's dead, but it's still swaying in the wind with the others. In the same way, I think if I die, I'll still be a part of life, come what may. Goodbye, my darling . . . (*Kisses her hand.*) Oh, those papers you gave me are lying on my desk, under the calendar.

IRINA. I'm coming with you.

TUZENBAKH (*hastily*). No, no. (*Walks off quickly, and stops in the avenue.*) Irina . . .

IRINA. Yes?

TUZENBAKH (*unsure what to say*). I haven't had coffee yet. Ask them to make me some, will you? (*Hurriedly exits.*)

IRINA *stands deep in thought, then goes upstage to sit on a swing.* ANDREI *enters, pushing the pram.* FERAPONT *then appears.*

FERAPONT. I mean, they're not my papers, sir, they're official. I didn't make them up.

ANDREI. Oh, where is it now, where's my past gone, eh? When I was young, and full of life, what's become of all those dreams and clever ideas, when my present and future were bright with hope? Why is it we become so dull, grey and uninteresting, when we've barely started to live? Why do we become lazy and apathetic, useless wretches . . . ? This town's been in existence now for two hundred years, with a hundred thousand inhabitants, and there isn't one of them any different from the rest, not a single great man, alive or dead. Not one scientist or artist, or anyone of the least significance, that might arouse envy, or a passionate desire to emulate him . . . All they do is eat, drink, sleep, and eventually die . . . Others are born, and they too eat, drink, sleep, and so as not to die of boredom, bring some variety into their lives with vicious backbiting, vodka, gambling, and lawsuits. Wives betray their husbands, and the husbands lie, and pretend they see nothing, hear nothing, while their vulgarity irresistibly influences the children, crushes the life out of them, extinguishes the divine spark, till they become just as pathetic, just as corpse-like, as their mothers and fathers . . . (*To* FERAPONT, *crossly.*) What is it you want?

FERAPONT. What? These papers have to be signed.

ANDREI. You're getting on my nerves.

FERAPONT (*hands over the papers*). The porter at the finance office was telling me just now . . . he says, last winter in St Petersburg they had two hundred degrees of frost.

ANDREI. I detest the life I lead now, but when I think about the future, well, that's something else! Everything seems so airy and bright, I can see a glimmer of light in the distance, I can see freedom, I can see myself and my children free, too – free from idleness, from perpetual stale beer, and goose and cabbage, from after-dinner naps, from all this vulgar dependency . . .

FERAPONT. Yes, they say two thousand people froze to death. Folks were scared stiff, they say. Either Petersburg or Moscow, I can't remember.

ANDREI (*overwhelmed with tenderness*). Oh, my dear sisters, my darling sisters! (*Tearfully.*) Dearest Masha . . .

NATASHA (*at the window*). Who's making all that noise out here? Is it you, Andrei? You'll waken Sophie. *Il ne faut pas faire du bruit, la Sophie est dormée déjà. Vous êtes un ours.* (*Getting annoyed.*) If you want to talk, give the pram to someone else. Ferapont, take the pram from the master!

FERAPONT. Yes, ma'am. (*Takes the pram.*)

ANDREI (*embarrassed*). I was talking quietly.

NATASHA (*cuddling her little boy at the window*). Bobik! Naughty Bobik! Who's a little rascal?

ANDREI (*looking over the papers*). All right, I'll look through these and sign what's necessary, then you can take them back to the council. (*Goes into the house, reading the papers. FERAPONT wheels the pram upstage.*)

NATASHA (*at the window*). What's Mummy's name, Bobik? Who's Mummy's clever boy! And who's that? That's Auntie Olya, say 'Hello, Auntie Olya!'

Some wandering musicians, a man and a girl, enter playing a violin and a harp. VERSHININ, OLGA *and* ANFISA *emerge from the house and listen a moment in silence.* IRINA *goes up to them.*

OLGA. Our garden's like a public thoroughfare, everybody uses it. Nanny, give these musicians something.

ANFISA (*gives the musicians some money*). God bless you, my dears.

The musicians bow and leave.

Poor things. You don't have to play round the streets if you're well fed. (*To* IRINA.) Irina, love! (*Embraces her.*) Oh, my darling girl, if you could see me now! What a life I have! I'm living in a school flat now with my lovely Olya – that's what the good Lord's granted me in my old age. I've never been so well off, old sinner that I am . . . It's a big flat, there's no rent to pay – it's school property, you see – and I've got my own little room and bed. I wake up at night sometimes, and I think, oh, Holy Mother of God, I must be the happiest person in the world!

VERSHININ (*glancing at his watch*). We'll be leaving soon, Olga. It's time I was going.

A pause.

I wish you all the very best . . . Where's Masha?

IRINA. She's in the garden somewhere . . . I'll go and find her.

VERSHININ. If you would, please. I'm in a hurry.

ANFISA. I'll look for her too. (*Shouts.*) Masha! Masha, dear! Coo-eee! (*Exits with* IRINA *to the far end of the garden.*) Coo-eee! Coo-eee!

VERSHININ. Well, all good things come to an end. And here we are, saying goodbye. (*Looks at his watch.*) The town threw a sort of official lunch for us. We had champagne, and the Mayor made a speech. I ate and listened, but my mind was elsewhere – here, with all of you. (*Looks round the garden.*) Yes, I've got so used to you.

OLGA. D'you think we'll see each other again?

VERSHININ. Probably not.

A pause.

My wife and my two little girls'll be staying on here for another month or two. Please, if anything should happen, or if they need . . .

OLGA. Yes, yes, of course. Don't worry.

A pause.

By tomorrow, there won't be a single officer left in the town – only memories. And we'll be starting a new life, of course.

A pause.

Nothing ever turns out the way we'd like. I didn't want to be a headmistress, but that's what I've become. That means I won't be going to Moscow.

VERSHININ. Anyway . . . Thank you for everything . . . I'm sorry if there's anything I've done . . . I've talked a lot, I know – far too much. Forgive me for that, and don't think ill of me . . .

OLGA (*wiping her eyes*). What on earth's keeping Masha?

VERSHININ. What else can I say to you before I go? What can I philosophise about? . . . (*Laughs.*) Yes, it's a hard life. To many of us it seems hopelessly dreary, but you must admit it's gradually getting easier, and clearer, and the time isn't far off when it'll shine out like a beacon. (*Looks at his watch.*) I really ought to be going. Yes, in the old days, mankind was obsessed with war, our entire existence was taken up with campaigns, invasions, victories – now that's all old hat, but it's left behind a great void, clamouring to be filled. Mankind is passionately searching for something, though, and we shall find it. But it can't come too soon, for me. (*Pause.*) If we could only find a means of injecting some culture into work, and some hard work into culture! (*Looks at his watch.*) I really must go . . .

OLGA. Here she comes now.

MASHA *enters.*

VERSHININ. I've come to say goodbye.

OLGA *walks a little way apart, so as not to inhibit their leavetaking.*

MASHA (*gazing into his eyes*). Goodbye. (*A prolonged embrace.*)

OLGA. Stop it, stop . . .

MASHA *sobs bitterly.*

VERSHININ. Write to me . . . Don't forget! Please, let me go, it's time . . . Olga, take her, please, I have to go . . . I'm late . . .

Deeply moved, he kisses OLGA's *hand, then embraces* MASHA *once again and hurriedly exits.*

OLGA. Masha, that's enough. Please don't, darling . . .

KULYGIN *enters.*

KULYGIN (*embarrassed*). Never mind, let her cry . . . Oh, my dearest Masha, my dear, good Masha . . . You're my wife, and I'm happy, no matter what . . . I'm not complaining, I wouldn't dream of reproaching you. Olga here is my witness . . . We'll go on living the way we used to, and I won't say a word, not a hint of blame . . .

MASHA (*restraining her sobs*). 'By a curving shore stands a green oak tree, hung with a golden chain . . . Hung with a golden chain . . . ' I'm going mad . . . 'By a curving shore . . . A green oak tree . . . '

OLGA. Masha, calm down . . . Please . . . Give her some water.

MASHA. No, I've stopped crying . . .

KULYGIN. She's stopped crying . . . She's a good woman . . .

In the distance, the muffled sound of a shot.

MASHA. 'By a curving shore stands a green oak tree, hung with a golden chain . . . A green cat . . . A green oak . . .

I'm getting all mixed up . . . (*Drinks some water.*) My life's ruined . . . I don't want anything . . . I'll be all right in a minute . . . It doesn't matter . . . What does that mean, a curving shore? Why do those words keep going through my mind? My thoughts are all mixed up.

IRINA *enters.*

OLGA. Masha, calm down, please. That's better, there's a good girl . . . Let's go inside.

MASHA (*angrily*). I'm not going in there. (*Begins sobbing, but stops almost immediately.*) I don't go in there any more, I'm never going back into that house . . .

IRINA. Let's just sit out here together, without speaking. You know I'm leaving tomorrow . . .

KULYGIN (*after a pause*). Look, I confiscated these whiskers from a lad in the Third Form yesterday. (*Dons a false beard and moustache.*) I look like our German teacher, don't you think? (*Laughs.*) They're so funny, those boys.

MASHA. Actually, you do look like the German teacher.

OLGA (*laughs*). Yes, you do.

MASHA *starts crying.*

IRINA. Masha, don't . . .

KULYGIN. Just like him.

NATASHA *enters.*

NATASHA (*to the* MAID). What? Oh yes, Mr Protopopov'll look after little Sophie, and the master can take Bobik out in the pram. Really, children are so much bother . . . (*To* IRINA.) Irina, you're leaving tomorrow – what a shame. Why don't you stay a few more days? (*Catching sight of* KULYGIN, *she lets out a shriek.* KULYGIN *laughs and takes off the false beard and moustache.*) Oh you – you gave me such a fright! (*To* IRINA.) You know, I've got so used to you, it's not going to be easy saying goodbye to you, believe me. I'll have them move Andrei into your room, along with his fiddle – he can saw away in there! – and

I'll put little Sophie into his room. She's such a delightful child, an absolute angel. You know, she looked up at me today with her darling little eyes, and said 'Mama!'

KULYGIN. She's a beautiful child, that's true.

NATASHA. So, tomorrow I'll be on my own. (*Sighs.*) The first thing I'll do is cut down that avenue of fir-trees, then the maple . . . it looks so ugly at nights . . . (*To* IRINA.) Really, my dear, that sash doesn't suit you at all . . . It looks awful, you need something a bit brighter. And I'll have flowers planted everywhere, lots of them, for the perfume . . . (*Sternly.*) What's this fork doing on the bench? (*Walks up to the house, shouting to the* MAID.) I want to know – what's this fork doing on the bench! (*Shrieks.*) Shut up!

KULYGIN. She's off again.

In the distance, a military band is playing a march. Everyone listens.

OLGA. They're leaving.

CHEBUTYKIN *enters.*

MASHA. Our men are leaving. Well . . . *Bon voyage* to them! (*To* KULYGIN.) We'd better go home . . . Where's my hat and cape?

KULYGIN. I took them inside . . . I'll go and fetch them. (*Goes into the house.*)

OLGA. Yes, we can all go home now. It's about time.

CHEBUTYKIN. Olga Sergeyevna . . .

OLGA. What is it? (*Pause.*) What's the matter?

CHEBUTYKIN. Nothing . . . I don't know how to tell you . . . (*Whispers in her ear.*)

OLGA (*horrified*). No, it's not possible!

CHEBUTYKIN. I'm afraid so . . . A nasty business . . . I've had enough, I'm sick of it all . . . I don't want to talk about it . . . (*Testily.*) Anyway, what does it matter?

MASHA. What's happened?

OLGA (*puts her arms round* IRINA). This is a dreadful day . . .
Oh, my dear, I don't know how to tell you . . .

IRINA. Tell me what? What's happened? What is it? For the
love of God, tell me! (*Starts crying.*)

CHEBUTYKIN. The Baron's been killed in a duel . . .

IRINA (*quietly weeping*). Oh, I knew it, I knew it . . .

CHEBUTYKIN (*sits down on a bench upstage*). I'm worn out . . .
(*Takes a newspaper out of his pocket.*) Well, let them cry for a
bit . . . (*Sings softly.*) 'Ta-ra-ra boom-dee-ay, ta-ra-ra boom-
dee-ay . . . ' Does it really matter?

The three sisters are standing with their arms around each other.

MASHA. Just listen to the band playing. They're leaving
us, one of them's already gone, gone forever, and we're
left alone, to begin life over again. We must live . . . we
must . . .

IRINA (*lays her head on* OLGA's *bosom*). One day . . . one day
people will know what all this was for, all this suffering,
there'll be no more mysteries, but until then we have to
carry on living . . . we must work, that's all we can do.
I'm leaving by myself tomorrow, I'll teach in a school,
and devote my whole life to people who need it. It's
autumn now, it'll soon be winter, and there'll be snow
everywhere, but I'll be working . . . yes, working.

OLGA (*embraces both her sisters*). The band's playing so cheerfully, and I want to live so much! Oh, dear Heaven . . .
Time will pass, and we'll be gone forever, we'll be forgotten, they'll forget our faces, our voices, even how many
of us there were. But our sufferings will turn into joy for
those who come after us, peace and happiness will reign
on earth, and we who live now will be remembered with
a kind word, and a blessing. No, my dear sisters, our lives
aren't over yet. We must live! The band plays on so
cheerfully, so joyously – it's as if any minute now we'll
discover why we live, and why we suffer . . . Oh, if only
we knew! If only we knew!

The music fades gradually into the distance. KULYGIN *enters in*

high spirits, smiling, carrying MASHA'*s hat and cape.* ANDREI
wheels Bobik past in the pram.

CHEBUTYKIN (*sings quietly*). 'Ta-ra-ra boom-dee-ay, ta-ra-ra
boom-dee-ay . . . ' (*Reads his newspaper.*) What does it
matter? What does anything matter?

OLGA. Oh, if only we knew! If only we knew!

Curtain.

THE CHERRY ORCHARD

212

Dramatis Personae

Lyubov RANEVSKAYA, *a landowner*

ANYA, *her daughter, aged 17*

VARYA, *her adopted daughter, aged 24*

Leonid GAEV, *Ranevskaya's brother*

Yermolai LOPAKHIN, *a merchant*

Pyotr TROFIMOV, *a student*

Boris SIMEONOV-PISHCHIK, *a landowner*

CHARLOTTA Ivanovna, *a governess*

Semyon YEPIKHODOV, *a clerk*

DUNYASHA, *a maid*

FIRS, *an old servant, aged 87*

YASHA, *a young servant*

A TRAMP, *a* STATIONMASTER, POST OFFICE CLERK, *various* GUESTS *and* SERVANTS

The action takes place on Madame Ranevskaya's estate.

For a Guide to Pronunciation of Names, see page 279.

ACT ONE

The action takes place on Mme RANEVSKAYA's *estate, and the scene is a room still referred to as the nursery. One of the doors leads to* ANYA's *room. It is daybreak, the sun is just coming up, a fine May morning with the cherry trees in blossom, but a little chilly yet, and all the windows are closed.* DUNYASHA *enters holding a candle, and* LOPAKHIN *with a book.*

LOPAKHIN. The train's arrived, thank goodness. What time is it?

DUNYASHA. Nearly two. (*Extinguishes the candle.*) It's getting light.

LOPAKHIN. So what does that make the train? A couple of hours late at least. (*Yawns and stretches.*) Well, I'm a fine one to talk, I've made a proper ass of myself. Rode over here specifically to meet them at the station, and just dozed off . . . Fell asleep in the chair. Damn nuisance . . . you might've wakened me.

DUNYASHA. I thought you'd already left. (*Pauses to listen.*) That'll be them now.

LOPAKHIN (*also listens*). No, they'll have to get their luggage out and so on.

A pause.

Madame Ranevskaya's lived abroad five years now, I've no idea what she'll be like . . . She's a fine woman. Straightforward, easy-going. I remember when I was a lad of about fifteen, my late father – he had a little shop in the village at that time – well, he hit me with his fist so hard my nose started bleeding. We'd come up here to the yard for something or other, and he'd been drinking. Anyway, Madame Ranevskaya – I remember even now –

she was just a slip of a girl, she took me over to the wash-basin in this very room, in the nursery. 'Now don't cry, little peasant, ' she said, 'It'll heal up in time for your wedding.'

A pause.

'Little peasant' . . . Well, true enough, my father was a peasant, but here I am now in a white waistcoat, and tan leather shoes. A silk purse out of a sow's ear, you might say. Plain fact is I'm rich, I've pots of money, but when you get right down to it, I'm a peasant through and through. (*Leafs through his book.*) Yes, I was reading this book, didn't understand a word of it. Fell asleep reading.

A pause.

DUNYASHA. Well, the dogs certainly got no sleep, they can sense their masters are coming.

LOPAKHIN. Dunyasha, what's up? You look as if you . . .

DUNYASHA. My hands are trembling. I think I'm going to faint.

LOPAKHIN. You're too sensitive, Dunyasha, that's your trouble. And you dress like a young lady. The way you do your hair, too. You shouldn't, you know – you've got to remember your place.

YEPIKHODOV *enters with a bunch of flowers. He is wearing a jacket, and highly-polished boots which squeak all the time. On entering, he drops the flowers.*

YEPIKHODOV (*picking up the flowers*). The gardener sent these over, he says to put them in the dining-room. (*Hands them to* DUNYASHA.)

LOPAKHIN. And you can bring me some *kvas*.

DUNYASHA. Yes, sir. (*Exits.*)

YEPIKHODOV. There's a frost this morning, three degrees below, and the cherry trees are in flower. I can't approve of this climate of ours. (*Sighs.*) No, not at all. Our climate isn't exactly conducive, I'm afraid. And if I might append,

Mr Lopakhin, I bought these shoes two days ago, and I can assure you, sir, that they squeak beyond the bounds of possibility. What should I oil them with?

LOPAKHIN. Oh, go away. You get on my nerves.

YEPIKHODOV. You know, some disaster happens to me every day. But I'm not complaining. I'm used to it, I can even smile.

DUNYASHA *enters, gives* LOPAKHIN *his kvas.*

All right, I'm going. (*Bumps into a chair, which topples over.*) You see? (*With a note of triumph.*) There you have it, if you'll excuse the expression . . . I mean, that's the sort of circumstance . . . It's quite extraordinary, there's no other word for it. (*Exits.*)

DUNYASHA. Actually, Mr Lopakhin . . . to tell you the truth, Yepikhodov's proposed to me.

LOPAKHIN. Oh?

DUNYASHA. I just don't know . . . I mean, he's harmless enough, but sometimes when he gets going, you just can't understand a word he says. It sounds fine, quite touching really, but it doesn't make any sense. I think I like him. And he loves me to distraction. He's a terribly unlucky man, some mishap or other every day. They all pull his leg about it: the walking disaster, they call him.

LOPAKHIN (*strains to listen*). That's them coming now, I think.

DUNYASHA. It's them! Oh, what's the matter with me? I've gone cold all over . . .

LOPAKHIN. Yes, it's them. We'll go and meet them. I wonder if she'll recognise me? We haven't seen each other for five years.

DUNYASHA (*agitated*). Oh God, I'm going to faint, I know I am!

Two carriages are heard drawing up outside. LOPAKHIN *and* DUNYASHA *hurriedly exit, leaving the stage empty. There is noisy activity in the outer room, and old* FIRS, *who has been to the station to greet Mme* RANEVSKAYA, *hobbles across the stage, leaning on a walking-stick. He is dressed in old-fashioned livery, and wearing a top hat, He is muttering to himself, but it is impossible to distinguish what he is saying. The noises offstage grow louder. A voice is heard: 'Let's go in this way . . . '.* Mme RANEVSKAYA, ANYA, *and* CHARLOTTA IVANOVNA, *leading a little dog on a leash, all enter in outdoor clothes.* VARYA *enters wearing an overcoat and headscarf, and* GAEV, SIMEONOV-PISHCHIK, LOPAKHIN *and* DUNYASHA, *carrying a parcel and an umbrella, and servants with luggage, all cross the stage.*

ANYA. We'll go through this way. You remember, Mama, what this room used to be?

RANEVSKAYA (*joyfully, deeply moved*). The nursery!

VARYA. It's so cold, my hands are quite numb. (*To* RANEVSKAYA.) Your rooms are just the way you left them, Mama, the violet and the white.

RANEVSKAYA. Ah yes, the nursery, my darling wonderful nursery! This is where I used to sleep, when I was little. (*Begins to weep.*) And now I'm like a little girl again . . . (*Kisses her brother and* VARYA, *then her brother again.*) And Varya hasn't changed a bit, she still looks like a nun. And I even recognise Dunyasha . . . (*Kisses* DUNYASHA.)

GAEV. The train was two hours late. What do you make of that, eh? Some organisation.

CHARLOTTA (*to* PISHCHIK). My little dog even eats nuts.

PISHCHIK (*astonished*). Fancy that!

All exit, save ANYA *and* DUNYASHA.

DUNYASHA. The time we've been waiting . . . (*Helps* ANYA *off with her coat and hat.*)

ANYA. I haven't slept the past four nights . . . now I'm freezing.

DUNYASHA. You left before Easter, and there was snow and frost then, and now look at it. Oh, dearest Anya!

(*Laughs, kisses her.*) I've waited so long for you, my precious darling . . . I must tell you this now, I can't hold back another second . . .

ANYA (*listlessly*). Not again . . .

DUNYASHA. Yepikhodov, the clerk, proposed to me just after Easter.

ANYA. The same old story . . . (*Fixing her hair.*) I've lost all my hairpins . . . (*She is very fatigued, almost staggering.*)

DUNYASHA. I mean, I don't know what to think. He's very much in love with me.

ANYA (*gazing fondly at her bedroom door*). My own room, my own windows, just as if I'd never left. I'm home! I'll get up tomorrow morning, and run into the garden . . . Oh, if only I could get to sleep! I haven't slept a wink the whole road, I'm worn out with worry.

DUNYASHA. Mr Trofimov arrived the day before yesterday.

ANYA (*joyfully*). Trofimov!

DUNYASHA. He's sleeping in the bath-house, that's where he's staying. He didn't want to put anybody out, he said. (*Glances at her pocket-watch.*) I really ought to wake him, but Miss Varya told me not to. Don't you dare wake him up, she says.

VARYA *enters, with a bunch of keys at her waist.*

VARYA. Dunyasha, what about that coffee? Mama's asking for coffee.

DUNYASHA. Right this minute. (*Exits.*)

VARYA. Well, thank heavens you're back. You're home again. (*Hugs her.*) My little darling's home again! My lovely girl's home!

ANYA. You've no idea what I've been through.

VARYA. I can imagine.

ANYA. I left here just before Easter, it was cold then. Charlotta never stopped talking the whole way, doing her

card tricks. What on earth possessed you to hang
Charlotta round my neck?

VARYA. Well, I couldn't let you travel alone, my darling,
not at seventeen.

ANYA. Anyway, when we got to Paris it was cold there too,
snowing. My French is abysmal. Mama was staying on
the fourth floor, and when I went to see her she had all
these French gentlemen with her, and ladies, and some
old Catholic priest with his little book, and the whole
place was full of tobacco smoke, very uncomfortable. I
suddenly felt so sorry for Mama, so terribly sorry, that I
put my arms round her, pressed her head to my breast,
and couldn't let go. And Mama couldn't stop hugging and
kissing me, and crying . . .

VARYA (*tearfully*). Don't . . . I don't want to hear . . .

ANYA. She's sold her villa at Menton, she's got nothing left,
absolutely nothing. And I haven't a kopeck either, we
barely managed to get home. And Mama has no idea! We
have dinner in the station buffet and she orders the most
expensive things on the menu, and tips the waiters a
whole rouble. Each! Charlotta does likewise. And Yasha
demands the same as us, it's just frightful. You know
Mama has a new servant, Yasha, we've brought him back
with us . . .

VARYA. Yes, I've seen him, the wretch.

ANYA. So, what's happening? Have you paid the interest?

VARYA. Huh, what with?

ANYA. Oh, my God . . .

VARYA. They're going to sell off the estate in August.

ANYA. Oh, my God . . .

LOPAKHIN (*pops his head round the door, and baas like a sheep*).
Baa-aa-aa . . . (*Exits.*)

VARYA (*tearfully*). Oh! If I get my hands on him . . . (*Shaking
her fist.*)

ANYA (*hugs* VARYA, *then gently*). Varya, has he proposed yet? (VARYA *shakes her head.*) After all, he does love you . . . Why don't you talk it over with him? What are you waiting for?

VARYA. Oh, I don't think anything'll come of it. He's so busy, he hasn't any time for me. He doesn't even notice me, God help him, but it's making life very difficult. Everybody keeps on about our wedding, congratulations and all that, but there's absolutely nothing, just a pipe-dream . . . (*Changing the subject.*) Mm, that brooch you've got on looks just like a bee.

ANYA (*sadly*). Mama bought it for me. (*Brightens up, almost a child again, goes into her bedroom.*) And I had a trip in a balloon in Paris!

VARYA. And my little to make him proud's home again! My lovely girl's home!

DUNYASHA *has re-entered with the coffee-pot, and is making the coffee.* VARYA *stands by the bedroom door.*

Oh yes, I go around doing housework all day, and I never stop dreaming. I'll marry you off to some rich man, and my mind'll be at rest, I could go away then to a retreat, go on a pilgrimage to Kiev, and Moscow, visit all the holy places . . . that's all I'd do. Sheer bliss!

ANYA. The birds are singing in the garden. What time is it now?

VARYA. Must be after two. Time you were in bed, my to make him proud. (*Goes into* ANYA's *room.*) Yes, sheer bliss!

YASHA *enters carrying a travel rug, and a bag.*

YASHA (*crossing the stage, affectedly*). May one pass this way?

DUNYASHA. Well, I'd hardly know you, Yasha. Being abroad's changed you all right.

YASHA. Er . . . and who might you be?

DUNYASHA. Oh, when you left here, I was only that high . . . (*Indicates from the floor.*) I'm Dunyasha – Fyodor Kozoyedov's daughter. You won't remember me.

YASHA. Mmm . . . quite a little peach! (*Looks round quickly and embraces her: she shrieks and drops a saucer. YASHA hurriedly exits.*)

VARYA (*appears in the doorway, displeased*). What's going on?

DUNYASHA (*tearfully*). I've broken a saucer . . .

VARYA. Oh well, that's good luck.

ANYA (*emerging from her room*). We'd better let Mama know Trofimov's here.

VARYA. I told them not to wake him.

ANYA (*thoughtfully*). Father died six years ago, and a month after that poor Grisha was drowned in the river, just seven, such a to make him proud little boy. Mama couldn't bear it, she just walked out, turned her back on it all . . . (*Shudders.*) I understand her, I really do, if she only knew.

A pause.

And Trofimov was poor Grisha's tutor, he'll bring it all back.

Old FIRS *enters, in a jacket and white waistcoat.*

FIRS (*goes up to the coffee-pot, anxiously*). The mistress is going to have it here . . . (*Pulls on white gloves.*) Is the coffee ready? (*Sternly, to* DUNYASHA.) Here, you – what about the cream?

DUNYASHA. Oh, God . . . (*Hurriedly exits.*)

FIRS (*fussing around the coffee-pot*). Damn silly girl . . . (*Muttering to himself.*) Come from Paris . . . Yes, the master used to go to Paris . . . used to go by coach . . . (*Laughs.*)

VARYA. What is it, Firs?

FIRS. Pardon, ma'am? (*Delightedly.*) And the mistress has come home, yes! I've been waiting so long. I can die happy now! (*Weeps from sheer joy.*)

Enter Mme RANEVSKAYA, GAEV, *and* SIMEONOV-PISHCHIK. *The latter is wearing a fine-quality sleeveless traditional overshirt, and breeches.* GAEV *enters in a crouch, arms outstretched as if playing a billiards shot.*

RANEVSKAYA. What is it they say? Wait, it'll come to me . . . Yes, red into the corner! Cannon into the middle!

GAEV. And screw back for the corner pocket! Yes, you and I used to sleep in this very room, sister, and now I'm fifty-one already, would you believe . . .

LOPAKHIN. Yes, time flies.

GAEV. What did you say?

LOPAKHIN. I said time flies.

GAEV. There's a smell of patchouli in here.

ANYA. Well, I'm off to bed. Goodnight, Mama. (*Kisses her mother.*)

RANEVSKAYA. Oh, my precious baby . . . (*Kisses her hands.*) Are you glad to be home? I still can't take it in.

ANYA. Goodnight, Uncle.

GAEV (*kisses her on the cheek, and hands*). God bless you. You're exactly like your mother. (*To* RANEVSKAYA.) You were just like that at her age, Lyuba.

ANYA *shakes hands with* LOPAKHIN *and* PISHCHIK, *and exits, closing the door behind her.*

RANEVSKAYA. She's exhausted.

PISHCHIK. Yes, it's a fair long road.

VARYA (*to* LOPAKHIN *and* PISHCHIK). Well, gentlemen . . . it's after two, time you were off.

RANEVSKAYA (*laughs*). Varya, you haven't changed a bit. (*Draws her close and kisses her.*) Right, I'll finish my coffee, then we'll all go. (FIRS *places a footstool under her feet.*) Thank you, my dear. Yes, I've got to have my coffee. I drink it night and day. Thank you, my dear old man. (*Kisses* FIRS.)

VARYA. I'd better make sure they've brought in all the luggage. (*Exits.*)

RANEVSKAYA. Am I really sitting down at last? (*Laughs.*) I want to jump up in the air, and wave my arms! (*Covers her face with her hands.*) What if this is just a dream? God knows, I love my country, love it so tenderly, I couldn't even look out of the train window, I kept crying all the time. (*Tearfully.*) Still, I must have my coffee. Thank you, Firs, thank you, old man. I'm so pleased you're still alive.

FIRS. The day before yesterday.

GAEV. He doesn't hear too well.

LOPAKHIN. Well, I'd better be off, I'm leaving for Kharkov just after four this morning. Damn nuisance, really. I'd have liked to look at you for a bit, have a chat . . . You're as beautiful as ever.

PISHCHIK (*sighing heavily*). Even more beautiful . . . and in the latest Paris fashion. Honestly, I don't know whether I'm coming or going.

LOPAKHIN. I'm afraid your brother here thinks I'm a scoundrel, a jumped-up peasant, but I couldn't care less. He can say what he likes. All I want is for you to believe in me the way you used to, to look on me with those wonderful, gentle eyes that same way . . . Oh, merciful God! My father was your grandfather's serf, and your father's after him, but you did so much for me in the old days, that I've forgotten all that, and I love you like a sister . . . more than a sister.

RANEVSKAYA. I can't sit still, I just can't . . . (*Jumps up and begins pacing the room excitedly.*) I'm so happy I could die . . . Oh, you'll laugh at me, I'm being silly . . . My darling little bookcase . . . (*Kisses the bookcase.*) And my own little table.

GAEV. I'm afraid Nanny died while you were away.

RANEVSKAYA (*sits down, sips her coffee again*). Oh yes, God rest her soul. They wrote to me about it.

GAEV. Anastasy's dead too. And Petrushka, the chap with the squint, he's left us. He's living in town now at the police inspector's place. (*Takes a box of sweets out of his pocket, pops one in his mouth.*)

PISHCHIK. My daughter, little Dasha . . . sends her regards . . .

LOPAKHIN. I've got something that'll cheer you up . . . (*Glances at his watch.*) I have to go now, no time for a chat . . . well, all right, just a word or two. You know, of course, that your cherry orchard's got to be sold off to pay your debts – the sale's been fixed for the 22nd of August – but don't worry, dear lady, you can rest easy, there's a way out . . . This is my plan. Pay attention, everybody! Your estate's only about fifteen miles from town, the railway runs past quite near, and if you break up the cherry orchard and the land along by the river into building lots, then rent them out for summer cottages, you'll have an income of at least twenty-five thousand a year.

GAEV. No, I'm sorry, that's nonsense.

RANEVSKAYA. I'm not sure what you mean, Mr Lopakhin.

LOPAKHIN. Look, you'll get at least twenty-five roubles a year from the tenants, for every acre, and if you advertise now, I guarantee they'll all be snapped up before autumn, there won't be a single patch of ground left. In a word, I congratulate you, you're saved! I mean, it's a marvellous site, with a good deep river. Of course, you'll have to tidy it up, do a bit of clearing . . . for instance, you'll have to demolish all the old buildings, like this house, which really isn't fit for anything now, and chop down the old cherry orchard . . .

RANEVSKAYA. Chop it down? No, excuse me, my dear, you don't know what you're saying. If there's anything at all of interest, or even remarkable, in this entire region, then it's our cherry orchard.

LOPAKHIN. The only thing remarkable about that orchard is that it's so big. It produces cherries every other year, that's all, and then you don't know what to do with them, nobody'll buy them.

GAEV. There's actually an entry in the Encyclopedia about that orchard.

LOPAKHIN (*looks at his watch again*). Well, if we can't think of something, and come to a decision before the 22nd of August, the whole estate, cherry orchard included, will be sold at auction. So, make up your mind! There's no other solution, believe me. Absolutely none.

FIRS. In the old days, forty, maybe fifty years ago, they used to dry the cherries, soak 'em and pickle 'em, make 'em into jam, and sometimes they'd . . .

GAEV. Oh, be quiet, Firs.

FIRS. Yes, they'd send the dried cherries, cartloads of 'em, to Moscow and Kharkov. Worth a fair bit, they were. And the dried cherries were soft and juicy, sweet, with a nice smell to 'em . . . They knew how to do that back then . . .

RANEVSKAYA. And why can't they do it now?

FIRS. Forgotten. Nobody can remember.

PISHCHIK (*to* RANEVSKAYA). So, how was Paris? What's it like? Did you eat frogs?

RANEVSKAYA. I ate crocodiles.

PISHCHIK. Fancy that!

LOPAKHIN. Yes, used to be only gentry and peasants that lived in the country, but now all these summer folk have appeared. All the towns these days, even quite small ones, are surrounded with cottages. And you can safely say these summer residents'll multiply out of sight, over the next twenty years or so. At the moment, all they do is drink tea on their verandas, but chances are they'll start working their little plots of land, and then that cherry orchard of yours'll really thrive, it'll grow rich and happy . . .

GAEV (*indignant*). Absolute rubbish!

VARYA *and* YASHA *enter.*

VARYA. Mama, there are two telegrams here for you. (*Selects a key from the bunch, and noisily unlocks the ancient cupboard.*) Here you are.

RANEVSKAYA. This is from Paris. (*Tears it up without reading it.*) I'm done with Paris . . .

GAEV. You know how old that bookcase is, Lyuba? That same bookcase? I pulled out one of the bottom drawers last week, and spotted some numbers burned into the wood. That bookcase was made exactly a hundred years ago. What d'you think of that, eh? We ought to celebrate its centenary. I mean, it's an inanimate object, but it's a bookcase nevertheless.

PISHCHIK (*astonished*). A hundred years . . . just fancy!

GAEV. Oh, yes . . . it's a . . . it's a wonderful thing. (*Feeling the bookcase.*) Dear, much respected bookcase! I salute your existence, which for over a century has been dedicated to the shining ideals of goodness and justice. Your silent service in the cause of fruitful toil has never once weakened throughout those hundred years, sustaining . . . (*Genuinely moved.*) from generation to generation of our family, good cheer, and faith in a better future, and instilling in us the ideals of virtue, and social consciousness . . .

A pause.

LOPAKHIN. Yes . . .

RANEVSKAYA. You haven't changed a bit, Leo.

GAEV (*slightly embarrassed*). Cannon into the right corner pocket! Screw back for the middle!

LOPAKHIN (*looks at his watch*). Well, it's time I was going.

YASHA (*hands* RANEVSKAYA *some medicine*). You might take your pills now, ma'am.

PISHCHIK. You shouldn't take any medicines, dear lady . . . they'll do you no harm, but no good either . . . Here, give them to me, dear friend. (*Takes the pills, pours them out onto his hand, blows on them, pops them in his mouth, and washes them down with a drink of kvas.*) There!

RANEVSKAYA (*alarmed*). Have you gone mad?

PISHCHIK. I've taken all the pills.

LOPAKHIN. Greedyguts!

They all laugh.

FIRS. Gentleman was here at Easter, too — ate half a bucket of pickles . . . (*Muttering.*)

RANEVSKAYA. What's he saying?

VARYA. Oh, he's been mumbling like that the past three years. We've got used to it.

YASHA. Mm . . . in his dotage.

CHARLOTTA *crosses the stage, very thin, and tightly laced into a white dress, with a lorgnette at her waist.*

LOPAKHIN. Charlotta Ivanovna, excuse me, I haven't had time to say hello . . . (*Attempts to kiss her hand.*)

CHARLOTTA (*pulling her hand away*). No, no, if I allow you to kiss my hand, next you'll want to kiss my elbow, then my shoulder . . .

LOPAKHIN. I'm out of luck today.

They all laugh.

Come on, Charlotta, show us a conjuring trick.

RANEVSKAYA. Yes, Charlotta, do — show us a trick.

CHARLOTTA. No, I can't. I want to sleep. (*Exits.*)

LOPAKHIN. Anyway, we'll meet again in three weeks. (*Kisses* RANEVSKAYA's *hand.*) Until then, goodbye. Time I was off. (*To* GAEV.) Goodbye, sir. (*Embraces* PISHCHIK.) Goodbye. (*Shakes hands with* VARYA, *then* FIRS *and* YASHA.) I really don't want to leave. (*To* RANEVSKAYA.) If you should come to a decision about the cottages, let me know and I can fix up a loan of fifty thousand or so. Do think about it, seriously.

VARYA (*angrily*). Oh, for God's sake go!

LOPAKHIN. I'm going, I'm going . . . (*Exits.*)

GAEV. Scoundrel! Oh, I beg your pardon . . . Varya's going to marry him, he's Varya's fiancé.

VARYA. You talk too much, Uncle dear.

RANEVSKAYA. Well, really, Varya, I'd be delighted. He's a fine man.

PISHCHIK. Oh yes, to give him his due . . . he's a thoroughly worthy . . . My little Dasha says . . . well, she says . . . oh, she says all sorts of things. (*Starts to snore, immediately wakes up again.*) Anyway, my dear lady, if you could oblige me . . . if you could lend me two hundred and forty roubles . . . I've got to pay the interest on my mortgage tomorrow.

VARYA (*alarmed*). No, no!

RANEVSKAYA. I really haven't any money.

PISHCHIK. Well, it'll turn up. (*Laughs.*) I never give up hope. I mean, I thought I was ruined before, really done for, then lo and behold, they ran the railway through my land, yes, and paid me for it. So you see, something's bound to turn up, if not today, tomorrow . . . My Dasha might even win two hundred thousand . . . she's got a lottery ticket.

RANEVSKAYA. Well, we've had our coffee, we can go to bed now.

FIRS (*brushing* GAEV *down, reprovingly*). You've put on the wrong trousers again. What are we going to do with you?

VARYA (*quietly*). Anya's asleep. (*Gently opens the window.*) The sun's up now, it's not so cold. Look, Mama – the trees are so lovely. Oh, and the fresh air! And the starlings are singing.

GAEV (*opening another window*). The orchard's completely white. You haven't forgotten, Lyuba? The way that long avenue runs straight on, absolutely straight, like a belt pulled tight, and how it shines white on moonlit nights? You remember? You haven't forgotten?

RANEVSKAYA (*looks out of the window at the orchard*). Oh, my childhood, my innocence! I used to sleep in this nursery, and look out at the orchard. My happiness would wake up with me every single morning, and the orchard looked exactly the same, nothing's changed. (*Laughs delightedly.*) White all over, absolutely white! Oh, my beautiful orchard! After the dark, rainy autumn, and the cold winter, you're young again, filled with happiness, the heavenly angels haven't abandoned you . . . Oh, if only I could cast aside this heavy stone that weighs on my heart, if only I could forget my past!

GAEV. Yes, and strange as it seems, the orchard'll have to be sold to pay off our debts.

RANEVSKAYA. Oh, look, look! It's my dear Mama . . . she's walking in the orchard . . . in a white dress! (*Overjoyed.*) It's her!

GAEV. Where?

VARYA. Mama, please . . .

RANEVSKAYA. No, there's no-one, I just imagined it. Look, over there to the right, where you turn towards the summerhouse, there's a little white tree bending over, it looks like a woman . . .

TROFIMOV *enters in his shabby student uniform, and spectacles.*

It's an amazing orchard! Masses of white flowers, the blue sky . . .

TROFIMOV. Madame Ranevskaya . . .

She looks round at him.

I'll just pay my respects and then I'll leave. (*Kisses her hand warmly.*) They told me to wait till morning, but I couldn't stop myself . . .

RANEVSKAYA *looks at him in bewilderment.*

VARYA (*tearfully*). It's Petya Trofimov . . .

TROFIMOV. Petya Trofimov, I used to be Grisha's tutor . . .
Surely I haven't changed that much?

RANEVSKAYA *embraces him, begins crying softly.*

GAEV *(embarrassed)*. Lyuba, don't . . .

VARYA *(crying)*. Petya, I told you to wait until tomorrow.

RANEVSKAYA. Oh, my little Grisha . . . my little boy . . .
Grisha, my son . . .

VARYA. It can't be helped, Mama. It was God's will.

TROFIMOV *(gently, deeply moved)*. There, there . . .

RANEVSKAYA. My little boy dead . . . drowned . . . Why?
What for, tell me, dear friend. *(Then quietly.)* Anya's asleep,
and I'm shouting . . . making a noise . . . Petya, what's
happened to your looks? Why have you grown so old?

TROFIMOV. A woman on the train said I looked mangy –
that mangy gentleman, she called me . . .

RANEVSKAYA. You were still just a boy then, a nice bright
student, and now your hair's thinning, and you're wearing
glasses. Don't tell me you're still a student? *(Walks over to
the door.)*

TROFIMOV. I think I'm the eternal student.

RANEVSKAYA *(kisses her brother, then VARYA)*. Well, time for
bed. You've aged too, Leonid.

PISHCHIK *(following her)*. So, it's time we were in bed . . .
Ouch, that gout of mine! I'll stay here, I think. And if you
could see your way, dear lady . . . you know, tomorrow
morning, dear heart . . . two hundred roubles?

GAEV. He has a one-track mind.

PISHCHIK. Two hundred roubles . . . it's to pay the
interest on my mortgage.

RANEVSKAYA. Darling, I haven't any money.

PISHCHIK. I'll pay it back . . . I mean, it's a trifling sum,
really.

RANEVSKAYA. Oh, all right, Leonid'll give it you . . . Do, Leonid, let him have it.

GAEV. Oh yes, for sure – here, open your pocket.

RANEVSKAYA. Leo, please, give it to him . . . He needs it . . . He'll pay it back.

RANEVSKAYA, TROFIMOV, PISHCHIK *and* FIRS *all exit, leaving behind* GAEV, VARYA *and* YASHA.

GAEV. My sister still hasn't got out of the habit of squandering her money. (*To* YASHA.) If you wouldn't mind, sir – a bit further off. You smell of chicken.

YASHA (*with a mocking smile*). Yes, my dear sir, you haven't changed one bit.

GAEV. What's that? (*To* VARYA.) What did he say?

VARYA (*to* YASHA). Your mother's come up from the village, she's been sitting since yesterday afternoon in the servants' hall, waiting to see you.

YASHA. So what? Let her wait.

VARYA. My God, you've no shame.

YASHA. That's all I need. Why couldn't she have come tomorrow? (*Exits.*)

VARYA. Mama's just the same as always, she hasn't changed. If she had her own way, she'd give away everything.

GAEV. Yes . . . (*A pause.*) You know, when people suggest all sorts of cures for some disease or other, it means it's incurable. I keep thinking, racking my brains, and I come up with plenty of solutions, plenty of remedies, and basically, that means none – not one. It'd be nice to inherit some money from somewhere, it'd be nice to marry our Anya off to some rich person, it'd be nice to go to Yaroslavl, and try my luck with my old aunt, the Countess. I mean, she's rich, extremely rich.

VARYA (*weeping*). If only God would help us.

GAEV. Oh, stop howling. Auntie's very rich, but she's no time for us. For a start, my sister happened to marry a lawyer, and not a nobleman . . .

ANYA *appears in the doorway.*

Yes, she married a commoner, and you can't say she's led a particularly virtuous life, quite honestly. Oh, she's a fine woman, charming and good-hearted, and I'm very fond of her, but whatever the extenuating circumstances, you've got to admit she's an immoral woman. You can sense it in her slightest movement.

VARYA (*in a whisper*). Anya's at the door . . .

GAEV. What?

A pause.

You know, it's funny – something's got into my eye . . . I can barely see. And on Thursday, when I was at the District Court . . .

ANYA *enters.*

VARYA. Why aren't you in bed, Anya?

ANYA. I can't sleep. I just can't.

GAEV. My dear little girl . . . (*Kisses* ANYA*'s face and hands.*) My sweet child . . . (*Emotionally.*) You're not just my niece, you're my angel, you're everything to me. Believe me, honestly . . .

ANYA. I believe you, Uncle. Everybody likes you, everybody respects you, but you really ought to keep quiet – just keep quiet. What were you saying just now about my mother, about your own sister? What made you say that?

GAEV. Yes, yes . . . (*Covers his face with his hands.*) You're right, it's terrible, actually. Oh, God. Save me, God! And that speech I made to the bookcase . . . so stupid! As soon as I'd done it I realised it was stupid.

VARYA. It's true, Uncle, you really should keep quiet. Just say nothing, and that's it.

ANYA. You'd feel a lot better yourself, if you did.

GAEV. I'll shut up. (*Kisses* ANYA *and* VARYA's *hands.*) Not a word. One point about business, though. I was at the District Court on Thursday, there was a crowd of people there, we started talking about this and that, one thing led to another, and apparently it would be possible to fix up a loan on a promissory note, to pay off the bank interest.

VARYA. Oh, if only God would help us!

GAEV. I'm going back in on Tuesday, I'll have another word about it. (*To* VARYA.) Oh, come on, stop howling. (*To* ANYA.) Your mother can speak to Lopakhin – he certainly won't turn her down . . . And as soon as you've had a rest you can go to Yaroslavl, to your great-aunt, the Countess. So we'll be active on three fronts, you see, and it's as good as done. We'll pay the interest, I'm convinced of it . . . (*Pops a sweet into his mouth.*) I give you my word of honour, whatever it takes, the estate won't be sold! (*Excitedly.*) I swear by my happiness! Look, here's my hand on it, you can call me a good-for-nothing scoundrel if I let it go to auction! I swear by my very soul!

ANYA (*her calm demeanour has returned, she is happy*). Oh, Uncle, you're such a good man, you're so clever! (*Embraces him.*) I feel at ease again. I'm so happy . . .

FIRS *enters.*

FIRS (*reproachfully*). Mr Gaev, sir, have you no fear of God? It's time you were in bed.

GAEV. In a moment, yes. Now go away, Firs. I'll manage . . . I can undress myself. Well, my dear children, bye-bye . . . We'll talk over the details tomorrow, but it's bedtime now. (*Kisses* ANYA *and* VARYA.) Yes, I'm a man of the 80's, I suppose . . . People aren't too impressed by those times now, but I must say I've taken a few knocks in my life, for my convictions. That's why the peasants like me. Yes, you've got to know the peasant, really understand what makes him . . .

ANYA. Uncle . . .

VARYA. Uncle dear, please be quiet.

FIRS (*crossly*). Mr Gaev, sir!

GAEV. I'm coming, I'm coming . . . Now go to bed, you two. Off two cushions into the middle pocket! I'll pot the white . . . (*Exits, with* FIRS *hobbling along behind him.*)

ANYA. I feel at peace now. I'd rather not go to Yaroslavl, I don't like great-aunt, but my mind's at rest now, thanks to Uncle. (*Sits down.*)

VARYA. You need some sleep. I'll go now. You know, while you were away, there was a bit of unpleasantness here, in the old servants' hall. It's only the older folk that live there, as you know, Yefim, Polya, Yevstignei, Karp and the rest of them. Well, they started taking in all sorts of strays, tramps, and so on, and I kept quiet about it. Next thing, I hear a rumour to the effect that I'd said they were to be given nothing but peas to eat! My meanness, you see . . . And this is all Yevstignei's doing. Right, I thought, if that's what you want, I'll just show you. So I send for Yevstignei . . . (*Yawns.*) And he comes in, and I say, 'What are you up to, Yevstignei?' I say, 'You're an old fool . . . (*Looks across at* ANYA.) Oh, Anya . . .

A pause.

She's fallen asleep. (*Takes* ANYA *by the arm.*) Come on, let's go to bed . . . Up you come . . . (*Leads her out.*) My little darling's asleep . . . Off we go . . .

They slowly exit. Far off beyond the orchard, a shepherd can be heard playing his pipe. TROFIMOV *crosses the stage, and catching sight of* VARYA *and* ANYA, *stops in his tracks.*

Ssshh . . . She's asleep . . . Fast asleep . . . Let's go, my darling.

ANYA (*drowsily*). I'm so tired . . . All the little bells . . . Uncle . . . so kind . . . and Mama . . . and Uncle . . .

VARYA. That's it, darling, there we go . . . (*They exit to* ANYA's *bedroom.*)

TROFIMOV (*tenderly*). My love . . . my spring sunshine . . .

Curtain.

ACT TWO

An old ramshackle shrine in the fields, long since abandoned; nearby a well, and some large stones, apparently old tombstone slabs, and an ancient bench. A road leading to GAEV's estate can be seen, and one side, dark poplars rising up, at the point where the cherry orchard begins. In the distance, there is a row of telegraph poles, and on the far horizon the vague outline of a big town, only visible in fine, clear weather. It will soon be sunset. CHARLOTTA, YASHA and DUNYASHA are seated on the bench; YEPIKHODOV is standing alongside, playing his guitar; they are all deep in thought. CHARLOTTA is wearing an old peaked cap; she has taken a rifle off her shoulder and is adjusting the strap buckle.

CHARLOTTA (*reflectively*). I don't have a proper passport, I don't know how old I am, but I think I'm quite young. When I was a little girl, my mother and father used to travel round all the country fairs, putting on shows, they were very good. And I used to do the *salto mortale*, and all sorts of tricks. Then when Mama and Papa died, a German lady took me in, and educated me. Very nice. I grew up, became a governess. But where I'm from, or who I am, I simply don't know. Who my parents were – maybe they weren't even married – I have no idea. (*Takes a cucumber from her pocket, begins eating it.*) Haven't a clue.

A pause.

It'd be nice to have a chat, but I've nobody to talk with . . . Not a soul.

YEPIKHODOV (*playing his guitar and singing*). 'What care I for this busy world? What's friend or foe to me . . . ?' Oh, it's so nice to play the mandolin!

DUNYASHA. That's a guitar, not a mandolin. (*Looks into a little hand-mirror and powders her nose.*)

YEPIKHODOV. To one who's madly in love, it's a mandolin . . . (*Sings.*) 'Oh, if only my heart were warmed with the fire of requited love . . . '

YASHA *joins in.*

CHARLOTTA. Ugh! These people sing so dreadfully. Like jackals.

DUNYASHA (*to* YASHA). Still, it must've been wonderful, being abroad.

YASHA. Oh, yes. I've got to agree with you on that score. (*Yawns, then lights up a cigar.*)

YEPIKHODOV. That goes without saying. I mean, everything abroad's been fully constituted for ages.

YASHA. Indeed it has.

YEPIKHODOV. I'm an educated man, I've read various remarkable books, but for the life of me I can't figure out my inclinations. I mean, whether I want to live, or else shoot myself, quite frankly, so I always carry a revolver with me just in case. Look . . . (*Shows them a revolver.*)

CHARLOTTA. There we are. I'll be off now. (*Slings on her rifle.*) Yepikhodov, you're a very clever man, and a very frightening one. Women ought to fall madly in love with you. Brrr! (*Makes to exit.*) These clever people are so stupid, there's nobody to talk to . . . I'm all on my own, absolutely, I don't have a soul, and who, or why I am, nobody knows . . . (*Exits unhurriedly.*)

YEPIKHODOV. Speaking personally, without touching on other issues, I feel bound to express the fact that, by and large, Fate deals with me pretty off-handedly, like a tempest with a not very large boat. And if I'm mistaken, well, all right, but why do I wake up this morning, for example, and look down, and there's a horrible huge spider sitting on my chest? This size, honestly . . . (*Indicates with both hands.*) And let's say you pick up your *kvas*, you go to drink it down, and you look, and there's something positively indecent in it, like a cockroach.

A pause.

Have you read Buckle?

Again, a pause.

If I might trouble you for a few words, Avdotiya?

DUNYASHA. Go on.

YEPIKHODOV. I'd like them in private, ideally . . . (*Sighs.*)

DUNYASHA (*embarrassed*). All right, then . . . but bring me my little cape first, it's beside the wardrobe. It's a bit damp out here.

YEPIKHODOV. Yes, of course, certainly. Now I know what to do with my revolver. (*He picks up his guitar and exits playing.*)

YASHA. The walking disaster! Between you and me, he's a stupid fellow.

DUNYASHA. God forbid he shoots himself. (*A pause.*) I've got so jumpy these days, I'm always in such a state. I was just a little girl when the mistress took me in, and I've grown quite unaccustomed to the simple life – I mean, look at my hands, they're as white as any lady's. I'm so highly-strung now, so delicate and refined, I'm frightened of the least thing . . . Terribly so. And if you deceive me, Yasha, well, I just don't know what it'll do to my nerves.

YASHA (*kisses her*). My little peach! Of course, a girl's got to mind her manners. If there's one thing I hate, it's a badly-behaved girl.

DUNYASHA. I'm terribly in love with you, Yasha – you're so well educated, you can talk about anything.

A pause.

YASHA (*yawns*). Mm . . . yes. Actually, the way I see it, if a girl loves a person, she must be immoral.

A pause.

Yes, it's very pleasant, a cigar in the fresh air . . . (*Listens.*) Someone's coming . . . it's the mistress . . .

DUNYASHA *impulsively embraces him.*

Walk home, as if you've just been for a swim in the river – take this path in case you bump into them and they get the idea it's me, that we've had some sort of rendezvous. I can't abide that.

DUNYASHA (*coughs a little*). Your cigar's given me a headache . . . (*Exits.*)

YASHA *remains sitting by the shrine. Enter* RANEVSKAYA, GAEV *and* LOPAKHIN.

LOPAKHIN. You've got to make up your mind, once and for all. Time won't stand still. I mean, it's a perfectly straightforward question. Do you agree to lease the land for cottages or not? You can answer in one word, yes or no. One word, that's all.

RANEVSKAYA. Who's been smoking those filthy cigars here? (*Sits down.*)

GAEV. Now that they've built the railway, it's made things very convenient. (*Sits down.*) We've been into town and had lunch . . . red to the middle pocket! I wouldn't mind going home first, have a game . . .

RANEVSKAYA. You've plenty of time.

LOPAKHIN. Just one word. (*Pleading.*) Answer me, please.

GAEV (*yawning*). What's that?

RANEVSKAYA (*looking into her purse*). You know, I had money yesterday, and now I've practically none. Poor dear Varya's feeding everybody milk soup, to make ends meet, the old folk in the kitchen get nothing but peas, and here I'm throwing money away like a mad thing. (*Drops her purse, scattering some gold coins.*) Oh God, it's gone everywhere . . . (*She is annoyed.*)

YASHA. Allow me, ma'am, I'll pick it up. (*Gathers up the coins.*)

RANEVSKAYA. Please do, Yasha. I mean, why did I go into town for lunch? That restaurant of yours with the

music was disgusting, the tablecloths smelled of soap. And
why do you drink so much, Leo? And eat so much? And
talk so much? You did it again at the restaurant today,
and it was quite out of place. All about the 70's, and the
Decadents, and to whom? Really, talking to waiters about
the Decadents!

LOPAKHIN. Yes.

GAEV (*waves his hand*). I'm incorrigible, I know . . . (*Then
irritably, to* YASHA.) What are you doing, spinning round
in front of me like that?

YASHA (*laughs*). I just can't hear your voice without
laughing.

GAEV (*to* RANEVSKAYA). Look, either he goes, or I . . .

RANEVSKAYA. Yasha, go away now, run along . . .

YASHA (*hands* RANEVSKAYA *back her purse*). Yes, I'm going . . .
(*Hardly able to keep from laughing.*) This very minute . . .
(*Exits.*)

LOPAKHIN. You know Deriganov's planning to buy your
estate, he's very rich. Apparently he's coming to the
auction in person.

RANEVSKAYA. Where did you hear that?

LOPAKHIN. That's what they're saying in town.

GAEV. Our aunt in Yaroslavl has promised to send some
money, but when, and how much, I don't know.

LOPAKHIN. And how much will she send? A hundred
thousand, say? Two hundred?

RANEVSKAYA. Well . . . Ten, or fifteen thousand, if we're
lucky.

LOPAKHIN. No, I'm sorry, but honestly, I've never met
such frivolous people as you two, you're so unbusinesslike,
it's bizarre. You're told in plain language your estate's
going to be sold off, and you just don't seem to understand.

RANEVSKAYA. But what on earth can we do? Tell us,
please!

LOPAKHIN. I am telling you. Every day I keep telling you the same thing. You've got to lease out the cherry orchard and the rest of the land for summer cottages – you've got to do it now, straightaway, the auction's practically upon us! Try and understand. Once you make up your mind about the cottages, you'll have all the money you want, and you'll be saved.

RANEVSKAYA. Summer cottages, summer residents – I'm sorry, it's all so vulgar.

GAEV. I couldn't agree more.

LOPAKHIN. I'll either start howling, or screaming, or faint dead on the spot. I can't stand this! You're wearing me out. (*To* GAEV.) And you – you're an old woman!

GAEV. I'm what?

LOPAKHIN. An old woman! (*Makes to exit.*)

RANEVSKAYA (*alarmed*). No, no, don't go – please. Please stay, my dear. Maybe we can work something out.

LOPAKHIN. Work what out!

RANEVSKAYA. Don't leave us, please, Lopakhin. I feel somehow more cheerful when you're here.

A pause.

I keep expecting something to happen, as if the house were about to cave in on top of us.

GAEV (*miles away*). In off to the corner . . . Double into the middle pocket . . .

RANEVSKAYA. We've so many sins to answer for.

LOPAKHIN. What sins can you have?

GAEV (*pops a sweet into his mouth*). They say I've eaten up my entire fortune in sweets . . . (*Laughs.*)

RANEVSKAYA. Oh, my sins . . . I've always flung my money away, like a madwoman, and I married a man who did nothing but run up debt. My husband died of champagne – he was a heavy drinker. Then I fell in love

with another man, worse luck, went off with him, and at
that point came my first punishment, a blow right to the
heart, here in this very river . . . my little boy was
drowned, and I went abroad, left it all behind, never to
return, never to see this river again . . . I just shut my
eyes to it, and ran off, almost out of my mind, but that
man followed me . . . mercilessly, cruelly. I bought a villa
near Menton, because he happened to fall ill there, and
for three years, night and day, I had no rest. That sick
man just wore me out, my very soul dried up. And then
last year, when the villa had to be sold to pay off our debts,
I left for Paris, and he robbed me of everything there,
flung me aside and went off with another woman – I tried
to poison myself . . . It was so stupid, so shameful . . .
And I suddenly felt a longing to come back to Russia, to
my own country, to my little girl . . . (*Wiping away tears.*)
Oh, God have mercy on me, forgive my sins! Don't
punish me any more! (*Takes a telegram out of her pocket.*) I got
this today from Paris . . . He asks my forgiveness, begs
me to go back . . . (*Tears up the telegram.*) That sounds like
music somewhere . . . (*Listens.*)

GAEV. Oh, that's our famous Jewish orchestra. You
remember? Four fiddles, a flute, and a double-bass.

RANEVSKAYA. They're still in existence? We should have
them to the house sometime, make an evening of it.

LOPAKHIN (*strains to hear*). I can't hear a thing . . .
(*Sings softly.*) 'The Germans can do it, isn't it funny? Turn
Russians to Frenchmen, if you give 'em some money . . . '
Yes, I saw a very funny play at the theatre yesterday.

RANEVSKAYA. It probably wasn't in the least funny. You
shouldn't go to plays, you should take a good look at
yourself. What a dreary life you all lead, so much
pointless chatter.

LOPAKHIN. That's true. It's a pretty stupid life, when you
get right down to it . . .

A pause.

My old man was a peasant, an idiot, frankly, who knew nothing, and taught me nothing. All he did was beat me when he was drunk, yes, with a stick. And deep down, I'm just as half-witted, just as much an idiot as he was. I've never learned anything, my writing's appalling. It's so bad I'm ashamed to show it to people, it's as if a pig could write.

RANEVSKAYA. You should get married, my friend.

LOPAKHIN. Yes . . . That's true.

RANEVSKAYA. You should marry our Varya. She's a nice girl.

LOPAKHIN. Yes.

RANEVSKAYA. She's from decent, simple folk, she works the whole day long, and she does love you, that's the main thing. And you've liked her for quite a while now.

LOPAKHIN. Yes, why not? I don't mind. She's a nice girl.

A pause.

GAEV. I've been offered a position at the bank. Six thousand a year . . . Have you heard about it?

RANEVSKAYA. You? In a bank? You'd better stay where you are.

FIRS *enters, carrying an overcoat.*

FIRS (*to* GAEV). Beg pardon, sir, but will you please put this on, it's getting damp.

GAEV (*puts on the coat*). Really, you're such a pest.

FIRS. That's as may be, sir, but you went off this morning without saying. (*Looks him over.*)

RANEVSKAYA. Oh, Firs, you've grown so old.

FIRS. Beg pardon, ma'am?

LOPAKHIN. She says you've got very old.

FIRS. Yes, I've been a long time alive. They were fixing to marry me off, and your Papa wasn't even born yet . . .

(*Laughs.*) When the Freedom came, I was already chief valet. And I wouldn't accept the Freedom, I stayed here with the master . . .

A pause.

Yes, I remember how happy they all were, and they didn't even know why.

LOPAKHIN. They were good times, back then. At least you could flog people.

FIRS (*mishears him*). Too true. The peasants had the masters, and the masters had the peasants, but it's all gone to the dogs now, you can't make head or tail of it.

GAEV. Oh, be quiet, Firs. I've got to go into town tomorrow. I've been promised an introduction to some general or other, who might give us a loan.

LOPAKHIN. You're wasting your time. You won't even be able to pay the interest, you can take my word for it.

RANEVSKAYA. He's raving, as usual. There isn't any general.

Enter TROFIMOV, ANYA *and* VARYA.

GAEV. Well, well, here come the girls.

ANYA. Mama's here.

RANEVSKAYA (*tenderly*). Oh, come here . . . come here, my dears . . . (*Hugs* ANYA *and* VARYA.) If you only knew how much I love you both. Sit beside me.

They all sit down.

LOPAKHIN. Our eternal student's always hanging around the young ladies.

TROFIMOV. It's none of your business.

LOPAKHIN. He'll soon be fifty, and he's still a student.

TROFIMOV. Oh, give it a rest, with your stupid jokes.

LOPAKHIN. What, losing our temper, are we, you funny creature?

TROFIMOV. Just leave me alone.

LOPAKHIN (*laughs*). All right, but permit me to ask, sir – what do you make of me, eh?

TROFIMOV. What do I make of you, Lopakhin? You're a rich man, you'll soon be a millionaire. And in the same way as a wild beast, devouring everything that crosses its path, is an essential link in the food chain, I suppose you're necessary too.

Everyone laughs.

VARYA. Petya, you'd be better talking about the planets.

RANEVSKAYA. No, let's continue the conversation we were having yesterday.

TROFIMOV. What about?

GAEV. About the proud man.

TROFIMOV. We spent a long time talking about it yesterday, without getting anywhere. In your understanding, there's some sort of mystique about a proud man. Well, that's how you see it, and you may be right, but if you take a simple view, without dressing it all up, what is there to be proud of, where's the sense in it, when man is so poorly constructed, physically, and when the vast majority of us are so coarse and unintelligent, and profoundly unhappy besides? We need to stop admiring ourselves, yes, and get down to some work.

GAEV. Well, we all die in the end.

TROFIMOV. Who knows? And what does it mean, to die? Quite possibly, man has a hundred senses, and only five of them perish with us at death, while the other ninety-five live on.

RANEVSKAYA. Oh, you're so clever, Petya!

LOPAKHIN (*ironically*). Brilliant!

TROFIMOV. Mankind marches on, constantly striving for perfection. And everything we find unattainable now, will one day be within reach, clearly understood – but we must work, we must exert all our energies to help those who seek after truth. Here in Russia, at the present time, very few people work. The vast majority of educated people, those I know, seek after nothing, do nothing, and are frankly incapable of work. They call themselves an intelligentsia, but they treat their servants as inferiors, they regard the peasants as domestic animals, they've no head for study, or serious reading, they do absolutely nothing, they talk about science, that's all, and they've little or no idea of art. They're all terribly grave, with such solemn faces, they discuss weighty matters, philosophise and so on, and meanwhile right in front of their eyes, ordinary working people eat like pigs, sleep without pillows, thirty or forty to a damp, stinking room, crawling with bedbugs, and rife with immorality . . . Well, obviously all our smart conversation is for the sole purpose of averting our eyes from that, a distraction, for ourselves and other people. Just show me where all these crèches are, that everybody keeps going on about – where are all these reading-rooms? People write about them in novels, yes, but they don't exist in fact. There's nothing but filth, vulgarity, Asiatic barbarism . . . No, I don't care for these serious faces, I'm afraid of them – them and their serious conversations. We'd do better to say nothing at all!

LOPAKHIN. You know, I get up just after four, I work from morning till night, I'm dealing constantly with my own or somebody else's money, and I see what kind of people there are around me. You only have to start doing something to realise how few decent, honest men there are. Now and again, when I can't get to sleep, I think, 'Oh, Lord, you have given us vast forests, boundless fields, endless horizons, and we who live here really ought to be a race of giants . . . '

RANEVSKAYA. That's all we need, giants . . . They're all very well in fairy stories, but elsewhere they're just frightening.

YEPIKHODOV *crosses upstage, playing a melancholy tune on his guitar.* RANEVSKAYA *is deep in thought.*

There goes Yepikhodov . . .

ANYA (*reflectively*). There goes Yepikhodov . . .

GAEV. Good people, the sun has set.

TROFIMOV. Yes.

GAEV (*quietly, but as if reciting*). O Nature, wondrous Nature, thou art radiant with eternal light, splendidly indifferent. Thou, whom we call Mother, dost unite within thyself both life and death, thou givest life, and thou takest it away . . .

VARYA (*imploring*). Uncle!

ANYA. You're at it again, Uncle!

TROFIMOV. You'd do better going in off the red, the middle pocket.

GAEV. All right, I'll shut up.

They all remain seated, deep in thought. The only sound is that of old FIRS, *muttering as usual. Suddenly a far-off noise is heard, as if in the heavens – like the sound of a breaking string, dying away, sadly.*

RANEVSKAYA. What's that?

LOPAKHIN. I don't know. Possibly a coal-tub broken loose somewhere, down the mines. A long way from here, anyway.

GAEV. Could be some sort of bird, like a heron.

TROFIMOV. Or an owl, perhaps . . .

RANEVSKAYA (*shudders*). It's horrible, whatever it is.

A pause.

FIRS. It was the same before the disaster. The owl started screeching, and the samovar wouldn't stop buzzing.

GAEV. Before what disaster?

FIRS. Before the Freedom.

A pause.

RANEVSKAYA. Well, anyway, let's go in, it's getting late. Anya dear, you're crying . . . what's the matter? (*Embraces her.*)

ANYA. It's all right, Mama, it's nothing.

TROFIMOV. Someone's coming.

A TRAMP *appears, wearing a shabby white peaked cap and an overcoat. He is slightly drunk.*

TRAMP. Beg pardon for asking, sir, but can I go through this way to the station?

GAEV. You may. Take this road.

TRAMP. I'm most deeply grateful to you, sir. (*Coughs.*) Splendid weather we're having . . . (*Recites.*) 'Brother of mine, my suffering brother . . . come forth to the Volga, whose groaning . . . ' (*To* VARYA.) Mademoiselle, spare a few kopecks for a starving Russian . . .

VARYA *is alarmed, cries out.*

LOPAKHIN (*angrily*). That's disgraceful. You know, there are limits!

RANEVSKAYA (*at a loss*). Here, here, take this . . . (*Searches in her purse.*) I've no silver . . . Oh, it doesn't matter, here's a rouble . . .

TRAMP. I'm most deeply grateful to you, ma'am! (*Exits.*)

Laughter.

VARYA (*frightened*). I'm going . . . I have to go . . . Oh, Mama, for heaven's sake, the servants have nothing to eat, and you've given him a rouble!

RANEVSKAYA. I know, I know, I'm so stupid, what can you do with me? I'll hand over everything to you when we get home. Lopakhin, lend me some more money, please.

LOPAKHIN. Yes, of course.

RANEVSKAYA. Now let's go home, it's time we were going. Incidentally, Varya, we've found you a husband – congratulations!

VARYA (*tearfully*). Mama, that's not funny.

LOPAKHIN. Okhmelia, get thee to a nunnery!

GAEV. Look, my hands are trembling. I haven't had a game of billiards in ages.

LOPAKHIN. Okhmelia, nymph, in thine orisons be all my sins remembered!

RANEVSKAYA. Come along – it'll soon be supper-time.

VARYA. He scared me. My heart's still thumping.

LOPAKHIN. Let me remind you, good people: they're selling off the cherry orchard on the 22nd of August. Bear that in mind! Think!

All exit, apart from TROFIMOV *and* ANYA.

ANYA (*laughs*). Well, thanks to that tramp giving Varya a fright – we're all alone now.

TROFIMOV. Varya's afraid we might suddenly fall in love, so she never leaves us, from one day to the next. She can't get it into that narrow mind of hers that we're above love – that the whole meaning and purpose of our life is to avoid everything petty and superficial, everything that stops us being truly free and happy. Forward! We're marching irresistibly towards that bright star, shining in the distance! Forward! Don't hang back, my friends!

ANYA (*clasping her hands*). Oh, how beautifully you speak, Petya!

A pause.

Isn't it just wonderful here today!

TROFIMOV. Yes, the weather's marvellous.

ANYA. Petya, what have you done to me? Why don't I love the cherry orchard the way I used to? I used to love it so dearly – I thought there was no place on earth like our garden.

TROFIMOV. The whole of Russia is our garden. It's a great land, a beautiful land, full of wonderful places.

A pause.

Just think, Anya, your father and grandfather, and all your ancestors were serf-owners, they owned living souls. And can't you see, looking out at you from every tree in that orchard, every leaf, every trunk, those human beings? Can't you hear their voices? Owning people – I mean, it's corrupted all of you, those who came before and now yourselves, so that neither you nor your mother, nor your uncle, are actually aware that you're living on credit, at the expense of people you wouldn't even let over your front door. We're at least two hundred years behind the times here, we still have absolutely nothing, no clearly defined attitude towards the past, all we do is philosophise, complain about being bored or drink vodka. It's quite obvious that in order to start living in the present, we first have to redeem our past, make an end of it, and we can only do that through suffering, through hard, unremitting toil. You must realise that, Anya.

ANYA. The house we live in hasn't been ours for a long time now, and I'm leaving it, I give you my word.

TROFIMOV. If you've got the house keys, fling them down the well and walk away. Be as free as the wind.

ANYA (*ecstatically*). Oh, you put it so beautifully!

TROFIMOV. You must believe me, Anya. I'm not thirty yet, I'm still a young man, still a student, but I've been through so much! As soon as winter comes, I go hungry, I get sick and anxious, as wretched as any beggar – I've been driven from pillar to post, at the mercy of fate. Yet even so, every minute of every day and every night, my soul is filled with an inexpressible feeling of anticipation – I can feel true happiness approaching, Anya, I can see it . . .

ANYA (*deep in thought*). The moon's rising.

YEPIKHODOV *is heard playing his guitar, the same melancholy song. The moon rises. Somewhere beyond the poplars* VARYA *is looking for* ANYA, *calling, 'Anya! Where are you?'*

TROFIMOV. Yes, the moon's rising.

A pause.

There it is, happiness – it's coming, it's drawing closer all the time, I can hear its footsteps already. And even if we never see it, if we never know it, well, what does it matter? Other people will!

VARYA (*offstage*). Anya! Where are you?

TROFIMOV. That Varya again! (*Angrily.*) Damned nuisance!

ANYA. Oh, never mind. Let's go down to the river. It's nice there.

TROFIMOV. All right. Let's go . . .

They exit.

VARYA (*offstage*). Anya! Anya!

Curtain.

ACT THREE

The drawing-room, separated from the ballroom by an arch. It is evening, the chandelier is lit, and the Jewish band mentioned in Act Two can be heard playing in the hall. A 'grand-rond' is being danced in the ballroom, and PISHCHIK *calls out, 'Promenade à une paire!' The dancers come into the drawing-room, with* PISHCHIK *and* CHARLOTTA *leading, followed by* TROFIMOV *and* RANEVSKAYA, *then* ANYA *and a post-office* CLERK, VARYA *and the* STATIONMASTER, *etc.* VARYA *is quietly crying, wiping away her tears as she dances.* DUNYASHA *is in the last pair, and as they pass through the drawing-room,* PISHCHIK *shouts: 'Grand-rond, balancez!' and 'Les cavaliers à genoux et remerciez vos dames!'* FIRS, *wearing a tail-coat, brings in seltzer water on a tray.* PISHCHIK *and* TROFIMOV *then re-enter the drawing-room . . .*

PISHCHIK. I've got rich blood, you see, I've already had two strokes – it makes dancing hard work, but you know what they say: if you run with the pack, you can bark if you like, but you've got to wag your tail. Anyway, I'm as strong as a horse. My late father, God rest him, was a great joker, and he used to say our ancestors, the original Simeonov-Pishchiks, were all descended from Caligula's horse, the one he made a senator. (*Sits.*) Yes, trouble is, we've no money. And a hungry dog can't think of anything but meat . . . (*Starts to snore, but instantly wakes up again.*) That's like me – all I can think about is money.

TROFIMOV. Actually, you do look a bit like a horse.

PISHCHIK. Well, a horse is a fine animal. You can sell a horse.

In the adjoining room, a game of billiards is in progress. VARYA *appears under the arch in the ballroom.*

TROFIMOV (*teasing*). Madame Lopakhin! Madame Lopakhin! . . .

VARYA (*angrily*). Huh, the mangy gent!

TROFIMOV. That's right – mangy, and proud of it!

VARYA (*bitterly*). Oh yes, we can hire musicians, but how are we going to pay them? (*Exits.*)

TROFIMOV (*to* PISHCHIK). You know, you've spent your whole life looking for money to pay the interest on your debts, but if you'd put all that wasted energy to some other use, you could've turned the world upside-down by now.

PISHCHIK. Actually Nietzsche – he's a famous philosopher, a great man, a huge intellect – he says somewhere that it's quite all right to forge banknotes.

TROFIMOV. You've read Nietzsche?

PISHCHIK. Well, no . . . it was my Dasha that told me. The position I'm in now, I'd forge them in a minute. I've got to pay out three hundred and ten roubles, day after tomorrow. I've managed to get a hundred and thirty so far . . . (*Feels in his pockets, alarmed.*) The money's gone! I've lost my money! (*In tears.*) Oh God, where is it! (*Then overjoyed.*) Here it is, it's inside the lining. Look, I've broken out in a sweat . . .

Enter RANEVSKAYA *and* CHARLOTTA.
RANEVSKAYA *is humming the 'Lezginka', a popular Caucasian folk-tune.*

RANEVSKAYA. I wonder what's keeping Leonid? What's he doing in town? Dunyasha, see if the musicians would like some tea.

TROFIMOV. The sale can't have gone ahead, most likely.

RANEVSKAYA. And the musicians came at the wrong time, we shouldn't have arranged this dance. Well, it doesn't matter . . . (*Sits down, and begins softly humming.*)

CHARLOTTA (*offers* PISHCHIK *a pack of cards*). Here you are, a pack of cards, think of a card, any one at all.

PISHCHIK. Right, I've thought of one.

CHARLOTTA. Now shuffle the pack. Good, that's fine. Now give it here, my dear Herr Pishchik. *Ein, zwei, drei!* There, now – look in your pocket . . .

PISHCHIK (*takes the card out of his breast pocket*). The eight of spades, that's absolutely right! Fancy that!

CHARLOTTA (*to* TROFIMOV, *holding the pack of cards on the palm of her hand*). Quickly, what's the top card?

TROFIMOV. What? Oh, the Queen of spades.

CHARLOTTA. That's right! (*To* PISHCHIK.) Now then, what's the top card?

PISHCHIK. Ace of hearts.

CHARLOTTA. Right! (*She claps her hands and the pack of cards vanishes.*) What lovely weather we're having!

She is answered by a mysterious female voice, apparently from under the floor: 'Oh yes, ma'am, it's magnificent.'

And you're so handsome, my ideal man . . .

And the voice responds: 'And I am liking you too, ma'am.'

STATIONMASTER (*applauds*). A lady ventriloquist, bravo!

PISHCHIK (*astonished*). Well, fancy that! Charlotta Ivanovna, you're an absolute charmer – I'm quite in love . . .

CHARLOTTA. In love? (*Shrugs.*) Can you love anybody? *Guter Mensch, aber schlechter Muzikant.*

TROFIMOV (*slaps* PISHCHIK *on the back*). Yes, you're a horse all right.

CHARLOTTA. Please, pay attention – one more trick. (*She picks up a travel-rug from a chair.*) Now, here's a rug, a fine travel rug for sale . . . (*Shakes it out.*) Would anyone care to buy it?

PISHCHIK. Fancy that!

CHARLOTTA. *Ein, zwei, drei!*

She quickly lifts up the rug to reveal ANYA *standing behind it. She curtseys and runs to her mother, gives her a hug, then runs back into the ballroom to everyone's delight.*

RANEVSKAYA (*applauds*). Bravo! Bravo!

CHARLOTTA. And now another one! *Ein, zwei, drei . . .*

She lifts up the rug to reveal VARYA, *who bows to the company.*

PISHCHIK. Fancy that!

CHARLOTTA. The end!

She flings the rug over PISHCHIK, *curtseys, and runs off to the ballroom.*

PISHCHIK (*following her out*). What a rascal! What a woman, eh? (*Exits.*)

RANEVSKAYA. Still no sign of Leonid. What on earth's taking him so long? I mean, it's all been settled, the estate's either sold, or else the auction hasn't gone ahead, why's he keeping us in suspense all this time?

VARYA (*attempting to console her*). Our uncle will have bought it, I'm sure of that.

TROFIMOV (*mockingly*). Oh, for sure.

VARYA. The Countess has given him power of attorney, to buy it in her name and take over the mortgage. She's done it for Anya's sake. God will help us, I'm sure of it – uncle'll buy it.

RANEVSKAYA. Your great-aunt in Yaroslavl sent fifteen thousand roubles, to buy the property in her name – that's how much she trusts us – and that's not even enough to pay off the interest. (*Covers her face with her hands.*) Well, my fate's being decided today, yes, indeed.

TROFIMOV (*teasing* VARYA). Madame Lopakhin!

VARYA (*angrily*). Eternal student! That's twice already you've been kicked out of university.

RANEVSKAYA. Varya, why are you so angry? He's only teasing about Lopakhin, what's wrong with that? Marry Lopakhin, if you like – he's very nice, an interesting man. And if you don't like, then don't marry him. Nobody's forcing you, my pet.

VARYA. Mama, I take this very seriously, and I'll say it straight out – yes, he's a good man, and I do like him.

RANEVSKAYA. Then marry him. I don't know what you're waiting for.

VARYA. Mama, I can't propose to him myself, can I. People have been talking about him for two years now, everybody has, but he either says nothing, or else he makes a joke about it. And I can see why. He's too busy getting rich, he's no time for me. And if I had any money, even just a little, a hundred roubles even, I'd give it all up and clear off. I'd go into a convent.

TROFIMOV. A life of bliss!

VARYA (*to* TROFIMOV). You'd think a student'd have more sense! (*Then gently, in tears.*) You've grown so ugly, Petya – so old. (*To* RANEVSKAYA, *no longer crying.*) But I can't stand to be idle, Mama. I need to be doing something, every minute of the day.

Enter YASHA.

YASHA (*trying not to laugh*). Yepikhodov's just broken a billiard cue! (*Exits.*)

VARYA. What's Yepikhodov doing here? Who gave him permission to play billiards? Honestly, I don't understand these people . . . (*Exits.*)

RANEVSKAYA. Petya, you shouldn't tease her – you can see she's got enough trouble.

TROFIMOV. Well, she makes such a fuss, she's always interfering in other people's business. She hasn't given us a minute's peace the whole summer, Anya and me. She's scared we might fall in love or something. And what's it got to do with her? It's not as if I've given her any grounds, I'm past all that vulgar rubbish. We're beyond love.

RANEVSKAYA. Then I suppose I must be beneath love. (*Extremely agitated.*) Why isn't Leonid here? If only I knew whether the estate's been sold or not! It's a disaster, it seems so incredible that I don't know what to think, I'm completely at a loss. I could start screaming right now, do something really stupid. Petya, you've got to save me. Talk to me, say something . . .

TROFIMOV. Whether it's been sold or not today, does it really matter? It's finished and done with, there's no way back – that path's long since overgrown. You might as well give up, dear lady. There's no point in deceiving yourself, you need to face the truth, even just once in your life.

RANEVSKAYA. What truth? Maybe you can see what's truth, and what isn't, but I've lost my sight, I can't see anything. Yes, you can solve all the great problems, but that's because you're too young to have suffered, to have experienced any problems of your own – isn't that so, darling? You can look boldly ahead, because you can't see anything to be frightened of, you're not expecting it, no, because life, real life, is still hidden from your young eyes. So you're braver, more honest, more profound than us, but just stop to think, if you have a generous bone in your whole body, show me some compassion. I was born here, you know, my mother and father, my grandfather lived here, and I love this house, I can't conceive of my life without the cherry orchard, and if it has to be sold now, well, you might as well sell me along with it . . . (*Embraces* TROFIMOV, *kisses him on the forehead.*) Good God, my son was drowned here . . . (*Weeps.*) Have pity on me, my dear, kind friend.

TROFIMOV. You know I feel for you with all my heart.

RANEVSKAYA. But you must say it, tell me some other way . . . (*She takes out her handkerchief, and a telegram falls onto the floor.*) I've got so much on my mind today, you can't imagine. It's so noisy in here, my heart jumps at every sound, I'm trembling all over, but I can't go to my own room, I'm afraid of the silence when I'm alone. Petya, don't be too hard on me . . . I love you like a son, and I'd willingly let you marry Anya, believe me I would, but, darling, you have to study, you have to finish your degree. You're not doing anything, you're just tossed by fate from one place to the next, it's very strange. Well, it's the truth, isn't it? And you really ought to do something about that beard, to make it grow a bit . . . (*Laughs.*) You look so funny!

TROFIMOV (*picking up the telegram*). I've no desire to be handsome.

RANEVSKAYA. That's a telegram from Paris. I get one every day. Yesterday and today. That crazy man's fallen sick again, he's in real trouble . . . He wants me to forgive him, begs me to return, and I really ought to go back to Paris, to be by his side. You look very grim, Petya, but what can I do, my darling, honestly, what can I do – he's ill, he's all alone and miserable, and who's going to look after him, who'll keep him out of harm's way, who'll give him his medicine on time? I love him, and that's that . . . He's a millstone round my neck, and he's dragging me down with him, but I love him just the same, I can't live without him. (*Squeezes* TROFIMOV's *hand*.) Don't think badly of me, Petya, don't say a word, please don't . . .

TROFIMOV (*emotionally*). God forgive me for speaking out, but I've got to – the man's robbing you blind!

RANEVSKAYA. No, no, don't say things like that!

TROFIMOV. He's a scoundrel, and you're the only one who can't see it! He's a worthless nonentity . . .

RANEVSKAYA (*angry, but in control of herself*). And you're twenty-six or twenty-seven, and still a schoolboy.

TROFIMOV. So what if I am?

RANEVSKAYA. It's time you grew up – at your age you ought to have some understanding of people in love.

You need to love someone yourself – yes, you need to fall in love, Petya! (*Angrily.*) That's right! And that purity of yours is nothing but a pose – you're a ridiculous crank, a freak . . .

TROFIMOV (*aghast*). How can you say that!

RANEVSKAYA. 'I'm beyond love!' No, you're not beyond love, you're just plain daft, as old Firs would say. At your age, not even to have a mistress!

TROFIMOV. This is dreadful! How can you say that! (*He hurries out to the ballroom, clutching his head.*) It's just dreadful . . . I can't stand it, I've got to go . . . (*Exits, then immediately re-enters.*) We're finished, do you hear! (*Exits to the hall.*)

RANEVSKAYA (*shouts after him*). Petya, wait! Don't be silly, I was only joking! Petya!

Outside in the hall, the sound of someone running upstairs, and suddenly falling back down with a great crash. ANYA and VARYA shriek, then immediately burst out laughing.

What's going on!

ANYA *rushes in, laughing.*

ANYA. It's Petya – he's fallen downstairs! (*Runs out again.*)

RANEVSKAYA. What a strange boy he is.

Meanwhile the STATIONMASTER stands in the middle of the ballroom, and begins reciting Aleksei Tolstoy's poem 'The Sinner'. Everyone stops to listen, but he has hardly spoken a few lines when a waltz is struck up in the hall, and the recital is interrupted, as the dancing begins. TROFIMOV, ANYA, VARYA and RANEVSKAYA come in from the hall.

Come on, Petya . . . pure of heart . . . please forgive me. Come, let's dance . . .

She begins dancing with TROFIMOV, and ANYA dances with VARYA. FIRS enters, and leans his walking-stick against the side door. YASHA also enters from the drawing-room, to watch the dancing.

YASHA. Well, how are things, old man?

FIRS. Not great. Time was, we had generals, and barons
and admirals at our dances, now we've got to send for the
post-office clerk and the stationmaster, yes, and they're
not that keen to come, neither. I'm feeling a bit weak,
myself. The old master, her granddad, he used to make us
take sealing-wax, for any sort of illness. I've taken sealing-
wax every day for the last twenty years or more. Maybe
it's that what's kept me alive.

YASHA. You give me a pain, old man. (*Yawns.*) It's about
time you snuffed it.

FIRS. Huh! And you're just daft! (*Mutters.*)

TROFIMOV *and* RANEVSKAYA *are dancing in the
ballroom, then move into the drawing-room.*

RANEVSKAYA. *Merci.* I'll sit down for bit . . . (*Sits down.*)
I'm tired.

Enter ANYA, *very agitated.*

ANYA. There was somebody in the kitchen just now – he
says the cherry orchard's been sold.

RANEVSKAYA. Sold to whom?

ANYA. He didn't say. And now he's gone.

She begins dancing with TROFIMOV, *and they exit to the
ballroom.*

YASHA. It was some old man raving on. Nobody we know.

FIRS. And the master's not home yet. He's wearing his light
overcoat, too – he'll catch cold, like as not. Huh, these
young people, they've no sense.

RANEVSKAYA. Honestly, I could die right now. Yasha, go
and find out who it was sold to.

YASHA. He's cleared off long ago, the old goat. (*Laughs.*)

RANEVSKAYA (*slightly irritated*). What are you laughing at?
What are you so happy about?

YASHA. It's that Yepikhodov – he really is a scream. He's so stupid – the walking disaster.

RANEVSKAYA. So, where will you go, Firs, if the estate's sold?

FIRS. I'll go wherever you tell me, ma'am.

RANEVSKAYA. Why are you looking like that? Are you unwell? You know, you really ought to be in bed . . .

FIRS. Oh, yes . . . (*With a hint of mockery.*) And if I go to bed, who's going to hand things round, and look after everybody? There's only me, in the whole house.

YASHA (*to* RANEVSKAYA). Madame, permit me to make a request of you, if you'd be so kind! If you're going back to Paris, please do me a favour and take me with you. I can't stay here, it's absolutely impossible. (*Looking round, in an aside.*) I mean, I don't need to tell you, you can see for yourself, this is a backward country, the people have no morals, and it's so boring! The food in the kitchen's disgusting, and that Firs creature goes round muttering the whole time, he doesn't make any sense. Take me with you, ma'am, please!

Enter PISHCHIK.

PISHCHIK. May I have the honour, fair lady, of this little waltz? (RANEVSKAYA *goes off with him.*) You're quite enchanting, but if I could borrow a hundred and eighty roubles from you . . . well, if I could . . . A hundred and eighty, that's all . . .

They begin dancing, and pass through into the ballroom.

YASHA (*sings softly*). 'Oh, can't you see how troubled is my heart . . . '

A figure appears in the ballroom, wearing a grey top-hat, and checked trousers. Shouts of 'Bravo, Charlotta Ivanovna!', as she flings her arms about and jumps in the air.

DUNYASHA (*stops to powder her nose*). Well, Firs Nikolaevich, the mistress ordered me to dance – there's too many gentlemen, and not enough ladies – but dancing makes me dizzy, and my heart's pounding. And that post-office clerk's just said something that's taken my breath away.

The music dies down.

FIRS. So what did he say?

DUNYASHA. You're like a little flower, he said.

YASHA (*yawns*). Ignorant peasant . . . (*Exits.*)

DUNYASHA. Like a flower . . . You know, I'm quite a sensitive person, I'm terribly fond of compliments.

FIRS. You'll get your head turned, you will.

Enter YEPIKHODOV.

YEPIKHODOV. It's obvious you don't want to see me, Dunyasha – it's as if I was some sort of insect. (*Sighs.*) Oh, what a life!

DUNYASHA. What do you want?

YEPIKHODOV. Well, no doubt you're right. (*Sighs.*) On the other hand, of course, looking at it from a point of view, then you – if I may permit myself to say so, and excuse my frankness – you've completely reduced me to a state of mind. I know my own destiny – every day some new disaster befalls me, I've got well used to it, so I can look upon my fate with a smile. But you gave me your word, and although I . . .

DUNYASHA. Please, let's talk later – just leave me in peace. I'm in a dream now. (*Toying with her fan.*)

YEPIKHODOV. Yes, some new mishap every day, and if you'll allow me to say so, I just smile – laugh, even.

VARYA enters from the ballroom.

VARYA. Are you still here, Yepikhodov? You really are an ill-mannered wretch. (*To* DUNYASHA.) You'd better go, Dunyasha. (*To* YEPIKHODOV.) First you break a cue playing billiards, now you're strolling round the drawing-room like an invited guest!

YEPIKHODOV. If you'll allow me to say so, I don't think you can sue me for damages.

VARYA. I'm not suing you, I'm telling you! You do nothing but wander from one place to the next, you never do any work. We employ a clerk, but God only knows what for.

YEPIKHODOV (*offended*). Whether I work or walk about, yes, or eat, or play billiards, that's a matter for older and wiser heads to judge – more understanding . . .

VARYA (*explodes*). You dare say that to me! You dare! You think I don't understand? Get out of here! Go on, get out!

YEPIKHODOV (*cringing*). Please express yourself a little more delicately . . .

VARYA (*beside herself*). If you don't get out of my sight this instant . . . Out! Out!

VARYA *pursues him to the door.*

Walking disaster! Now get out and stay out! Don't let me see you in this house ever again!

YEPIKHODOV *exits, shouts from behind the door: 'I'm going to complain about you!'*

Oho, coming back in, are you? (*Seizes* FIRS' *walking-stick from beside the door.*) Come on . . . Come on, then, and I'll show you . . . Are you coming in? Eh? Take that! (*Swings the stick just as* LOPAKHIN *comes through the door.*)

LOPAKHIN. Why, thank you, most humbly!

VARYA (*annoyed, sarcastically*). I beg your pardon.

LOPAKHIN. Don't mention it. I'm most grateful for such a warm reception.

VARYA. It's not worth your gratitude. (*Walks away, then looks round and asks gently.*) I didn't hurt you, did I?

LOPAKHIN. No, not at all. I'll have an enormous bump, that's all.

Voices are heard in the ballroom: 'Lopakhin's arrived! He's here now!'

PISHCHIK. The very same, large as life! (*Embraces* LOPAKHIN.) There's a faint whiff of brandy about you, my dear chap. And we've been enjoying ourselves here too.

Enter RANEVSKAYA.

RANEVSKAYA. Lopakhin, is that you? What kept you so long? Where's Leonid?

LOPAKHIN. He came home with me, he's just . . .

RANEVSKAYA (*agitated*). Well, what happened? Was it sold? Tell me!

LOPAKHIN (*embarrassed, trying not to show his delight*). The auction was over by four o'clock . . . We missed the train, so we had to wait till half-past nine . . . (*A deep sigh.*) Phew, I feel a bit dizzy . . .

Enter GAEV. *He is carrying some parcels in one hand, and wiping away tears with the other.*

RANEVSKAYA. What's the matter, Leo? Leo, what is it? (*Impatiently, in tears.*) For God's sake, tell me!

GAEV *doesn't answer, waves his hand despairingly.*

GAEV (*to* FIRS, *weeping*). Here, take these . . . There's some anchovies, and fresh herrings . . . I've had nothing to eat all day . . . Oh, God, what I've gone through . . .

The billiard room door is open, and we can hear the click of billiard balls, and the voice of YASHA: *'That's seven, and eighteen!'* GAEV's *expression has changed, and he is no longer weeping.*

I'm dreadfully tired. Help me get changed, Firs. (*Exits to his own room through the ballroom, followed by* FIRS.)

PISHCHIK. So, what about the auction? Come on, tell us!

RANEVSKAYA. Has the cherry orchard been sold?

LOPAKHIN. Yes.

RANEVSKAYA. Who bought it?

LOPAKHIN. I did.

A silence. RANEVSKAYA *is overwhelmed. If it weren't for the table and chair beside her, she would fall down.* VARYA *detaches the keys from her belt, flings them to the floor in the middle of the drawing-room, and walks out.*

I bought it! Ladies and gentlemen, please, wait – I've a
bit of a thick head, I can't speak . . . (*Laughs.*) When we
got to the auction, Deriganov was already there. Leonid
Andreyich had only fifteen thousand, and straight away
Deriganov bid another thirty, on top of the mortgage.
Well, I could see how things were going, so I waded in
with forty thousand. He went up to forty-five, so I bid
fifty-five. He would go up by five, you see, and I'd bid
another ten. Well, it finished eventually. I bid ninety
thousand roubles over and above the mortgage, and it
was knocked down to me. The cherry orchard's mine
now. All mine! (*Laughs.*) Tell me I'm drunk, or crazy, tell
me I'm imagining all this . . . (*Stamps his feet.*) No, don't
laugh at me! If only my father and grandfather could rise
up out of their graves, and see all that's happened – how
their little Yermolai, their abused, semi-literate Yermolai,
who used to run around barefoot in winter – how that
same Yermolai has bought this estate, the most beautiful
spot on earth. Yes, I've bought the land on which my
father and grandfather were slaves, where they weren't
even allowed into the kitchen. I must be asleep, it's all just
a dream, it's all in the mind . . . It's your imagination at
work, shrouded in mystery . . . (*Picks up the keys, smiling
affectionately.*) She threw down the keys, to show she's no
longer mistress of this house. (*Jingles the keys.*) Well, it
doesn't matter.

The musicians are heard tuning up.

Hey, musicians, let's hear you play! Come on in, all of
you, and watch Yermolai Lopakhin take his axe to the
cherry orchard, see the trees falling down! We're going to
build cottages here, and our grandsons and great-
grandsons'll see a whole new life . . . Come on, let's have
some music!

The orchestra starts playing. RANEVSKAYA *slumps into a
chair, weeping bitterly.* LOPAKHIN *reproaches her.*

Why didn't you listen to me, eh? Why not? Oh, my poor
dear lady, there's no going back now. (*A catch in his voice.*)
God, I wish all this was over and done with, I wish our
miserable, disjointed lives could be somehow changed.

PISHCHIK (*takes him by the arm, whispers*). She's crying. Let's go into the ballroom, and leave her be . . . Come on . . . (*Leads* LOPAKHIN *towards the ballroom.*)

LOPAKHIN. What's going on? Hey, musicians, play up so we can hear you! Everything's to be as I want it. (*Ironically.*) Come on, here comes the new landlord, the owner of the cherry orchard! (*Accidentally bumps into a table, almost knocks over the candelabra.*) What the hell, I can pay for it! (*Exits with* PISHCHIK.)

There is no-one left now in the ballroom or drawing-room, apart from RANEVSKAYA, *who sits hunched up, still weeping bitterly. The orchestra plays quietly in the background.* ANYA *and* TROFIMOV *come running in.* ANYA *goes up to her mother and kneels down before her.* TROFIMOV *remains by the ballroom door.*

ANYA. Mama! Mama, you're crying! Oh, my dear, kind, good Mama, darling Mama, I love you so much . . . God bless you, Mama. The cherry orchard's sold, it's all gone now, it's true, it's true, but don't cry, Mama, please – you still have your life in front of you, you still have your good, pure heart . . . Come with me, darling Mama, we'll leave here, we'll go away together. We can plant a new orchard somewhere, even more beautiful, and when you see it, you'll understand, and joy – a deep, quiet joy will descend on your soul, Mama, like the sun in the evening, and you'll smile again . . . Come, my darling . . . Come . . .

Curtain.

ACT FOUR

The stage is set as in Act One. There are no curtains on the windows, no pictures on the walls, and only a few items of furniture, piled into one corner, as if for a sale. A sense of emptiness. There are various pieces of luggage, suitcases, bundles, etc., lying by the outer door and upstage. The door to the left is open, and we can hear the voices of VARYA *and* ANYA. LOPAKHIN *stands waiting.* YASHA *is holding a tray of glasses, filled with champagne.* YEPIKHODOV *is tying up a box in the hallway. A buzz of voices in the background off-stage – the peasants have arrived to say goodbye.* GAEV *is heard:* 'Thank you, my lads, thank you.'

YASHA. That's the common folk come to say goodbye. The way I see it, Mr Lopakhin, they're decent people, but they're none too bright.

The buzz subsides. RANEVSKAYA *and* GAEV *enter through the hall; she is no longer crying, but she is very pale, her cheeks are trembling, and she can scarcely speak.*

GAEV. Lyuba, you've given them your purse. You shouldn't have done that, you really shouldn't.

RANEVSKAYA. I couldn't help it. I couldn't stop myself.

They exit. LOPAKHIN *calls after them.*

LOPAKHIN. Please! Won't you have a glass before you leave? Just one glass, please! I didn't think to bring any from town, and I could only find one bottle at the station. Come on, please.

A pause.

Ladies, gentlemen, please – don't you want a drink? (*Steps back from the door.*) If I'd known that I wouldn't have bought it. Well, I'm not going to drink either.

YASHA *sets the tray carefully down on a chair.*

Have a drink, Yasha, you might as well.

YASHA. Here's to us, we're on our way! And good luck to them left behind! (*Drinks.*) Hm – this isn't genuine champagne, I can tell you that.

LOPAKHIN. It was eight roubles the bottle.

A pause.

It's damnably cold in here.

YASHA. They haven't lit the stoves, we're leaving anyway. (*Laughs.*)

LOPAKHIN. What is it?

YASHA. I'm just pleased.

LOPAKHIN. It's October outside, but it's sunny and mild, like a summer's day. Good building weather. (*Looks at his watch, then at the door.*) Hello, listen, the train goes in exactly forty-six minutes! So you'll have to leave for the station in twenty minutes. Better get a move on.

TROFIMOV *enters from outside, wearing an overcoat.*

TROFIMOV. I think it's time we were going now. The horses are ready. I'm damned if I know where my galoshes are. Must've lost them. (*Calls through the door.*) Anya, my galoshes aren't here! I can't find them!

LOPAKHIN. And I've got to go to Kharkov. I'll be coming with you in the same train. I'll be spending the whole winter in Kharkov. I've been loafing around with you people all the time, I can't stand doing nothing. I can't live without work, I don't know what to do with my hands. It's strange the way they flap about , as if they belong to somebody else.

TROFIMOV. Well we're leaving now, so you'll be able to get back to your useful labours.

LOPAKHIN. Look, have a drink.

TROFIMOV. No, I won't.

LOPAKHIN. So, you're off to Moscow now?

TROFIMOV. Yes, I'll see them into town, and tomorrow I'll head for Moscow.

LOPAKHIN. Yes . . . I suppose the professors won't be giving any lectures – they'll be waiting till you turn up.

TROFIMOV. That's none of your business.

LOPAKHIN. And how many years have you spent at university?

TROFIMOV. Why don't you think up something new? That's pretty stale beer. (*Looking for his galoshes.*) You know, we probably won't ever see each other again, so you'll forgive me if I offer you some advice: don't keep waving your arms. You want to get out of that habit, flapping your arms, you really do. And all that stuff about building cottages, calculating how you're going to make freeholders out of summer residents, that's just flapping your arms as well . . . Even so, I like you. You have very fine, delicate fingers, like an artist – you have a fine, delicate soul . . .

LOPAKHIN (*embraces him*). Goodbye, my dear chap. Thanks for everything. Here, take some money for the road, if you want.

TROFIMOV. What for? I don't need it.

LOPAKHIN. But you haven't got any.

TROFIMOV. Yes, I have. Thanks, anyway. I got some money for a translation. Look, here it is, in my pocket. (*Anxiously.*) But I still haven't found my galoshes!

VARYA (*from the adjoining room*). Here, take your rubbish away! (*Flings a pair of rubber galoshes onto the stage.*)

TROFIMOV. Varya, why are you so angry? Hm . . . And these aren't my galoshes either!

LOPAKHIN. You know, I sowed nearly three thousand acres of poppies in the spring, and that's forty thousand clear profit now. And when my poppies were in flower, well, that was some sight! Yes, as I was saying, I've made forty thousand, so I'm offering you a loan, if you like, because I can afford to. So why turn up your nose at it? I'm a peasant, let's face it . . .

TROFIMOV. Your father was a peasant, mine had a chemist's shop − that proves absolutely nothing.

LOPAKHIN *takes out his wallet.*

No, no, stop, put that away . . . Supposing you were to offer me two hundred thousand, I wouldn't take it. I'm a free man. And everything you people value so highly, rich and poor alike, hasn't the slightest power over me − it's just so much fluff, carried along on the wind. I can get along without you, I can walk right by you, strong and proud. Yes, mankind is marching towards the highest truth, the highest form of happiness possible on this earth, and I'm in the front ranks!

LOPAKHIN. But will you get there?

TROFIMOV. Yes, I shall.

A pause.

I'll get there, or I'll show other people the way.

In the distance, the sound of axes at work.

LOPAKHIN. Anyway, goodbye, dear chap. It's time we were going. We're standing here scoring points off one another, and life's just passing us by. You know, when I put in a hard day's work, without getting tired, I feel easier in my mind, and it's as if I know why I exist. But you just think, my friend, how many people there are in Russia, and they've no idea what they're living for. Well, no matter, the wheels circulate just the same, eh? I hear Gaev's got himself a job, he's taken a post at the bank, six thousand a year . . . He won't stick it out, though − he's bone idle . . .

ANYA (*in the doorway*). Mama's asking if you would mind not cutting the orchard down till she's gone.

TROFIMOV. Really, you'd think you might've had a bit of tact . . . (*Exits through the hall.*)

LOPAKHIN. Yes, yes, of course, right away . . . Idiots, honestly. (*Follows them out.*)

ANYA. Have they sent Firs to the hospital?

YASHA. I told them this morning. I expect they have.

ANYA (*to* YEPIKHODOV, *crossing the drawing-room*). Yepikhodov, please check if they've taken Firs to the hospital yet.

YASHA (*annoyed*). I told Yegor this morning. Honestly, that's the tenth time you've asked.

YEPIKHODOV. In my conclusive opinion, the venerable old Firs isn't worth repairing, it's time he joined his ancestors. And frankly, I can only envy him. (*Puts a suitcase down on top of a hatbox and crushes it.*) Oh yes, of course. I knew that would happen. (*Exits.*)

YASHA (*mockingly*). Walking disaster . . .

VARYA (*offstage*). Have they taken Firs to the hospital?

ANYA. Yes.

VARYA. So why didn't they take this letter for the doctor?

ANYA. Well, we'd better send it after them . . . (*Exits.*)

VARYA (*from the adjoining room*). Where's Yasha? Tell him his mother's arrived, she wants to say goodbye to him.

YASHA (*waves his arm dismissively*). Honestly, they'd try anyone's patience.

DUNYASHA *is fussing around with the luggage. Seeing* YASHA *alone, she goes up to him.*

DUNYASHA. You might at least look at me, Yasha, even just once. You're going away . . . abandoning me . . . (*Begins to cry, and flings her arms round his neck.*)

YASHA. What on earth is there to cry for? (*Drinks champagne.*) In six days' time I'll be back in Paris. Tomorrow we'll get on the express train and take off, and that'll be the last you'll see of us. I can hardly believe it. *Vive la France!* I can't be doing with this place, it's not my style . . . there's no help for it. I'm sick to death of ignorance – yes, I've had my fill. (*Drinks champagne.*) So, what are you crying for? Have a bit of decorum, then you won't cry.

DUNYASHA (*fixes her make-up, looking into a pocket-mirror*). You'll send me a letter from Paris, won't you? I mean, I did love you, Yasha, I truly did. And I'm a sensitive person, Yasha.

YASHA. There's someone coming. (*Starts busying himself with the luggage, quietly humming a tune.*)

Enter RANEVSKAYA, GAEV, ANYA *and* CHARLOTTA.

GAEV. We ought to be on our way. We haven't much time. (*Looks at* YASHA.) Someone stinks of herrings.

RANEVSKAYA. We should be getting into the carriages in ten minutes . . . (*Looks round the room.*) Goodbye, dear house, goodbye, old grandfather. The winter will pass, and then it'll be spring, but you won't be here, they'll have pulled you down. Yes, the things these old walls have seen! (*Kisses her daughter warmly.*) Oh, my precious darling, you look radiant, your eyes are sparkling like diamonds. Are you happy? Truly?

ANYA. Yes, yes! We're beginning a new life, Mama!

GAEV (*gaily*). Indeed we are, everything's fine now. We were all so anxious and upset before the sale of the orchard, but afterwards, when the business was settled once and for all, we were able to relax, we even cheered up a bit . . . I'm an employee of the bank now, yes, a financial type . . . Red to the middle pocket – and you're looking much better yourself, Lyuba, you can't deny it.

RANEVSKAYA. Yes. My nerves are better, that's true.

They help her on with her hat and coat.

I'm sleeping well now. Yasha, take out my things. It's time we were going. (*To* ANYA.) My darling girl, we'll meet again soon . . . I'm going to Paris, I can live there on the money your great-aunt in Yaroslavl sent us to buy the property – three cheers for the Countess! – but I'm afraid it won't last very long.

ANYA. You'll come back, Mama, you'll come back soon, won't you. I've got to take my exams at the high school, and then I'll work, I'll be able to help you. We can read all sorts of books together, Mama, you and I, can't we. (*Kisses her mother's hand.*) We'll sit reading in the autumn evenings, we'll read lots of books, and a whole new, wonderful life'll open up for us . . . (*Dreamily.*) Mama, come home soon . . .

RANEVSKAYA. Yes, yes, I'll come home, my treasure. (*Hugs her daughter.*)

Enter LOPAKHIN. CHARLOTTA *begins quietly humming a tune.*

GAEV. Charlotta's happy – she's singing!

CHARLOTTA (*picks up a bundle, resembling a baby all wrapped up*). There, there – bye-bye, my baby . . .

We hear a baby's cry: 'Wah! Wah!'

There now, hush, my lovely boy, my little darling.

Wah! Wah!

Oh, you get on my nerves! (*Flings the bundle down on the floor.*) So – you'll find me a new position, won't you. I can't stay here like this.

LOPAKHIN. We'll find you something, Charlotta, don't worry.

GAEV. They're all abandoning us, Varya's leaving . . . we've suddenly become superfluous.

CHARLOTTA. I've nowhere to stay in town. I'll have to go . . . (*Starts humming.*) Well, who cares?

Enter PISHCHIK.

LOPAKHIN. Huh, wonders'll never cease! . . .

PISHCHIK (*out of breath, panting*). Oh, let me catch my breath . . . I'm completely exhausted . . . Dearest good friends . . . Please . . . Give me some water . . .

GAEV. You'll be after money, I suppose? Well, if you'll
excuse me, I'll get out of harm's way . . . (*Exits.*)

PISHCHIK. It's been ages since I was last here . . .
My dearest lady . . . (*To* LOPAKHIN.) And you're here
too, sir . . . I'm delighted to see you . . . a hugely clever
man, yes . . . here, take it, take it . . . (*Offers* LOPAKHIN
money.) There's four hundred roubles . . . That means I
still owe you eight hundred and forty . . .

LOPAKHIN (*shrugs his shoulders in bewilderment*). I must be
dreaming . . . Where on earth did you get this?

PISHCHIK. Wait, wait . . . Oh, it's so hot . . . Yes, a most
extraordinary event. Some Englishmen just turned up, and
found some sort of white clay on my land . . . (*To*
RANEVSKAYA.) And here's four hundred for you . . .
lovely, wonderful creature . . . (*Gives her the money.*) You'll
get the rest later. (*Has a drink of water.*) Yes, a young chap
was telling us on the carriage just now, it seems there's
some great philosopher or other, telling us we should all
jump off the roof . . . 'Go on and jump!' he says, it'll
solve all your problems. (*Wonderingly.*) Fancy that! More
water, please!

LOPAKHIN. So who exactly are these Englishmen?

PISHCHIK. I've leased them the plot with the clay for
twenty-four years . . . And now, if you'll excuse me . . .
I must dash . . . I've got to go and see Znoikov, then on
to Kardamonov . . . I owe money to everybody . . .
(*Drinks.*) I wish you all good health . . . I'll look in again
on Thursday . . .

RANEVSKAYA. We're moving into town right now, and
tomorrow I'll be going abroad . . .

PISHCHIK (*alarmed*). What? What are you going into town
for? Ah, I see now – the furniture . . . all these cases . . .
Oh, well, it can't helped . . . (*Tearfully.*) No, it's too bad . . .
You know, they're highly intelligent people . . . these
Englishmen . . . Well, it doesn't matter . . . I hope
you'll be happy . . . God will look after you . . . Never
mind . . . All good things come to an end . . . (*Kisses*

RANEVSKAYA's *hand*.) And if word reaches you that I've
come to my end, you'll perhaps remember this old . . .
this old horse, and you'll say: 'Well, there was a man like
that once . . . Simeonov-Pishchik his name was . . . God
rest his soul.' . . . What remarkable weather we're having,
really extraordinary . . . Yes . . . (*Exits, deeply moved, but
almost immediately returns and speaks from the doorway*.) My little
Dasha sends you her compliments! (*Exits*.)

RANEVSKAYA. We can go now. Though I'm leaving with
two things still on my mind. One of them is poor Firs,
he's not well. (*Looks at her watch*.) We can wait another five
minutes.

ANYA. They've taken Firs to the hospital. Yasha sent him
this morning.

RANEVSKAYA. And my second worry is poor Varya. She's
so used to rising early and working, and now she's got
no work to do, she's like a fish out of water. She's grown
so thin, and pale, and she cries all the time, the poor
darling . . .

A pause.

You know all this perfectly well, Yermolai. I used to
dream of seeing her married to you, and indeed all the
signs were that you two would get married. (*Whispers to
ANYA, who then nods to CHARLOTTA, and both exit*.) She
loves you, and you obviously like her, and for the life of
me I can't see why you steer clear of each other, I just
don't understand it.

LOPAKHIN. I don't understand it either, to tell you the
truth. It's all so funny . . . If we've still time, well, I'm
ready now . . . Let's settle it once and for all – if you're
not here, I don't think I'll ever propose.

RANEVSKAYA. Excellent! It'll only take a minute, I'm sure.
I'll call her right now . . .

LOPAKHIN. And there's champagne handy too. (*Looks at the
glasses*.) Huh – empty, somebody's drunk it all.

YASHA *coughs.*

Lapping it up, that's called . . .

RANEVSKAYA (*animatedly*). Wonderful. We can all go out . . .
Yasha, *allez*! I'll call her in . . . (*At the door.*) Varya, leave
all that, and come here. Come on! (*Exits with* YASHA.)

LOPAKHIN (*looks at his watch*). Yes . . .

A pause. Offstage, a stifled laugh and whispering, VARYA *finally
enters.*

VARYA (*inspects the luggage at some length*). That's strange,
I can't find it anywhere . . .

LOPAKHIN. What are you looking for?

VARYA. I packed these myself, and now I can't remember.

A pause.

LOPAKHIN. So where are you off to now, Miss Varvara?

VARYA. Me? I'm going to the Ragulins' . . . I've agreed to
look after the house for them . . . I'll be a sort of
housekeeper.

LOPAKHIN. And that's at Yashnevo? That'll be about fifty
miles from here.

A pause.

So, life in this house is over now.

VARYA (*examining the luggage*). Where on earth is it? . . .
Maybe I packed it away in the trunk . . . Yes, life's
finished in this house . . . there'll be nothing left . . .

LOPAKHIN. And I'm off to Kharkov now . . . by the same
train. I've a lot of business on hand. I'm leaving
Yepikhodov here to look after the place. I've taken him
on.

VARYA. Not really!

LOPAKHIN. This time last year we'd already had snow, if
you remember, and now it's so mild and sunny. It's cold
nonetheless . . . three degrees below.

VARYA. I haven't looked.

A pause.

Our thermometer's broken anyway.

A pause.

Someone calls through the door from outside: 'Mr Lopakhin!'

LOPAKHIN (*as if he had been waiting for this call*). Just coming! (*Hurriedly exits.*)

VARYA *is sitting on the floor, lays her head on a bundle of dresses, and begins quietly sobbing. The door opens, and* RANEVSKAYA *tentatively enters.*

RANEVSKAYA. Well?

A pause.

We have to go.

VARYA (*has stopped crying, dried her eyes*). Yes, Mama dear, it's time. I'll manage to get to the Ragulins' today, as long as I don't miss the train . . .

RANYEVSKAYA (*calls offstage*). Anya, put on your things, please.

ANYA *enters, followed by* GAEV *and* CHARLOTTA. GAEV *is wearing a warm overcoat with a hood. The servants and coachmen assemble.* YEPIKHODOV *is fussing around with the luggage.*

Well, now we can get on our way.

ANYA (*delightedly*). Yes, we're on our way!

GAEV. My friends, my dearly beloved friends! Now that we're leaving this house for ever, how can I keep silent, how can I restrain myself from giving vent, at parting, to those emotions which fill up my entire being . . .

ANYA (*pleading*). Uncle!

VARYA. Dearest uncle, please don't.

GAEV (*glumly*). Double the red to the middle pocket . . . I'll be quiet . . .

Enter TROFIMOV, *followed by* LOPAKHIN.

TROFIMOV. Come along, folks, it's time we were going.

LOPAKHIN. Yepikhodov, my coat.

RANEVSKAYA. I'll sit here for another minute. It's as if I've never noticed what the walls of this house were like, or the ceilings, and now I'm looking at them so longingly, with such tender love . . .

GAEV. I can remember when I was six years old, sitting on this window-sill on Trinity Sunday, watching my father going out to church . . .

RANEVSKAYA. Have they taken everything out?

LOPAKHIN. I think so. (*To* YEPIKHODOV, *helping him on with his overcoat.*) Off you go, Yepikhodov, make sure everything's in order.

YEPIKHODOV (*hoarse-voiced*). Don't worry, Mr Lopakhin.

LOPAKHIN. What's the matter with your voice?

YEPIKHODOV. I had a drink of water just now, and I think I've swallowed something.

YASHA (*contemptuously*). Peasants . . .

RANEVSKAYA. We're going – and there won't be a living soul left here . . .

LOPAKHIN. No, not until the spring.

VARYA *jerks an umbrella out of a bundle, almost as if she were about to strike somebody with it;* LOPAKHIN *pretends to be alarmed.*

VARYA. Don't be silly. As if I would . . .

TROFIMOV. Come on, people, let's get into the carriages . . . It's time! The train'll be arriving any second.

VARYA. Petya, look, there they are – your galoshes, beside that suitcase. (*Touched.*) Oh, and they're so old and dirty . . .

TROFIMOV (*putting on his galoshes*). Right, come on, let's go!

GAEV (*deeply moved, on the verge of tears*). The train . . . the station . . . Cannon to the middle pocket, double the white to the corner . . .

RANEVSKAYA. Let's go . . .

LOPAKHIN. Is everyone here? Nobody left behind? (*Locks the door on the left.*) There's stuff packed away in there, I'll need to lock it. Right, we're off!

ANYA. Goodbye, house! Goodbye, old life!

TROFIMOV. And hello, new life! (*Exits with* ANYA.)

VARYA *takes a last look round the room and unhurriedly exits, followed by* YASHA, *and* CHARLOTTA *carrying her little dog.*

LOPAKHIN. So – that's it until the spring. Out you go, ladies and gentlemen . . . Goodbye . . . (*Exits.*)

RANEVSKAYA *and* GAEV *remain alone together. It is as if they have been waiting for this moment, and they fling their arms around each other, sobbing quietly and restrainedly, so as not to be overheard.*

GAEV (*despairingly*). My sister, my dear sister . . .

RANEVSKAYA. Oh, my dearest darling, wonderful cherry orchard! My life, my youth, my happiness, goodbye! Goodbye!

Offstage, ANYA *gaily calling her: 'Mama!', and* TROFIMOV, *calling excitedly: 'Hall-oo!'*

One last look round these walls, these windows . . . Our dear mother loved just walking about in this room . . .

GAEV. Oh, sister, sister . . .

Offstage, the voices of ANYA: *'Mama!', and* TROFIMOV: *'Hall-oo!'*

RANEVSKAYA. We're coming! (*They exit.*)

The stage is empty. We hear all the doors being locked, then the carriages departing. Everything is quiet – the silence broken only by the sombre sound of an axe, dully thudding against a tree. We hear footsteps. FIRS *appears, entering from the door to the right, dressed as usual in his jacket and white waistcoat, with slippers on his feet. He is very ill.*

FIRS (*goes up to the door, tries the handle*). Locked . . . They've all gone. (*Sits down on the settee.*) They've forgotten about me . . . Well, no matter . . . I'll just sit here for a bit . . . I don't suppose the master'll have put on his furs, he'll have gone off in his overcoat . . . (*Sighs anxiously.*) Didn't have me to look after him . . . Young folks these days . . . (*Mumbles something incoherently.*) Yes, life's gone by, it's as if I've never lived. (*Lies down.*) I'll lie down for a while . . . You've got no strength left in you, not a bit . . . No, you're not worth a light . . . (*Lies motionless.*)

From far away, as if coming from the sky, the sound of a breaking string – a melancholy, dying fall. Silence descends then, and the only thing we hear is a distant axe, striking a tree in the orchard.

Curtain.

Guide to Pronunciation of Names

Where the stress in English polysyllables tends to fall on the penultimate syllable, Russian stress, which is also heavier, is less predictable, and this gives rise to pronunciation difficulties, quite apart from its unfamiliar consonant clusters. The following is an approximation of those names and places which might present difficulty in the spoken text, with the stressed syllables clearly marked:

Aivazovsky   Aye-vah-ZAWF-ski
Aleko   Ah-LEH-ko
Alekseevich   Ah-lek-SAY-yeh-vitch
Alexandrovna   Ah-lek-SAHN-drov-nah
Alexeyevich   Ah-lek-SAY-yeh-vitch
Anastasy   Ah-nah-STAH-say
Andrei   Ahn-DRAY
Andreyevna   An-DRAY-yehv-nah
Andreyich   An-DRAY-itch
Andryusha   An-DRYOO-sha
Anfisa   An-FEE-sa
Anya   AH-nyah
Arkadina   Ar-KAH-dee-nah
Astrov   AH-stroff
Avdotiya   Ahv-DAW-tee-yah
Basmanny   Bass-MAH-ny
Batyushkov   BAH-tyoosh-koff
Berdichev   Ber-DEE-tcheff
Bobik   BAW-bik
Boris   Baw-REES
Chadin   CHAH-deen
Chekhartmà   Cheh-khart-MAH
Cheremshà   Cheh-rem-SHAH
Dasha   DAH-shah
Deriganov   Deh-ree-GAH-noff
Dobrolyubov   Doh-bro-LYOO-boff
Dunyasha   Doon-YAH-shah

Fedotik   Feh-DAW-tik
Ferapont   Feh-Yah-PAWNT
Firs   FEERS
Fyodor   FYAW-dor
Gaev   GAH-yeff
Gogol   GOH-gol
Grigory   Gree-GOH-ree
Grisha   GREE-shah
Grokholsky   Gro-KHAWL-skee
Ignatyevich, Ignatych   Ig-NAH-tyeh-vitch, Ig-NAH-titch
Ilya   Eel-YAH
Ilyich   Eel-YEETCH
Irina Sergeyevna   Ee-REE-na Ser-GAY-evna
Ismailov   Ees-MY-loff
Ivan   Ee-VAHN
Ivan Romanych   Ee-VAHN Ro-MAH-nitch
Ivanovna   Ee-VAH-noff-nah
Ivanych   Ee-VAH-nitch
Kardamonov   Kar-dah-MOH-noff
Kharkov   KHAR-koff
Kirsanov   Keer-SAH-noff
Kohane   Ko-HAH-nay
Kolotilin   Koh-loh-TEE-lin
Konstantin   Kawn-stahn-TEEN
Kostya   KAW-styah
Kozoyedov   KAW-zoh-YAY-doff
Kozyrev   KAW-zeer-yeff
Krasny   KRASS-ni
Kulygin   Koo-LEE-ghin
Kursk   KOORSK
Lakedemonov   Lah-keh-day-MOH-noff
Lena   LAY-nah
Leonid   Lay-oh-NEED
Lermontov   LEHR-mon-toff
Lopakhin   Loh-PAH-kheen
Lyuba   LYOO-bah
Malitskoye   MAH-lits-kaw-yeh
Marina   Mah-REE-nah
Matryona   Mah-TRYAW-nah
Medvedenko   Med-vay-DYEN-koh
Mikhail Potapych   Mee-KHAIL ('ai' pron. 'eye') Po-TAH-pitch
Molchanovka   Mol-CHAH-noff-kah
Nekrasov   Nyeh-KRAH-soff
Nemetsky   Nyeh-MET-ski

Novo-Devichy   NAW-vo-DYEH-vitchy
Olga Sergeyevna   AWL-ga Ser-GAY-ev-nah ('gay' as English)
Ostrovsky   Aw-STRAWF-ski
Papa and Mama   accented on the first syllable
Pavel   PAH-vel
Petrovich   Peh-TRAW-vitch
Petrovna   Peh-TRAWV-nah
Petrushka   Peh-TROOSH-kah
Petya   PEH-tyah
Pishchik   PEE-shchik
Polina   Paw-LEE-nah
Polya   PAW-lyah
Protopopov   Pro-toh-PAW-poff
Prozorov   PROH-zoh-roff
Ragulin   Rah-GOO-lin
Ranevskaya   Rah-NYEFF-ska-yah
Rasplyuev   Rah-SPLYOO-yeff
Rodé   Raw-DAY
Rozhdestvennoye   Rawzh-DYEHST-veh-naw-yeh
Rusalka   Roo-SAHL-kah
Sadovsky   Sah-DOFF-skee
Saratov   Sa-RAH-toff
Semyon   Sehm-YAWN
Serebryakov   Seh-reh-bryah-KOFF
Sergeyich   Ser-GAY-itch
Shamraev   Sham-RAH-yeff
Simeonov   Sim-YAW-noff
Skvortsov   SkvorTSOHFF
Slavyansky   Slah-VYAHN-skee
Sofya   SOH-fyah
Soliony   Sol-YAW-ny
Sonya   SAW-nyah
Sorin   SAW-reen
Suzdaltsev   SOOZ-dal-tseff
Telegin   Tell-YAY-ghin
Trigorin   Tree-GAW-reen
Trofimov   Troh-FEE-moff
Trofimovich   Troh-FEE-moh-vitch
Tsitsikar   Tseet-see-KAHR
Tula   TOO-lah
Turgenev   Toor-GAY-nyeff
Tyestov   TYEH-stoff
Vanya   VAH-nyah
Varvara   Var-VAH-rah

Varya   VAH-ryah
Vasilievna   Vah-SEEL-yehv-nah
Vera   VAY-rah
Vershinin   Ver-SHEE-nin
Voinitsky   Voy-NEET-ski
Yakov   YAH-koff
Yaroslavl   Yah-roh-SLAH-vl
Yasha   YAH-shah
Yashnevo   YASH-nyeh-vo
Yefim   Yeh-FEEM
Yefim   Yeh-FEEM
Yegor   YEH-gor
Yelena   Yeh-LAY-nah
Yelets   Yell-YETS
Yelisavetgrad   Yeh-lee-sah-vyet-GRAD
Yepikhodov   Yeh-pee-KHAW-doff
Yermolai   Yehr-moh-LIE
Yevgeny   Yev-GAY-nee
Yevstignei   Yehff-steeg-NAY
Zasyp   ZAH-sip
Znoikov   ZNOY-koff